DAVID J. RYDER

34th and 39th Director of the United States Mint

PRESENTS

American Silver Eagles

FIFTH EDITION

A Guide to the U.S. Bullion Coin Program

Celebrating 40 years of America's Favorite Silver Bullion Coin

BY JOHN M. MERCANTI

Chief Engraver, United States Mint (ret.)

Whitman

SINCE 1934

American Silver Eagles FIFTH EDITION

A Guide to the U.S. Bullion Coin Program

Whitman™
SINCE 1934

4001 Helton Dr., Florence, AL 35630
whitman.com

ISBN: 978-07948-54294 / WW1905 08/25 / Ebook ISBN: 978-07948-55208
Printed in the United States of America.

CONTENTS

Foreword *by David J. Ryder, 34th and 39th Director, United States Mint* vii

Introduction ix

Chapter 1: History of the U.S. Bullion Coin Program 1

Chapter 2: Behind the Scenes at the U.S. Mint 11

Chapter 3: Date-by-Date Study of American Silver Eagles 47

Appendix A: Check List of American Silver Eagles 197

Appendix B: Illustrated Catalog of John Mercanti's Numismatic Work 202

Notes 211

About the Authors 211

Credits and Acknowledgments 212

Index 212

On July 9, 1985, President Ronald Reagan signed the Liberty Coin Act, which gave birth to the American Silver Eagle.

FOREWORD

It is with immense pride that I pen this foreword to the fifth edition of the *American Silver Eagles: A Guide to the U.S. Bullion Coin Program*. For those new to numismatics, I have always felt education is an important first step in understanding the wonderful hobby of coin collecting. This book serves as both a guide and a historical perspective. You will discover the beauty and intricacy of U.S. coin designs, the historical contexts behind mintages, and the processes that have preserved these objects for generations. For those of you who are seasoned collectors, I hope the updated content will offer fresh insights about the American Silver Eagles.

In 1980, I was asked by an old friend to be a volunteer for California's then-governor, Ronald Reagan, when he kicked off his presidential campaign at Liberty Island State Park in Jersey City, New Jersey. Little did I know that volunteering at this important political event would open up numerous opportunities for me professionally later in life. After Reagan won the presidency, I went to work in his new administration, eventually going to work for his vice president, George H.W. Bush, in the White House. Several years later, President Reagan signed the Liberty Coin Act of 1985; little did I know that many years later, President Bush would appoint me to become the 34th United States Mint director. Then, 26 years later, President Donald Trump reappointed me as the 39th director. And it all started that day in 1980 at Liberty Island State Park under the watchful eyes of Lady Liberty.

Since 1986, the American Silver Eagle has become not just a symbol of American coinage, but a powerful icon that represents the ideals of liberty, freedom, and patriotism. The obverse of the coin features a refreshed depiction of Adolph A. Weinman's full-length figure of Lady Liberty in full stride, enveloped in folds of the flag, with her right hand extended and her left hand holding branches of laurel and oak. The reverse until 2021 featured the iconic and beautiful heraldic eagle motif by my dear friend, former chief engraver John M. Mercanti. His design adorned the American Silver Eagle from the program's inception through 2021, with almost 700 hundred million of the coins struck by the Mint.

In 2019, when I began discussions about redesigning the American Silver Eagle, I felt it was my duty to first reach out to John to explain my plan, and more importantly, to seek his approval for a redesign of the Silver Eagle. Without hesitation, John gave me his endorsement, saying, "It would be wonderful if a new artist had the same design opportunity that I had back in 1986." Between that conversation and the hundreds of hours of work by many people within the Mint, the new, innovative design was introduced and won overwhelming approval by the secretary of the Treasury, the Citizens Coinage Advisory Committee, and the Commission of Fine Arts, as well as by the global coin-collecting community. The newly redesigned obverse returned to its original beauty, while the reverse, created by U.S. Mint Artistic Infusion Program designer Emily Damstra, features an eagle as it prepares to land, carrying an oak branch as if to add it to a nest. Retired U.S. Mint medallic artist Michael Gaudioso sculpted the design.

When I first set out to recreate the new reverse for the Silver Eagle coin, I wanted to capture not only the beauty and majesty of our nation's symbol, but also the eagle's dominance as a symbol of American strength and resilience. It was an ambitious project, but one that filled me with immense pride. I honestly believe this innovative design will become an enduring symbol of what it means to be an American and a true believer in freedom, just as John's original Heraldic Eagle reverse has done since 1986.

As you turn the pages of this edition, you will discover the history of these and other remarkable coins—their artistry, their craftsmanship, and their place within the broader narrative of U.S. coinage. The American Eagle series stands as a testament to both the artistic vision and the precision of American coinage, and I believe this edition of *American Silver Eagles* encapsulates that journey beautifully.

It is truly an honor to be a part of this moment in the history of the American Silver Eagle, and I hope that this edition of the book brings you the same sense of pride, excitement, and appreciation for American artistry and craftsmanship that it has brought me.

With sincere appreciation and gratitude,
David J. Ryder
34th and 39th Director, United States Mint

Introduction

How to Collect Silver Eagles

American Silver Eagles are highly collectible, thanks to a myriad of rare and exciting issues, a multitude of different strike finishes, and diverse methods and platforms for assembling sets of these popular coins. While many people regard the Silver Eagle as a modern bullion series aimed squarely at precious-metals investors, those who dive deeper will better understand why this coin is alluring to so many collectors. The American Silver Eagle has matured into a series with more than 100 different issues, including bullion strikes, Proofs, and other numismatic offerings, not to mention intriguing varieties and privy-marked pieces.

A series that continues growing larger by the year may intimidate some collectors, especially those who might feel overwhelmed by the notion of buying decades of back-catalog coins just to catch up to "current." However, the reality is that American Silver Eagles afford collectors many feasible options for building sets that are suitable for their individual budget and the level of numismatic challenge they desire.

Professional grading services will, for a fee, authenticate and grade a coin, then encapsulate it in a protective holder known as a slab; an identifying label is included inside the holder.

Determining Your Collecting Strategy

So many Silver Eagles, so many options! Which do you choose?

Consider the following:

- Collect slabbed (certified and encapsulated) or raw (uncertified)?
- Go for Variety 1 (John Mercanti's Heraldic Eagle reverse), Variety 2 (Emily S. Damstra's Flying Eagle reverse), or both?
- Seek bullion strikes, numismatic strikes, or both?
- Build a set of Silver Eagles via a third-party set registry or not?

How you maneuver these four forks in the numismatic road will greatly dictate your journey in collecting American Silver Eagles. Let's further review the options.

Go Slabbed or Raw?

Slabbed coins have their advantages, such as an independent grade awarded by a third party and protection in tamper-evident holders that help shield them from the elements. But they also tend to cost more than similar, raw coins and require more storage space. Conversely, raw coins usually sell for lower prices and can be compactly stored in standard albums or coin tubes. However, buying raw coins doesn't provide the physical protection, security, authenticity, and grade guarantees derived from purchasing certified specimens.

Variety 1 and Variety 2 Options

This book goes into extensive detail on the backgrounds of both the Mercanti and Damstra designs. Many collectors start with the 1986-dated Variety 1 Silver

Eagles and proceed from there. However, the introduction of Damstra's Variety 2 design in 2021 not only serves as an organic bookend for the Variety 1 design, it gives collectors on smaller budgets a natural starting point for building sets with coins of much more recent vintage.

Different Strikes for Different Folks

Collecting just the bullion strikes is the simplest and most affordable method for building an American Silver Eagle set. However, adding in the Proofs and Reverse Proofs, and/or the Burnished, Enhanced Uncirculated, and Enhanced Reverse Proof strikes provides a much more visually compelling and numismatically challenging set.

Registry Sets Are a Popular Choice

The major third-party grading services offer their own iterations of the collecting platform known as a *registry set*. In its most practical function, a registry set serves as a type of glorified inventory system for notching which certified coins you have within the context of a predetermined set and what grade those coins are. However, what really makes registry sets popular among so many collectors is that they give collectors the opportunity to display their collections to the public in a safe, secure, and (if desired) anonymous fashion. Many set registries offer awards and recognition for sets based on the cumulative grade-point average of coins within the set and its overall completion, as well as other metrics.

Ideas for Set Building

There are a variety of ways a collector can assemble an organized set of American Silver Eagles. Many collectors build sets composed of only the bullion strikes. Since only 2021 has seen more than one design type, this method effectively results in something of a simple year set. Intriguingly, a set consisting of bullion Silver Eagles offers collectors the only way to include a 2009-dated coin in their collection, since silver-planchet shortages that year led to a complete absence of Proofs and of pieces with other numismatic finishes.

Those who want to augment their Silver Eagle sets beyond the bullion strikes usually turn to the Proofs, which present few challenges during the first years of the series but become much a more expensive and complex endeavor as the series moves along. The big stopper for many collectors is the 1995-W Proof, which is a four-figure coin in PF-69 and reaches into the five figures for a PF-70 example.

The release of Reverse Proofs and Enhanced Reverse Proofs in more recent years creates opportunities and dilemmas for collectors: Do they restrict themselves to only the regular Proofs or expand into other Proof variants? What about including Burnished specimens and the (to date) sole Enhanced Uncirculated issue? Adventuresome collectors might begin with the bullion strikes and eventually add in the numismatic strikes. They also must decide whether they should get the 1995-W Proof and 2019-S Enhanced Reverse Proof out of the way first, then pursue the less-expensive issues, or vice versa—build out the majority of the set and save the big keys for last.

Toning on silver coins can be quite beautiful, and some collectors specialize in toned coins.

A popular destination for 70-graded American Silver Eagles is the realm of the registry set, which Professional Coin Grading Service (PCGS) launched in the 1990's and brought to the Internet in 2001. Numismatic Guaranty Company (NGC) and Certified Acceptance Corporation (CAC) also have registry sets.

Then there is the subject of toned coins. There are many American Silver Eagle collectors who pursue sets composed of only toned coins. Yet, toning is often a controversial thing in some circles. Some collectors want rainbow-hued Silver Eagles while others prefer blast-white examples. Those who prefer toned coins need to avoid *artificial toning*, which is rampant in the numismatic world. Purchasing toned coins encapsulated by major third-party graders can help reduce the apprehension and risk associated with buying coins that may carry artificial toning.

Special Labels

PCGS, NGC, and other third-party graders have been encapsulating American Silver Eagles with many different types of labels for years. The labels either call out a specific characteristic or feature of the coin itself or carry a special design or attribute that connects with the coin.

Some critics think collecting coins based on the presence of a special label emphasizes the holder over the coin. However, what special labels do, in essence, is enhance the encapsulated coin's collectability by symbolizing a tangible or intangible quality of the coin itself, and/or by placing it within the grander numismatic or historical context of the coin's production.

In other words, special labels may elevate the collectability of the Silver Eagles and can expand their appeal beyond numismatics. Special labels can connect coins to landmark moments in history or a widely recognized figure. Here is an inexhaustive list of different types of special labels:

- *first-strike or early-release labels*—Typically awarded only to coins verified to have been struck during the first 30 days of an issue's production.
- *emergency-issue labels*—These may designate production of a coin at a facility that would not ordinarily produce it; for Silver Eagles, emergency labels generally relate to COVID-era strikings of bullion-finish coins at the Philadelphia and San Francisco Mints.
- *parenthetical-mintmark labels*—These indicate Silver Eagles that were struck at a facility other than their usual point of origin (which is normally the West Point Mint). The parenthetical mintmark is ascertained by inspection of the shipment labels that wrap sealed boxes of bullion Silver Eagles and describe the mint of origin for the coins within. Coins qualifying for this type of label must be contained within their original, unopened box so the grading service can properly verify the mint of origin.

Typical slab labels include the denomination, date, mintmark, strike, and any special finish (e.g., Enhanced Uncirculated). For a fee, most grading services will include special identifying information on the label. The NGC and CAC labels shown here guarantee the coins to have been first strikes or from the first day of delivery, respectively; the NGC label was signed by Silver Eagle obverse designer Michael Gaudioso. The PCGS-graded coin merits labels on both sides; the one on the front has been signed by Silver Eagle reverse designer John Mercanti, the author of this book.

- *hand-signed labels*—Hand-signed labels contain autographs of individuals connected in some way to the encapsulated coin; such figures may include Mint directors, coin designers or sculptors, political figures, or hobby luminaries involved with or serving during the era of the coin's production.
- *World Trade Center labels*—These labels denote coins that were recovered from bank vaults at the World Trade Center in New York City, which was destroyed on September 11, 2001; many different types of coins from around the world were stored in vaults at that location, including multitudes of American Silver Eagles.

There are various other kinds of special labels. Among them are labels awarded to coins that were ceremoniously encapsulated for certain coin shows, numismatic events, or other landmark occasions. These are quite popular with many collectors, and some are quite rare.

Storage and Display Options

How will you store your American Silver Eagles? While some regard the topic as more of an afterthought, you should consider this before you even begin collecting them. Why? Because your preferred method of coin storage might determine what type of set you ultimately build. Let's review some of the most popular methods of storing Silver Eagles and how these storage options can drive set-building decisions.

- *albums*—Collecting Silver Eagles within albums can dictate the scope of a given set, due to the specific coins accommodated by the album.
- *certified holders*—Buying Silver Eagles in slabs permits inclusion of those coins within registry sets; collectors can still go the date-and-mintmark route or may pursue a so-called Box of 20 set, defined by the number of coins that can fit in a typical storage box offered by the major grading companies.
- *display cases*—Coin-supply companies manufacture all manner of special presentation cases designed to hold certain types of sets and arrangements of American Silver Eagles.
- *original U.S. Mint holders*—Many collectors keep their American Silver Eagles in their original packaging as issued by the U.S. Mint; while this can get bulky and unwieldy, especially in a collection of many coins from across the series, it satisfies the desire of collectors who want their coins as they were originally issued and sold.
- *rolls and tubes*—One of the most efficient ways to store Silver Eagles is in rigid, inert rolls and tubes—a widely preferred method among bullion "stackers" and precious-metals investors. The big downside to this type of storage is the lack of visual presentation and dearth of aesthetic appeal.
- *capsules, flips, and 2x2's*—Capsules, flips, and 2x2's offer varying forms of protection, from the nearly air-tight security provided by the capsule to the efficient, if temporary, protection of a standard cardboard 2" x 2" holder. An inert vinyl flip can ensure longer-term protection and be used for storing coins in row boxes or in pocketed pages, with the latter being great for organizing coins within three-ring binders.

Whichever methods you choose for storing your Silver Eagles, avoid any options that may contain harmful chemicals, such as polyvinylchloride (PVC). Seek chemically inert holders from major, reputable coin-supply manufacturers and distributors who stand behind their products. And always store your coins in a cool, dry place away from light and fumes to provide further long-term protection.

Buying American Silver Eagles

There is no shortage of suppliers with American Silver Eagles for sale. The most popular silver bullion coin in the world can be found in everything from direct-mail dealer advertisements to

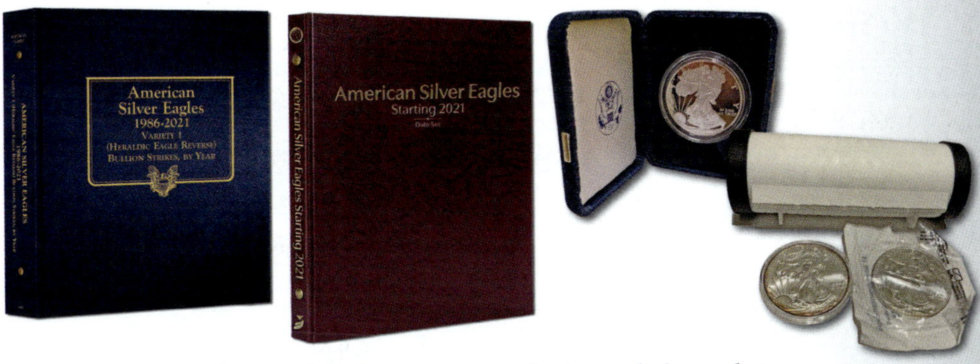

Albums, original government packaging, and aftermarket holders are among the storage options for your collection.

television infomercials, magazine advertorials, and pop-up ads online. However, the best resources for buying American Silver Eagles are reputable coin and bullion dealers. Many sell coins in brick-and-mortar storefronts, via mail-order, in magazines, and through points of sale online and on social media platforms.

Some people get themselves in trouble when searching for "cheap deals" on American Silver Eagles. You generally will not find legitimate American Silver Eagles in retail settings for prices lower than their spot value. Many people have wound up with fake goods or stolen property looking for lower-than-spot American Silver Eagles online, whether buying through overseas e-commerce sites or engaging in parking-lot deals arranged through swap-meet websites or online marketplaces.

Buy Silver Eagles only from coin dealers and bullion brokers who have a solid word-of-mouth reputation or many (and mostly) positive customer reviews online. Another line of defense when buying Silver Eagles is to search for dealers through the *Greysheet* (greysheet.com/dealerdirectory), the Professional Numismatists Guild (PNG, at pngdealers.org/af_memberDirectory_Custom.asp), or the National Coin and Bullion Association (ncbassoc.org/AF_MemberDirectory.asp).

You can also choose dealers who are affiliated with numismatic organizations like the American Numismatic Association (ANA, at coin-dealer-directory.money.org/), PCGS (pcgs.com/dealers), NGC (ngccoin.com/coin-dealer-locator/), or CAC (cacgrading.com/dealers).

Beware of Counterfeits

Not enough can be said about the rampant dangers of counterfeits. The risk of buying counterfeit Silver Eagles is rising as bad players get their hands on increasingly sophisticated counterfeiting equipment. Some of these modern counterfeits are fooling advanced collectors and investors. Yet even crude fakes can deceive buyers who have little to no background in buying or collecting American Silver Eagles. Knowledge is always power.

Unfortunately, a great many Silver Eagle buyers lack numismatic understanding of these coins and are buying them only because they heard about them somewhere or someone may have told them "they make great investments"—or some such. Many of these newbie buyers innocently walk right into scams involving fake Silver Eagles because they're looking for the cheapest deals online and inadvertently end up purchasing fakes, many of which could look convincing to the unknowing buyer.

Conventional wisdom for buying rare and valuable coins is to purchase only those that have been certified and encapsulated by major third-party graders. However, even the slabs are getting faked today. This is why those who purchase encapsulated coins should refer to certificate-verification resources to ensure that the holdered coins they are buying are the real deal.

A Word on Milk Spots

Some years back, collectors began noticing white splotches forming on some of their American Silver Eagles. These unsightly marks, known as *milk spots*, can take the form of a single, tiny, whitish blotch or cloudy mottling across the entire surface of the coin. It is theorized that milk spots may arise as part of the planchet preparation process at the mint, most likely by way of a wash or rinse.

As then-editor of *Coin World* Paul Gilkes wrote in its December 17, 2012, issue,

> During her less than 18 months as the U.S. Mint's quality division chief, Stacy Kelley-Scherer has focused her attention on a problem that has plagued the American Silver Eagle silver bullion coin almost since its 1986 inception—spots. So far, a solution that prevents spotting from occurring has eluded mint officials. . . . Each year of the program, collectors and dealers of the American Eagle silver dollars have reported spots or blotches on the obverse and reverse, on all finishes—bullion, proof, and uncirculated—and on coins from all mints. The spotting is random and can appear as a single spot, multiple spots crossing the field and devices, or in large blotches or patches consuming significant portions of a coin's design.

Milk spots are not confined only to American Silver Eagles. They have also been reported on similar .999-fine silver coins from other nations, such as Australia, Canada, and China. The major third-party grading firms have their own guidelines for grading coins that contain milk spots, and each company has criteria for how this issue may affect grading and guarantees. Buyers are urged to check with the grading companies for their current policies on milk spots.

How to Use the GSID Numbers

The *Greysheet* Identification system represents unique catalog numbers for more than 275,000 items of U.S. and world coinage and paper money, and it is the bedrock of the vast CDN–Whitman database. Comprising tens of millions of records of pricing, auction prices realized, metadata, and images, it grows and changes on a daily basis. The GSID number allows the user to quickly search this database and enables seamless identification across Whitman's family of products.

1

History of the U.S. Bullion Coin Program

The American Silver Eagle bullion program was launched in the 1980's. Its debut was influenced by numerous factors on the national and world scenes. In many ways, however, the stage had been set 50 years earlier, during the Great Depression.

From the mid-1930's to the mid-1960's, the value of gold was pegged by the U.S. government at a steady $35 an ounce. Silver, meanwhile, fluctuated between roughly $0.30 and $0.90 an ounce up to the early 1960's.

In 1933 President Franklin Roosevelt signed Executive Order 6102, forbidding the hoarding of gold. The order required "all persons" to "deliver on or before May 1, 1933 all gold coin, gold bullion, and Gold Certificates now owned by them to a Federal Reserve Bank, branch or agency, or to any member bank of the Federal Reserve System." Criminal penalties for violation of the order were a fine of up to $10,000 or jail time of up to 10 years—or both. (Exceptions were made for reasonable amounts of gold used in industry, professions like dentistry, and the arts; rare coins owned by collectors; and a few other special cases. Also, individuals could personally hold an allowed amount of gold coinage—up to $100 but no more.) The president's order was designed to protect the nation's banking system, which was fragile and wounded in the early years of the Great Depression.

As instructed, Americans turned in millions of gold coins. These were melted and eventually stored as bars at the United States Bullion Depository, Fort Knox. The value of the gold held by the Federal Reserve tripled between 1933 and 1937.

It was the Gold Reserve Act of 1934 that changed the dollar value of gold from $20.67 to $35 per ounce. This official government price remained in effect until August 15, 1971, when President Richard Nixon announced that the United States would no longer convert dollars to gold at a fixed value. With that, the country was off the gold standard (which it had been on officially since 1900, and de facto for decades before that).

In 1974 Congress and President Gerald Ford re-legalized the private ownership of gold coins, bars, and certificates, effective December 31. After more than 40 years, Americans could once again legally own as much gold as they wanted.

POSTMASTER: PLEASE POST IN A CONSPICUOUS PLACE.—JAMES A. FARLEY, Postmaster General

UNDER EXECUTIVE ORDER OF THE PRESIDENT

issued April 5, 1933

all persons are required to deliver

ON OR BEFORE MAY 1, 1933

all GOLD COIN, GOLD BULLION, AND GOLD CERTIFICATES now owned by them to a Federal Reserve Bank, branch or agency, or to any member bank of the Federal Reserve System.

Executive Order

FORBIDDING THE HOARDING OF GOLD COIN, GOLD BULLION AND GOLD CERTIFICATES.

By virtue of the authority vested in me by Section 5(b) of the Act of October 6, 1917, as amended by Section 2 of the Act of March 9, 1933, entitled "An Act to provide relief in the existing national emergency in banking, and for other purposes", in which amendatory Act Congress declared that a serious emergency exists, I, Franklin D. Roosevelt, President of the United States of America, do declare that said national emergency still continues to exist and pursuant to said section do hereby prohibit the hoarding of gold coin, gold bullion, and gold certificates within the continental United States by individuals, partnerships, associations and corporations and hereby prescribe the following regulations for carrying out the purposes of this order:

Section 1. For the purposes of this regulation, the term "hoarding" means the withdrawal and withholding of gold coin, gold bullion or gold certificates from the recognized and customary channels of trade. The term "person" means any individual, partnership, association or corporation.

Section 2. All persons are hereby required to deliver on or before May 1, 1933, to a Federal reserve bank or a branch or agency thereof or to any member bank of the Federal Reserve System all gold coin, gold bullion and gold certificates now owned by them or coming into their ownership on or before April 28, 1933, except the following:

(a) Such amount of gold as may be required for legitimate and customary use in industry, profession or art within a reasonable time, including gold prior to refining and stocks of gold in reasonable amounts for the usual trade requirements of owners mining and refining such gold.

(b) Gold coin and gold certificates in an amount not exceeding in the aggregate $100.00 belonging to any one person; and gold coins having a recognized special value to collectors of rare and unusual coins.

(c) Gold coin and bullion earmarked or held in trust for a recognized foreign government or foreign central bank or the Bank for International Settlements.

(d) Gold coin and bullion licensed for other proper transactions (not involving hoarding) including gold coin and bullion imported for reexport or held pending action on applications for export licenses.

Section 3. Until otherwise ordered any person becoming the owner of any gold coin, gold bullion, or gold certificates after April 28, 1933, shall, within three days after receipt thereof, deliver the same in the manner prescribed in Section 2; unless such gold coin, gold bullion or gold certificates are held for any of the purposes specified in paragraphs (a), (b) or (c) of Section 2; or unless such gold coin or gold bullion is held for purposes specified in paragraph (d) of Section 2 and the person holding it is, with respect to such gold coin or bullion, a licensee or applicant for license pending action thereon.

Section 4. Upon receipt of gold coin, gold bullion or gold certificates delivered to it in accordance with Sections 2 or 3, the Federal reserve bank or member bank will pay therefor an equivalent amount of any other form of coin or currency coined or issued under the laws of the United States.

Section 5. Member banks shall deliver all gold coin, gold bullion and gold certificates owned or received by them (other than as exempted under the provisions of Section 2) to the Federal reserve banks of their respective districts and receive credit or payment therefor.

Section 6. The Secretary of the Treasury, out of the sum made available to the President by Section 501 of the Act of March 9, 1933, will in all proper cases pay the reasonable costs of transportation of gold coin, gold bullion or gold certificates delivered to a member bank or Federal reserve bank in accordance with Sections 2, 3, or 5 hereof, including the cost of insurance, protection, and such other incidental costs as may be necessary, upon production of satisfactory evidence of such costs. Voucher forms for this purpose may be procured from Federal reserve banks.

Section 7. In cases where the delivery of gold coin, gold bullion or gold certificates by the owners thereof within the time set forth above will involve extraordinary hardship or difficulty, the Secretary of the Treasury may, in his discretion, extend the time within which such delivery must be made. Applications for such extensions must be made in writing under oath, addressed to the Secretary of the Treasury and filed with a Federal reserve bank. Each application must state the date to which the extension is desired, the amount and location of the gold coin, gold bullion and gold certificates in respect of which such application is made and the facts showing extension to be necessary to avoid extraordinary hardship or difficulty.

Section 8. The Secretary of the Treasury is hereby authorized and empowered to issue such further regulations as he may deem necessary to carry out the purposes of this order and to issue licenses thereunder, through such officers or agencies as he may designate, including licenses permitting the Federal reserve banks and member banks of the Federal Reserve System, in return for an equivalent amount of other coin, currency or credit, to deliver, earmark or hold in trust gold coin and bullion to or for persons showing the need for the same for any of the purposes specified in paragraphs (a), (c) and (d) of Section 2 of these regulations.

Section 9. Whoever willfully violates any provision of this Executive Order or of these regulations or of any rule, regulation or license issued thereunder may be fined not more than $10,000, or, if a natural person, may be imprisoned for not more than ten years, or both; and any officer, director, or agent of any corporation who knowingly participates in any such violation may be punished by a like fine, imprisonment, or both.

This order and these regulations may be modified or revoked at any time.

THE WHITE HOUSE
April 5, 1933.

FRANKLIN D ROOSEVELT

For Further Information Consult Your Local Bank

GOLD CERTIFICATES may be identified by the words "GOLD CERTIFICATE" appearing thereon. The serial number and the Treasury seal on the face of a GOLD CERTIFICATE are printed in YELLOW. Be careful not to confuse GOLD CERTIFICATES with other issues which are redeemable in gold but which are not GOLD CERTIFICATES. Federal Reserve Notes and United States Notes are "redeemable in gold" but are not "GOLD CERTIFICATES" and are not required to be surrendered

Special attention is directed to the exceptions allowed under Section 2 of the Executive Order

CRIMINAL PENALTIES FOR VIOLATION OF EXECUTIVE ORDER $10,000 fine or 10 years imprisonment, or both, as provided in Section 9 of the order

Secretary of the Treasury.

U.S. Government Printing Office: 1933 2-16064

Millions of U.S. gold coins coins (shown here enlarged) were turned in to the Federal Reserve following Executive Order 6102.

President Gerald Ford revoked Roosevelt's prohibition, lifting earlier restrictions on gold ownership.

International Competition in Gold

A few years after President Ford's 1974 executive order revoked the ban on gold, the United States would begin offering silver, gold, and platinum coins for sale to collectors and investors. Before that, however, several other nations (notably South Africa, Canada, China, Mexico, and Australia) were minting their own gold bullion coins.

South Africa's Krugerrand was first struck in 1967; it proved very popular and by 1980 had captured 90 percent of the world's gold-coin market. (In the United States, importing Krugerrands was illegal starting in 1985. This was an economic sanction against the South African government, to punish and discourage its racial-segregation policies. The sanction was lifted in 1994 when South Africa officially abandoned apartheid.)

The Krugerrand's success encouraged other gold-producing countries to develop their own bullion programs. Canada launched the gold Maple Leaf in 1979. Mexico, with a long tradition of minting gold and silver coins, started its Libertad in 1981. China's Panda series began in 1982. Australia introduced its gold Nugget in 1986, and the United Kingdom debuted the Britannia in 1987. Austria began its Vienna Philharmonic gold-coin program in 1989, and it quickly became a best-seller. All of these coins, as well as the Krugerrand, had official legal-tender status backed by their issuing governments.

Other gold-producing nations saw the success of South Africa's Krugerrand starting in the 1960's and were inspired to introduce their own bullion coins. The United States would eventually enter the market.

Starting in 1980, the United States attempted to compete with these international products and capture some of the market in gold. The congressionally mandated vehicle was the "American Arts Commemorative Series" of gold medals. Unlike the Krugerrand and other international coins, these medals were not legal tender—in fact, they were at first designed specifically not to resemble traditional U.S. coinage. Sales were slow from the start; the marketing was clumsy, and buyers were confronted by constantly changing prices based on daily bullion values. Even a rejuvenated marketing effort in 1982 failed to boost the program. It sputtered out and ended in 1984. These medals are explored in detail in *American Gold and Silver: U.S. Mint Collector and Investor Coins and Medals, Bicentennial to Date*, by Dennis Tucker.

In December 1985 the Gold Bullion Coin Act of 1985 finally established a truly competitive American product, with full legal-tender status—the American Gold Eagle. Meanwhile, on the silver scene, events had been set in motion that would bring about an equally historic coin.

The United States' first post–Executive Order 6102 entry into the gold market was the American Arts Commemorative Series. Its half-ounce and one-ounce medals honored Willa Cather, Mark Twain, and other American writers, artists, and musicians.

The U.S. Mint's bullion coinage program has grown to include silver, gold, platinum, and palladium in various formats. The Mint defines a bullion coin thus: "A bullion coin is a coin that is valued by its weight in a specific precious metal. Unlike commemorative or numismatic coins valued by limited mintage, rarity, condition and age, bullion coins are purchased by investors seeking a simple and tangible means to own and invest in the gold, silver, platinum, and palladium markets."

THE DOMESTIC SITUATION IN SILVER

In the 1970's and early 1980's executive plans were afoot to sell off precious metal from the Defense National Stockpile Center (a branch of the federal Defense Logistics Agency, whose purpose is to store, secure, and sell raw materials). Several presidential administrations were convinced that domestic production of silver was far greater than any strategic need for the metal, and sought—mostly unsuccessfully—to liquidate part of the nation's stockpile. Powerful forces in the mining states resisted such selloffs, fearing that they would flood the market with silver and decrease its value. (A September 1976 *Wall Street Journal* article noted that "When the US government makes noises about selling silver from the federal stockpile, futures traders start unloading futures contracts in speculation that such a sale would depress prices."[1]) Certain military-minded lawmakers also opposed the sale of stockpiled silver, wanting guarantees that the proceeds would be used not simply to reduce the federal debt, but to buy other materials needed for national defense.

A sampling of *Wall Street Journal* headlines from the era illustrates the challenges various presidents faced in selling off the stockpiled silver:

> "Nixon Plan to Sell Stockpiled Commodities Could Be Slowed by Market, Legal Snags," March 16, 1973
>
> "House Committee Rejects Sales of Silver from Government's Strategic Stockpile," September 12, 1979
>
> "House Refuses to Sell Any Silver in U.S. Stockpile: Compromise That Called for Sale of 5 Million Ounces Loses by Lopsided Margin," December 13, 1979
>
> "House Panel Rejects Reagan Bid to Sell All of Silver in Stockpile," June 5, 1981

For more than 170 years, many U.S. coins, like the half dollar seen here, were made of .900 fine silver. By the 1960's the precious metal was too expensive to use for coinage, and the Mint introduced a new composition of copper and nickel. Still, Uncle Sam held massive reserves of silver as part of the national-defense stockpile.

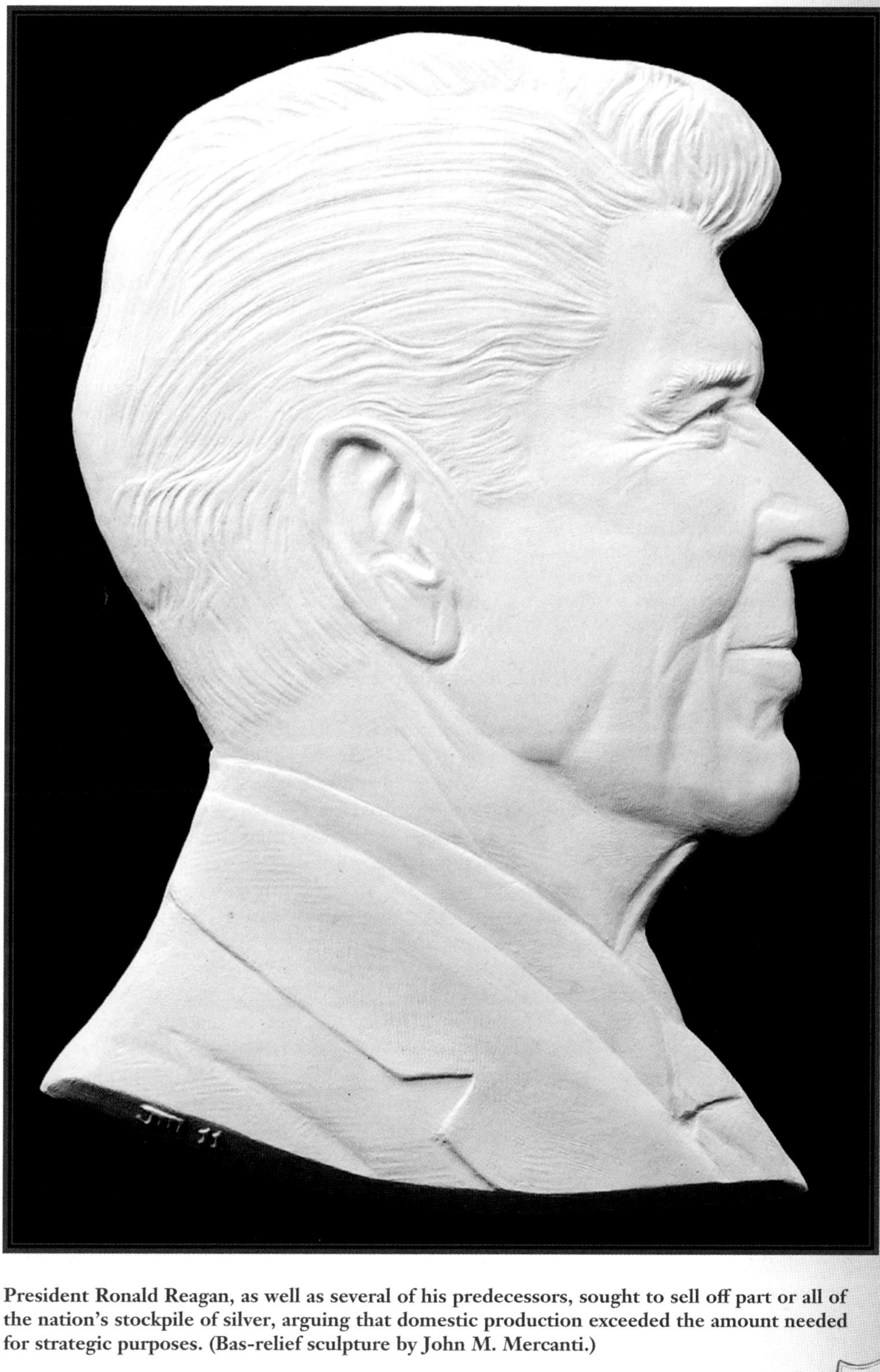

President Ronald Reagan, as well as several of his predecessors, sought to sell off part or all of the nation's stockpile of silver, arguing that domestic production exceeded the amount needed for strategic purposes. (Bas-relief sculpture by John M. Mercanti.)

Senator James McClure of Idaho sought to protect his state's mining interests—in particular, keeping the price of silver as high as possible. McClure was the influential chairman of the Senate Energy and Natural Resources Committee. Toward the end of his political career, he was described by Senator Malcolm Wallop of Wyoming: "There is no major piece of energy, public lands, or natural resources legislation passed in recent years on which he has not left an imprint."[2]

President Ronald Reagan.

Despite such opposition, the government did sell portions of its silver. On June 10, 1981, the House Armed Services Committee decided to approve the Reagan administration's request to sell federal silver, beginning in fiscal year 1982, to help balance the budget. The next month, Congress agreed to allow the sale of three-quarters of the stockpiled silver—105.1 million troy ounces—over a three-year period. When news got out, investors balked, and that September the market value of silver fell 11 percent. (Gold prices also dropped.) A group of politicians from Idaho, a major silver-mining state, tried to block the silver sales, the first of which was held in October 1981. On December 3 they proposed an amendment to the 1982 Department of Defense appropriation bill to end the federal sale of silver "until the President, not later than July 1, 1982, redetermines that the silver authorized for disposal is excess to the requirements of the stockpile." When the appropriations bill was signed into law with the amendment still attached, further sales of the silver were effectively blocked.

On May 27, 1982, Senator James McClure and Representative Larry Craig (both of Idaho) introduced identical bills in the Senate and House "to provide for the disposal of silver from the National Defense Stockpile through the issuance of silver coins." Their thinking appears to have been, "We can't fight the silver selloff forever; if it has to occur, at least we can try to control it." Presumably the sale of, say, 10 million ounces of silver coins to hundreds of thousands of Americans would depress the price of silver less than the same weight sold in bulk to a few large wholesale buyers. The bills' stated objectives were to "redirect the sale of silver from our national defense stockpile in an effort to minimize its [effect] on the already depressed price of silver."

The bills were both referred to committee and never enacted.

That June the price of silver soared when Secretary of the Interior James Watt announced that the federal sale of stockpiled silver would be indefinitely postponed. (The government's mandated study on potential methods of selling the silver had been delayed.)

On January 27, 1983, Senator McClure introduced another bill that was nearly identical to the May 1982 proposal. "If we are forced to accept a sale," McClure asked, "why use the method guaranteed to depress the price and dispose of the silver with the lowest possible return to the taxpayers? Why not instead, if we must sell, at least get as much for it as we can?" His solution: "legislation which provides that in the event the President proposes and Congress authorizes the sale of silver from the strategic stockpile, this silver would be sold through the minting and distribution of a silver-bearing coin."[3] Like the 1982 bill, this one was referred to committee; hearings were held, but it was not enacted.

The authorization for a new bullion coinage program in 1986 was tacked on to the law that authorized these Statue of Liberty coins, part of the United States' commemorative coin program. Mint engraver John Mercanti designed the Statue of Liberty silver dollar as well as the reverse of the American Silver Eagle.

Sales of the silver remained suspended for more than two years. Finally, Senator McClure on June 21, 1985, proposed the Liberty Coin Act—an amendment to the Statue of Liberty–Ellis Island Commemorative Coin Act, then being considered in the House of Representatives. The Senate agreed to the amendment, the House approved the amended bill, and on July 9 President Ronald Reagan signed it into law.

The Liberty Coin Act:

- authorized the secretary of the Treasury to mint and issue silver bullion coins
- specified the diameter, weight, fineness, general design, inscriptions, and edge format of the coins
- established the formula for pricing the coins
- defined the coins as having both numismatic and legal-tender status
- specified that the silver would come from the national stockpiles
- set the act in effect as of October 1, 1985
- stipulated that no coins would be issued or sold before September 1, 1986

Secretary of the Treasury James Baker presided over the striking of the first American Silver Eagle on October 29, 1986, in a special ceremony in San Francisco (at the U.S. Mint's Assay Office). As Baker "reached for the electronic button on press No. 105, he turned to the audience and said, 'I don't need a pick and shovel to start the San Francisco Silver Rush of 1986.'"[4]

James Baker was secretary of the Treasury when the American Silver Eagle program began.

Secretary Baker's analogy to an old-time gold rush was apt. The United States' bullion program started quietly but over the years has grown into a case of "silver fever." Between the bullion coins and various collectible formats, more than 725 million ounces have been sold since 1986. The coins are readily available in the numismatic marketplace and also from banks, investment firms, and other mainstream channels. In the nearly 40 years since the American Silver Eagle was launched, the coin has become one of the most popular silver-investment vehicles in the world.

Partway through 2021 the Mint introduced a new reverse design. John Mercanti's classic rendition of a heraldic eagle took its place in the realm of historical coins, and Emily S. Damstra's motif of a flying eagle became the new reverse of America's best-selling silver coin.

The American Silver Eagle (face value $1, actual silver weight one ounce) is a legal-tender bullion coin with weight, content, and purity guaranteed by the United States government. It is one of very few silver coins allowed in individual retirement accounts (IRAs).The obverse features Adolph A. Weinman's Liberty Walking design, as used \on the circulating half dollar of 1916 to 1947. The reverse from 1986 to 2021 featured a heraldic eagle, the work of John Mercanti. In 2021 a new design by Emily S. Damstra, showing an eagle in flight, became the reverse motif.

2
Behind the Scenes at the U.S. Mint

I've often been asked, "What is the coin design process like? How do you design a coin? Who selects the final design?" So let's take some time to explore that aspect of the coining process, along with some of my personal experiences, with special emphasis on the American Silver Eagle.

My Breakthrough Into Engraving

There were five engravers plus the chief engraver on staff when I came to the Mint in 1974. At the time Frank Gasparro had been chief engraver for a number of years. He had been appointed to the position on February 23, 1965, and would hold it until his retirement on January 16, 1981.

Toward the end of 1973 I had been working as an illustrator for a federal agency that supported all the military services—Army, Navy, Air Force, Marines, and Coast Guard. I had been with the federal government almost six years. I was married, with an infant son, working three jobs to make ends meet, and I wasn't happy with the position I held at the time because I saw no future advancement.

One afternoon I was reviewing competitive open positions within the federal government. I saw that there was an opening for an apprentice at the United States Mint, and I decided to apply.

I filled out the required paperwork and waited.

I was called a few weeks later and was told that I would be interviewed by Mr. Gasparro and that I should call him for an appointment.

I immediately called to set up a meeting date. Frank was cordial and asked me if I had ever done anything related to medallic art.

"Most of my training to date has been in drawing and illustrating," I replied. He told me that was great, because a large amount of time would be spent on the board creating designs. He also requested I model something in relief and bring it to him—in two days.

Needless to say, panic alarms went off all around me. What would I do?

I immediately went to my library and opened a coffee-table book on Michelangelo. I sketched one of the prophets from the painting on the Sistine Chapel ceiling (Zechariah, to be exact). Now all I had to do was model it in clay. Piece of cake!

I happened to have on hand in my workshop a piece of wood about seven inches in diameter. I gessoed it white (gesso is a paint mixture, a binder combined with chalk, gypsum, or pigment). Then I transferred the drawing onto it and began building up the clay portrait.

I've heard of people having epiphanies in their lives where an event or experience changed them forever. I never thought I would ever have such an experience. I loved illustrating, I had learned from the best, and I knew I would spend the rest of my life creating images on paper. But when I began modeling that one portrait and the image began to take shape, I knew there

U.S. Mint Chief Engraver Frank Gasparro

Frank Gasparro was born August 26, 1909, in Philadelphia. His father was a musician and wanted his son to follow in his footsteps, but young Frank had another calling: the visual arts. He apprenticed under sculptor Giuseppe Donato, who had worked for the legendary Auguste Rodin. After studying at the Fleisher Art Memorial school and the Pennsylvania Academy of Fine Arts, he won two scholarships and continued to learn and practice his craft in France, Italy, Germany, England, and Sweden.

Starting in 1937 Gasparro worked as a sculptor for the Federal Arts Administration. He joined the Philadelphia Mint in December 1942, working under Chief Engraver John R. Sinnock (who later would design the Roosevelt dime and the Franklin half dollar, among other coins), and then under Chief Engraver Gilroy Roberts (who designed the obverse of the Kennedy half dollar). His projects included various medals as well as coins struck for other countries.

In 1959 Assistant Engraver Gasparro's first major U.S. coinage design debuted: a new reverse for the Lincoln cent. The coin, like Gasparro, had been born in 1909, a hundred years after the birth of Abraham Lincoln, and in its 50th year its famous "wheat ears" reverse was replaced by Gasparro's rendition of the Lincoln Memorial. His design entry was chosen from among 23 reviewed at the Mint.

He created the reverse of the John F. Kennedy half dollar after the president was assassinated in late 1963.

Gasparro was appointed chief engraver in 1965. Among his later coinage designs are the Eisenhower and Susan B. Anthony dollars. He created medals honoring Winston Churchill, Douglas MacArthur, John Wayne, and other famous people, and also the presidential medals for every chief executive from Lyndon Johnson to Ronald Reagan.

was no going back. I had to have this job. At that point I wanted nothing else but to be a medallic sculptor.

I still have that portrait and it's still in clay. I've never cast it.

I finished the portrait as best I could, packed it up with my portfolio, and kept my appointment with Frank.

The sculpture of Zechariah that John Mercanti modeled for his interview at the U.S. Mint.

Joining the U.S. Mint

Frank Gasparro was always a hard person to read. Serious, but never angry. At that first meeting, as I showed him my work, all he said was, "Very nice, very nice, yes, yes, very nice." That's it. That's all he said. Never introduced me to the staff or showed me around the department. He politely asked if I had any questions. He answered them and said he'd call me and let me know about the position. Then he sent me on my way.

I left not knowing what kind of impression I'd made.

A month went by and I hadn't heard anything from the Mint so I decided to call and check the status of the position. That call was a life changer. Human Resources told me that Frank had selected me for the apprenticeship and that they'd been trying to reach me for a week, but they must have had the wrong contact number.

And that's it—that's how I got the position.

After 15 years as chief engraver, Frank Gasparro retired from the U.S. Mint in January 1981. He continued to design medals for private and public groups and also taught at the Fleisher Art Memorial, where he had studied in his youth. He was 92 years old when he passed away on September 29, 2001.

"More than any other chief engraver up to that time," writes Q. David Bowers in the *Guide Book of Lincoln Cents*, "Gasparro was a warm, friendly, outgoing man who loved numismatics and enjoyed meeting members of the coin collecting community."[1]

In his obituary, the *New York Times* noted: "His daughter said her father, a slight man with a Jimmy Durante profile, had strong, large hands and liked to work in alabaster. When he introduced himself to strangers as a sculptor, he had a ready reply when they asked where they might find his work. 'It's in your pocket,' he said."[2] His artistry was coined on more than 100 billion Lincoln cents.

John Mercanti: first week on the job as a sculptor-engraver at the U.S. Mint, 1974.

I'll always be grateful to Frank for hiring me. He was a great teacher and a great friend. I have many, many funny stories about him, including those he told me about himself. A few weeks after he retired in 1981, I met him for lunch. I took along a tape recorder and he told me all the stories about his life and career related to the Mint, and stories of his early life. But that's for another time and another book.

The Mint's Engravers and Designers

At the time I came on board at the U.S. Mint, in 1974, there were five engravers on staff.

There was Edgar Z. Steever—a brilliant mind—who had two parents who were physicians, and could have been one himself.

Michael G. Iacocca, who was one of the best portrait artists I ever met.

Sherl Joseph Winter, an incredible portraitist and numismatic sculptor and designer, who taught me so much.

John Mercanti, circa 1975, about one year into his long career at the Philadelphia Mint.

Philip J. Fowler, who was, for want of a better word, one of the great "characters" in my early career, introducing me to the arts, music, and some of the finest wine and cuisine in Philadelphia and New York.

And finally, Matthew Peloso, who came to the Mint soon after I arrived. Matt was the biggest man I had ever met, well over six feet tall, with hands that dwarfed everyone else's, but when he picked up a tool he could sculpt the finest detail. He had the touch of an angel.

These men were so instrumental to me in my early career that no story of me and my accomplishments is complete without them. Some never had a design selected for a circulating coin, but nonetheless they are a vital part of numismatic history.

A gathering of Mint staff celebrating Frank Gasparro's 70th birthday, August 1979. All of the Philadelphia Mint's engravers are present. Gasparro is standing fourth from the left, in jacket and tie. Matthew Peloso is second from the left; Michael Iacocco stands behind him. Sherl Winter is the mustachioed man in the back, center. In the necktie, directly above the portrait of John Wayne, is Philip Fowler; in the back, behind him, is Edgar Steever. John Mercanti stands at far right.

Many years later, in 2003, the Mint would launch its Artistic Infusion Program. The program is composed of two categories of artists: master designers and associate designers. At the start of the program there was another category, for student artists, but it was discontinued a few years later.

The purpose of the program is to add to the Mint's design portfolio artists with unique and varied disciplines such as illustrating, painting, and sculpture. As of this writing, it has proven to be highly successful, and from the program have emerged some of the best designers in the country.

The design process evolved into an in-house competition that still exists today. There were times, but very infrequently, when an engraver would be assigned to develop a design for a specific program. I, as chief engraver, did at times delegate a specific engraver to work on an obverse or reverse design, or a particular program, especially if I felt his or her talents and strengths lent themselves to that project.

In the past, under the management of Frank Gasparro and chief engravers before him, it was extremely hard for a staff engraver to have his design selected for any coin. (I say *his* because in those days the staff was all male.) The chief engraver had first pick at every program. That was just the way the system ran: it was a hierarchy, with the chief engraver at the top. You either accepted it or you moved on—and yes, there were a few engravers who were very unhappy with the situation and moved on very quickly. If the staff were lucky, they might be assigned a reverse design. This is a fact that is easily documented by checking the Mint medal catalog. The majority of significant programs were designed and sculpted by chief engravers.

I particularly remember designing for the J. Edgar Hoover medal. Frank Gasparro called a staff meeting advising us that he was designing and sculpting the obverse and that we, the staff, would be graced by being allowed to submit reverse designs. (The Hoover reverse was

Frank Gasparro autographing a photo of his Susan B. Anthony dollar design at the coin's launch, February 2, 1979.

the first of my designs selected for a production medal.) This was the same procedure Gasparro used for presidential medals.

This system ultimately began evolving into something different. In time it was requested that engravers submit designs for both obverses and reverses of coins and medal programs. We were generally allotted two weeks to submit several obverse designs and another two weeks for reverse designs. I'm not sure what precipitated this change, but I feel the Mint wanted to begin using the diversity of its in-house talent. In my early years with the Mint, the mid-1970's and early 1980's, I had the privilege of working with some of the most talented sculptors and numismatic artists in the country, and it was great to see that they were getting a chance to display their talents.

Designing a Coin or Medal

There are many factors related to design that go into the production of a coin or medal. As examples: The relationship of elements working in harmony with each other. The attitude of the subject or main element. Is the figure looking in the right direction? Is the pose conveying the necessary message? Or the flow of the text: Does the text intersect or overlap the main or secondary elements? Will the text run over or under, around or through, any of the elements?

The sum of all these factors is what makes an artistically pleasing design and, ultimately, sculpture.

In my experience there are designers, good designers, and great designers. I've worked with them all. Some would answer the design questions and meet the criteria above and consider the final product adequate. Others had and still have a certain passion in them—that passion that prohibits satisfaction with a product until the day of the deadline is upon them and designs are due. They constantly tweak, searching for perfection.

John Mercanti working on the reverse of the J. Edgar Hoover medal, around 1975.

Any form of art is a lifestyle. You can't leave it after eight or ten hours. It stays with you, it is you and who you are. You're a painter, a sculptor, a designer, a potter. Whatever form of art you practice, you live it and breathe it. It's who you are as a person. It's your identity.

I've had members of my staff tell me that an idea for a particular program came to them in the shower, or that in the middle of the night they had a dream with a design resolution. It's a passion and a fire in your soul that's never extinguished.

A portrait of Frank Gasparro, sculpted by John Mercanti.

Elements of Good Design

The following are a few examples of what I consider good coin and medal designs. I have not included any of my own work in these examples. Please understand that these are my personal opinions based on nearly 50 years of work in the industry, and might not reflect the opinions of numismatic writers and scholars. They may completely disagree with me; I'm okay with that. Let's get started:

The **Liberty Cap half cent coins of 1793 and 1794** to me are the perfect example of Primitive American Folk Art. They beautifully display simplicity and balance. The artwork on the obverse and reverse is simply rendered with no extraneous detail and is a delight to behold.

The original **1913 Buffalo nickel**. Most people don't know that the original artwork is only a little over four inches in diameter. The coin is perfectly designed to scale. The size of the portrait and the buffalo beautifully fill the basin, and the design is instantly readable. It's the perfect coin.

The **Little Rock Central High School Desegregation commemorative** obverse. This coin was designed by Richard Masters, who worked with me as an AIP (Artistic Infusion Program) designer. When Rick first submitted his initial drafts they were completely different from the winning design. There were full figures, with readable faces. We didn't want to be person-specific; the figures had to be generic. After a few rounds I suggested that Rick submit a draft showing figures from the waist down only. He did, and the final design eventually evolved. This coin received a COTY (Coin of the Year) award and I'm extremely proud of what Rick accomplished.

1999 George Washington Death Bicentennial $5 gold commemorative, by Laura Gardin Fraser. This design, to me, should have been the 1932 quarter dollar. It won the competition but it was deemed unworthy maybe because it was designed by a woman. It is, in my opinion, far superior to the selected design submitted by John Flanagan. Fraser's is a far better rendered portrait. It's more powerful and fills the basin better. Her reverse is more heraldic and powerful. Flanagan's eagle has no strength and resembles a pigeon. The injustice that her design was not selected irritates me to this day.

The **Congressional Gold Medal commemorating the Dalai Lama**. The obverse is a beautiful portrait designed and rendered by Don Everhart. Don was my second-in-command and could model a portrait faster than anyone I ever knew. He is also one of the premier medallic artists in the industry. This is a wonderfully balanced piece. The simplicity of the reverse perfectly reflects the simple life of the Dalai Lama. It was rendered by staff sculptor, and now chief engraver, Joseph Menna.

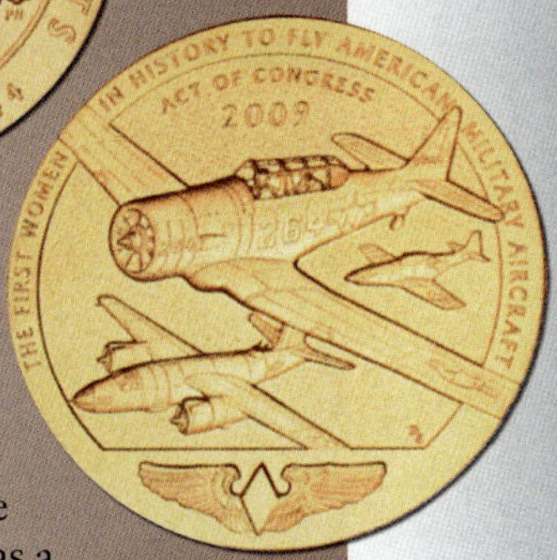

The **commemorative gold medal honoring Women Airforce Service Pilots (WASP)**. The obverse was designed by Joel Iskowitz (of the Artistic Infusion Program) and rendered by Mint staff sculptor Phebe Hemphill. Since being selected as an AIP designer, Joel has evolved into one of the best designers in the program. He has had many designs selected for coins and medals and I'm happy to have had the privilege of working with him. Phebe's execution of the clay model, the sensitivity in the way she's rendered the portrait and the figures, is breathtakingly beautiful. As far as low-relief sculpture goes, Phebe is the twenty-first-century John Sinnock. There's no one better. Once I saw Phebe's work, I knew immediately I wanted her on the Mint's staff. I stole her from McFarlane Toys, where she was a staff sculptor, and to this day have no regrets about it. Don Everhart's perfectly balanced reverse design beautifully describes the story of the WASP fliers.

Design Selection

Let's now turn to design selection.

Before 2003, when the Citizens Coinage Advisory Committee was formed, all designs were vetted in-house at the Mint. Included in the evaluation process were representatives from sales and marketing and the legal department, the Mint director, and his or her associates.

Any form of design evaluation, be it in-house or by committee, can be, for want of a better word, challenging. In my personal experience with committees, people are appointed to serve who generally don't have the full depth of experience to make a sound design decision, because they come from various backgrounds and occupations not related to the arts. Lawyers, doctors, accountants, coin collectors. They lack the eye and background of the designer—although that doesn't mean they don't have the passion to produce the best product possible. A great deal of diplomacy is required in officiating these meetings.

Once the designs were selected, they would be forwarded to the U.S. Commission of Fine Arts in Washington. The CFA is a federal commission made up of representatives from various sectors of the arts. They're responsible for overseeing, evaluating, and approving everything in the federal government related to art and architecture. Nothing that has anything to do with the federal government (outside of some areas managed by the Architect of the Capitol) gets built, issued, sculpted, or painted unless it's first reviewed, modified, and finally approved by this committee. For coins and medals, they submit formal recommendations to the secretary of the Treasury. The Commission of Fine Arts is chaired by the best and brightest in the country.

Once all committee recommendations, modifications, and redraws were approved, modeling could begin.

With any coin or medal program, the process begins with legislation. The American Silver Eagle program was no exception. The law as written stated that the coin would have a design symbolic of Liberty on the obverse and an eagle on the reverse. Such instructions, as written in coinage laws, can be more or less ambiguous and not always well defined. This of course leaves many options for the designers in their interpretations of design elements.

The Citizens Coinage Advisory Committee

The CCAC was established by Congress in 2003, under Public Law 108-15, to advise the secretary of the Treasury on the themes and designs of all U.S. coins and medals. This includes circulating coinage, commemoratives, bullion, Congressional Gold Medals, and national and other medals. The committee advises on the events, persons, and places to be honored by the issuance of commemorative coins, and makes recommendations with respect to their mintage levels. It serves as an informed, experienced, and impartial resource to the secretary of the Treasury and represents the interests of American citizens and coin collectors. CCAC meetings are public. Minutes and letters are submitted to the secretary of the Treasury after each gathering, and an annual report is sent to Congress. More information is available online at ccac.gov.

The design process for the American Silver Eagle program began immediately after the staff completed designs for the Statue of Liberty–Ellis Island coins. As I think back, we may have worked on both programs simultaneously, since both were attached to the same legislation with the same issue date.

As fate would have it, my designs were selected for the Statue of Liberty–Ellis Island silver dollar obverse and reverse. This was an honor I never expected. My grandparents came to this country as immigrants from Sicily early in the twentieth century, and it made me proud that I could honor them with this coin.

Not every coin design makes its way into final production, of course—not even if its artist is the Mint's chief engraver. Frank Gasparro's favorite design was his 1977 proposal for a small-diameter dollar coin, featuring a rendition of Miss Liberty. The design was not used because Congress mandated that the coin portray American women's rights leader Susan B. Anthony. This bronzed plaster of Gasparro's Liberty is in the archives of the National Numismatic Collection in the Smithsonian Institution—a reminder of "what might have been."

The U.S. Commission of Fine Arts

The Commission of Fine Arts, established in 1910 by Act of Congress, is charged with giving expert advice to the president, Congress, and the heads of departments and agencies of the federal and District of Columbia governments on matters of design and aesthetics, "as they affect the federal interest and preserve the dignity of the nation's capital," per the Commission's official literature. The Commission consists of seven "well qualified judges of the fine arts" who are appointed by the president and serve for a term of four years; they may also be reappointed.

The Commission advises the U.S. Mint on the design of coins and medals, in accordance with Executive Order 3524 (of July 1921). Its members review sketches such as the ones pictured here, developed for the Filipino Veterans of World War II Congressional Gold Medal.

The Liberty Coin Act

The Liberty Coin Act was tacked onto the 1985 legislation that authorized the Statue of Liberty commemorative coins. With this act, the American Silver Eagle was written into law.

Title II — LIBERTY COINS[3]

Sec. 201. Short Title.

This title may be cited as the "Liberty Coin Act."

Sec. 202. Minting of Silver Coins.

Section 5112 of title 31, United States Code, is amended by striking out subsections (e) and (f) and inserting in lieu thereof the following new subsections:

(e) Notwithstanding any other provision of law, the Secretary shall mint and issue, in quantities sufficient to meet public demand, coins which—

(1) are 40.6 millimeters in diameter and weigh 31.103 grams;

(2) contain .999 fine silver;

(3) have a design—

(A) symbolic of Liberty on the obverse side; and

(B) of an eagle on the reverse side;

(4) have inscriptions of the year of minting or issuance, and the words 'Liberty,' 'In God We Trust,' 'United States of America,' '1 Oz. Fine Silver,' 'E Pluribus Unum,' and 'One Dollar'; and

(5) have reeded edges.

(f) The Secretary shall sell the coins minted under subsection (e) to the public at a price equal to the market value of the bullion at the time of sale, plus the cost of minting, marketing, and distributing such coins (including labor, materials, dyes [*sic*], use of machinery, and overhead expenses).

(g) For purposes of section 5132(a)(1) of this title, all coins minted under subsection (e) of this section shall be considered to be numismatic items.

(h) The coins issued under this title shall be legal tender as provided in section 5103 of title 31, United States Code.

Sec. 203. Purchase of Silver.

Section 5116(b) of title 31, United States Code, is amended—

(1) in the first sentence of paragraph (1), by striking out "The Secretary shall" and inserting in lieu thereof "The Secretary may";

(2) by striking out the second sentence of paragraph (1); and

(3) by inserting after the first sentence of paragraph (2) the following new sentence: "The Secretary shall obtain the silver for the coins authorized under section 5112(e) of this title by purchase from stockpiles established under the Strategic and Critical Materials Stock Piling Act (50 U.S.C. 98 et seq.)."

Sec. 204. Conforming Amendment.

The third sentence of section 5132(a)(1) of title 31, United States Code, is amended by inserting "minted under section 5112(a) of this title" after "proof coins."

Sec. 205. Effective Date.

This title shall take effect on October 1, 1985, except that no coins may be issued or sold under subsection (e) of section 5112 of title 31, United States Code, before September 1, 1986, or before the date on which all coins minted under title I of this Act have been sold, whichever is earlier.

Approved July 9, 1985.

The Statue of Liberty commemorative silver dollar has special significance to the families of immigrants. John Mercanti's paternal grandparents (seen here on their wedding day) came to the United States in the early 1900's. Also pictured: his grandmother and mother.

Design and Preparation of the American Silver Eagle Obverse and Reverse

Preparation of the Obverse

The obverse design of the American Silver Eagle was predetermined: it would be Adolph A. Weinman's Walking Liberty, originally issued on the half dollar in 1916 and in production until 1947. I have no idea who made that decision. It could have come from the Mint director, from sales and marketing, or from someone lobbying for it.

What the average collector may not know, but the numismatic scholar does, is that the master plaster for the Weinman Walking Liberty obverse is only six inches in diameter. When you consider the amount of fine detail of the piece and its sculptural beauty, you appreciate the skill and knowledge required to achieve what Weinman did on such a scale. The final product is an absolute masterpiece.

There were some technical problems that had to be addressed. At that period in time, when a medallic sculptor modeled a coin in clay, the basin (a concave plaster model that the sculptor models the portraits, figures, text, or various other elements on) was made by hand. I know this because in my formative years at the Mint I was required to make them, in various sizes from three inches to twelve inches. The process was simple but not so easy. It went something like this:

I had a metal ellipse guide that was half the diameter of a circle, made so that it had a cylindrical vertical rod about an eighth of an inch in diameter ground to a point at the end.

Adolph A. Weinman

Adolph Alexander Weinman was born in Karlsruhe, in the German grand duchy of Baden, on December 11, 1870. He came to the United States at the age of 10, and at 15 he attended evening classes at Cooper Union in Manhattan's East Village. Later he studied at the Art Students League of New York under renowned sculptors Augustus Saint-Gaudens and Philip Martiny. The young artist served as an assistant to Charles Niehaus, Olin Warner, and Daniel Chester French before opening his own studio in 1904. Weinman was a talented and in-demand creator of architectural and monumental works, with many important large sculptures to his credit—but he is perhaps best known for his smaller-sized artistry on medals and coins. His personifications of American Liberty were minted on billions of silver dimes and half dollars from 1916 into the late 1940's.

The curve of the arc on the ellipse guide was lower on the end where the vertical bar was than on the opposite end (which would eventually be what is known as the inside diameter of the coin; in numismatic technical circles this is referred to as the ID).

On a 14-inch-square piece of wood with a hole drilled in the center, I would build up a one-inch mound of Plastaline oil-based clay. Then I would rake the top of the clay so that it was as flat and even across the top surface as I could make it.

I would then roughly cut an 11-inch-diameter circle around the outside of the clay using a circle compass with a long arm, from the center of the board where the hole was drilled. At this point I had a circular mound of clay approximately one inch thick on the wooden board, with a center hole.

I would then take the ellipse guide, center it over a predetermined center point of the clay, insert the pointed rod through the clay and into the hole in the board, and begin swinging it around, scraping the clay as I swiped. I kept at this until I had formed a concave basin in the clay three-eighths to one-half inch thick, depending on the curvature of the ellipse guide.

Once this was completed I placed a metal band around the concave clay basin, fastened it, and poured plaster over it. After the plaster had dried it was separated, exposing a convex negative model. This model was then sanded and smoothed and refined, creating what was believed to be a smooth negative basin. It was then put on a lathe and trued up to the best of our abilities.

If, in fact, measurements were then taken North, South, East, and West on that basin, you probably would have found variations in measurements as great as 30 or 40 thousandths of an inch. In the world of minting, thousandths of an inch are mountains—and at that time, trying to achieve a true basin (one that was even on all four axes, North, South, East, and West) was virtually impossible. We would get close but we could never achieve a true basin. Later on we manufactured ellipse guides that were half the diameter of a circle and mounted them on lathes to true up the convex negative models, but even that did not make a perfect basin because they had to be touched up by hand—and once you sand a plaster basin by hand it's virtually impossible to true up.

Sculptors Adolph A. Weinman (front left) and Charles Keck (seated, front, in vest) pose with artists and a model, possibly at the Art Students League of New York, circa 1897.

Weinman's Walking Liberty

"The winner of the 1916 design contest for a new half dollar was A.A. Weinman, also the winner of the competition for the dime," numismatic historians Ron Guth and Jeff Garrett write in *United States Coinage: A Study by Type*. "The grace and beauty of Weinman's half dollar design makes it one of the most popular of all American types." These beautiful coins were minted from 1916 through 1947 (except for some years during the Great Depression), at the Philadelphia, Denver, and San Francisco mints.

The coin debuted at a time when Europe was at battle. Great Britain, France, and their allies were fighting the German and Austrian empires and the other Central Powers. The United States had not yet declared war (we would remain neutral until April 1917). Weinman's imagery captures some of the spirit of the era: Miss Liberty is proudly draped in the American flag, walking toward the rising sun and holding a bouquet of laurel and oak—symbolic of civil and military glory. Her outstretched hand represents the bestowal of freedom. At the same time, the American eagle strikes a defiant pose, apparently ready to do battle if necessary. The secretary of the Treasury, William Gibbs McAdoo, described the coin thus: "The design of the half dollar bears a full-length figure of Liberty, the folds of the Stars and Stripes flying to the breeze as a background, progressing in full stride toward the dawn of a new day. . . . The reverse of the half dollar shows an eagle perched high upon a mountain crag, his wings unfolded, fearless in spirit and conscious of his power. Springing from a rift in the rock is a sapling of mountain pine, symbolical of America."[4]

Adolph A. Weinman, designer of the Walking Liberty half dollar, at work in his studio (below, from *Mehl's Numismatic Monthly*, March 1917) and (left) later in life.

Guth and Garrett note some technical challenges caused by the design: "Strike is always an issue with this type, especially for those coins struck at the San Francisco Mint. The highest point on the obverse is Liberty's hand; the highest point on the reverse is the eagle's chest and foreleg. Unfortunately, these points oppose each other directly, making it very difficult for metal to flow into the deepest recesses of not one, but two dies. Thus, many of the San Francisco Mint issues, because they were struck with insufficient pressure, looked worn the moment they fell from the dies."[5]

Despite any mechanical troubles in the minting process, Weinman's work stands as a triumph of American numismatics. Art historian Cornelius Vermeule calls it "one of the greatest coins of the United States," noting its "surfaces are formal, like a well-carved marble or precisely cast bronze relief for a war memorial," the detail of the eagle's feathers "is a miraculous coup de force," and as a whole the coin has a "combination of naturalism, classicism, and dignified inner balance, a generally suave figure style in the midst of traditional poses, costumes, and attributes."[6]

Perfect basins would come much later, with the introduction of digital technology. But more about that later.

The basin is critical in the production of a coin. It determines the path where the metal will flow under pressure. If the basin is too deep, the metal won't flow to the edge and fill the cavities of the peripheral design elements (for example, the text). If it's too shallow, or less deep, then the elements on the periphery will fill too soon and the main element in the center of the coin will not fill properly. The harder you strike the coin to get the center element to fill, the more metal will flow to the edge, and you risk getting what's called a fin. A fin is when the metal has no place to go and squeezes out around the die above the top shelf of the coin.

Chief Engraver Gilroy Roberts working on the Kennedy half dollar.

As far as basins go, I particularly remember the John F. Kennedy half dollar. Gilroy Roberts first made the clay basin, but did not cast it. He began modeling the portrait on the clay basin, and once the portrait was complete he cast them both as one. I wasn't at the Mint at the time but I've seen the model in the Mint's vault.

When the half dollar was minted it became a problem getting the top of Kennedy's head and the hair to form properly because the basin was too deep where his head met the border. I worked on the top of Kennedy's head (as did every engraver at one time or another), scraping away the detail of the hair and then recutting it at a lower relief in order to get it to fill properly. Then I made a negative model and adjusted the basin.

Gilroy Roberts's obverse design for the John F. Kennedy half dollar.

You can tell after a few setup strikes whether the metal is flowing properly and there is even metal flow all around the coin.

Coin dies typically are processed with two or three alternative basins and tested in pretrial strikes to determine which die, with which basin, gives the best fill so that all elements are clear.

For the first few years of American Silver Eagle production, Weinman's obverse Walking Liberty was used without any modifications, and there were what is referred to in the industry as "fill problems" related to modeling and basin issues. Also, the cry from headquarters was, "We need to see more detail."

There is something in sculpture referred to as "lost and found." This means that you don't have to model all the detail on a piece. All you need to do is create the impression or illusion of an element.

I've never personally been a proponent of going back over a classic model and sharpening the detail. This was how and why John Flanagan's beautiful original obverse quarter portrait (of George Washington) was later referred to as the "Spaghetti Hair." Someone made the determination that they wanted to see every hair on Washington's head.

John Flanagan's portrait of George Washington: the original (top), and the modified "Spaghetti Hair" version, redesigned for use on the Mint's State quarters starting in 1999.

Nonetheless, detail modifications were made to Weinman's model by defining all the stars in the flag, the oak leaves, the lines in Miss Liberty's skirt, and her sandals, so that everything was as clear as we could make it at that scale.

Production was begun and dies were cut. Unfortunately, the modification hadn't been enough to get the level of detail requested.

Because we were working with six-inch models for both the obverse and reverse, and because we were still using Janvier reducing machines and hadn't yet moved into the digital arena, the artwork was too small for the tracing stylus to get into small areas of the model to pick up fine detail.

Our only option was to enlarge the original model.

The problem with the Janvier machine is that it's made for reducing, not enlarging. It will create a perfect reduction if the ratios are correct and the artwork is large enough for the stylus to get into the finest element to pick up the detail, but when it comes to enlarging, it's a whole different ball game. Enlargements produced on the Janvier machine look like, for want of a better word, "donuts." All the artwork is overblown and blurred because you can't achieve the proper ratios, thereby requiring recutting and redefining all elements of the model. And that's exactly what we had to do to achieve more detail in the master models.

About 10 years or so into production of the American Silver Eagle, we began working with epoxies. Epoxy models were introduced after OSHA deemed it unsafe to use copper or galvano models for Janvier reductions. (Galvanos were the product of electric plating.)

In the older galvano method, first a negative master plaster was made and dried in the oven overnight. The next day, after the model had dried and cooled, it was dusted with copper powder and submerged in a copper electroplating tank filled with active plating fluid. Copper bars hung on one side of the tank and the plaster model (dusted with the copper powder) hung on the opposite side. Copper from the bars found its way to the dusted model and then would adhere to the copper dust and begin to build up.

The model stayed submerged in the electroplating tank for three days, and then it was removed. The plaster was then separated from the copper and you had a positive galvano, which was next cleaned and mounted on the Janvier, where it produced a positive steel reduction.

The problem with galvanos is that you could only use them twice at the most, because copper is soft and the stylus would soften detail. The galvano would be removed from the machine and sent to the engravers for touchup and cleaning (which entailed using files and sandpaper). It was a laborious process that took an inordinate amount of time.

Epoxies, on the other hand, were very easily cast and cleaned, and they could be used three or four times without losing detail. We now could refine the plasters and that refinement was reflected in the epoxy—no touchup required.

In order to increase the size of the American Silver Eagle, we cast two 12-inch blank epoxy models and mounted them onto the Janviers. Tents were constructed around the machines because it was determined that there would be a great amount of dust generated from the cutting process.

A Janvier reducing machine in action.

A hub being engraved for the 2001 Kentucky State quarter.

The models were first cut in epoxy and cast in negative plaster, then recast to finally produce a positive plaster that then could be redefined with detail restored.

In order for me to reproduce the new master, I literally had to counterfeit my own coin. To accomplish this I constructed a grid to fit over the original model, then made another grid proportional to the larger model, laid it over the artwork, and, working in small quadrants, I began to redefine all the lost detail.

It took me about two weeks to finally produce a new larger master model that represented the six-inch original American Silver Eagle reverse. The same was done for the obverse, with another staff engraver restoring detail. Once this was completed, we cut new dies that reflected a visual increase in detail.

This page and following: Note the differences in definition in Miss Liberty's skirt, the flag, and other design details.

This process was used until we transitioned into the digital arena.

I want to take a moment here to clarify something. I've often read numismatic articles, talking about dies going into production, using the phrase "dies were sunk." The proper phrase should be "dies were cut." In the 1970's we did sink dies, but we did it for better fill. Dies are case hardened, which means that they're softer in the middle than they are on the periphery. At that time, when we ran trial strikes prior to production, in some cases we would find that the center element was filling far too fast and the text on the periphery was very light. If tonnage on the press was increased too much we risked the spreading or doubling of the portrait. To clarify: There is a cavity in the center of the die with the portrait. It takes a certain amount of pressure from the press to fill that cavity. If too much pressure is applied then the metal has nowhere to go and begins to back up. A doubling or spread becomes visible around the portrait and related elements within close proximity. All this is taking place and the text on the edge of the coin is still not formed. This is all related to the height of the basin. That means that the convex dome of the die is too high and had to be lowered so that metal would flow more evenly, enabling the coin to form equally across the surface. To remedy this problem we would "sink the die." The die was tempered or softened and placed in a press. A piece of lead or soft steel was placed on top of it and pressure applied. If done correctly, you could drop the basin enough to increase even metal flow. You could also explode the die or crack it. It's not a recommended procedure, but under time constraints it was quicker than going back and making a new reduction. It didn't always work but sometimes it did. If it worked a positive metal hub could be manufactured and from that corrected dies with proper basins could be made for production.

In 2021, along with the introduction of the new Flying Eagle reverse, the Mint would again modify the obverse design of the American Silver Eagle. The main motif would stay, but with certain details tweaked, as illustrated later in this book.

A Sampling of American Eagles

Reverse of Augustin Dupré's 1792 Diplomatic medal, commemorating the Declaration of Independence.

Reverse of the half disme of 1792, possibly engraved by Robert Birch.

Reverse of the Draped Bust, Small Eagle silver dollar, by Robert Scot.

Reverse of the Draped Bust, Heraldic Eagle silver dollar, by Robert Scot.

Reverse of the Capped Bust half dollar, early 1800's, by John Reich.

Reverse of Christian Gobrecht's silver dollar of 1836.

Design and Preparation of the Reverse

Throughout numismatic history the eagle has probably been the one element interpreted and reinterpreted more than any other.

Reverse of the Classic Head half eagle ($5 gold coin) of the 1830's, designed by Christian Gobrecht.

A pattern half dollar, by Gobrecht, 1839.

Reverse of the Liberty Seated dollar (1840's–1870's), by Gobrecht.

Reverse of the trade dollar of the 1870's and 1880's, designed by William Barber.

Reverse of the 1878–1921 silver dollar, designed by George T. Morgan.

Reverse of the quarter dollar of 1892–1916, by Charles E. Barber.

The Mint Act of 1792 stated that the reverse of the first coin would depict an eagle, the national bird of the United States. Since then the eagle has appeared a multitude of times on U.S. coins and medals. Early eagles have a beautiful folk-art look. They're extremely primitive and reflect the artwork of that period.

Reverse of the half eagle of 1908–1929, by Bela Lyon Pratt.

Reverse of the Standing Liberty quarter dollar of 1916–1930, by Hermon A. MacNeil.

Reverse of Adolph A. Weinman's half dollar of 1916–1947.

Reverse of the 1921–1935 Peace silver dollar, designed by Anthony de Francisci.

Reverse of the double eagle ($20 gold coin) of 1907–1933, by Augustus Saint-Gaudens.

Reverse of the 1918 Illinois Centennial half dollar, by John R. Sinnock.

The eagle has been installed on shields, over shields, and around shields. Flying, soaring, sitting perched, holding laurel and holly and arrows, looking left, looking right, and (in the case of my 1991 Mount Rushmore Golden Anniversary $5 gold coin) carrying carving tools to the mountain.

Reverse of the 1921 Alabama Centennial half dollar, by Laura Gardin Fraser.

Reverse of the Washington quarter dollar (1932–1998), by John Flanagan.

"What might have been": a study for the reverse of the Washington quarter, by John Flanagan.

Obverse of the 1934–1938 Texas Independence Centennial half dollar, by Pompeo Coppini.

Obverse of the 1935 Connecticut Tercentenary half dollar, by Henry G. Kreis.

Reverse of the 1936 Bridgeport, Connecticut, Centennial half dollar, by Kreis.

I didn't want a flying eagle for the American Silver Eagle coin. I didn't go in the direction of soaring eagles with sun rays behind them because it had been done so many times before. I wanted something more formal, more heraldic.

As I think back on the program, I may have submitted an eagle in flight. The drawings are gone and probably lost forever.

Just a bit of an aside: Many years ago I noticed that drawings that I and the staff were submitting to headquarters were never being returned to the Philadelphia engraving office. One day when I was down in Washington on business I inquired to someone about the problem. They took me aside and quietly whispered in my ear that someday we might be famous and the originals would fetch a good price from collectors, so they were keeping them aside. Needless to say, they never received an original from me after that. This happened at the beginning of my career and since then things have changed dramatically; I know that all our original drawings are now on file where they should be. (Today there are no "original drawings," so to speak; all drawings are produced on computer using Photoshop and Illustrator.)

I submitted two variations of the eagle that ultimately was produced. The first was as it appears on the coin today: formal, facing forward with wings spread wide, 13 stars in a reversed triangle over the eagle's head. This was always my favorite. The second version was the same pose but the eagle was turned slightly to the right, giving it a little perspective.

A sketch for the American Silver Eagle reverse—very close to the design ultimately chosen for the coin.

A related sketch, with the heraldic eagle turned slightly to the viewer's right.

Another sketch, with the legends moved around.

I don't recall how long we had to work on the American Silver Eagle designs. I would say that, because of the extremely tight deadline, we were allotted no longer than two weeks for finished designs to be submitted.

After completing the designs, the established protocol was followed and they were sent to headquarters for review and modification requests. I was notified that my formal design with the eagle facing forward was selected with no modifications and that I should proceed with generating a model for production.

Knowing that the Weinman obverse was six inches required that I make my model the same size, so that we would get the same quality on both sides when we made the Janvier reductions. It was no easy task modeling something so intricate at that scale. It took about two weeks. Dies were then produced and cleaned, and we went into production.

A model of the American Silver Eagle reverse (cropped).

John Mercanti at work on a large model of the American Silver Eagle reverse.

Engraving, Die Preparation, and Cleaning

After Frank Gasparro left the Mint in 1981 I was, at that time, the last hand engraver on staff. (In more recent years there were two steel-die engravers on staff, also highly skilled at hand-engraving, who cleaned all production-coinage dies.)

The Mint staff in the early 1970's did a large amount of hand engraving directly on medals, where we would engrave the recipient's name. We engraved on bronze, silver, and gold. Not an easy skill to master, but once you do it's extremely rewarding.

Unbeknownst to most, metal is like clay. It can be moved. Holes can be filled and errors can be corrected, if not too severe. These corrections are made with various punches. There's much tapping, a lot of metal movement, and a fair amount of sanding.

Frank Gasparro, in a relief medallion by Michael Iacocca.

If a particular program would require the staff to engrave medals, we would first mount them in nests on engraver's vises. The room was always quiet. It took all our concentration to manipulate the vise and swing the graver. Our tools were extremely sharp, and in the process of engraving a particular recipient's name on a medal the tools would dull to some degree and would have to be resharpened. Silver wasn't too bad; we might be able to get through the whole name without retouching the tool. But gold was another story. Gold dulls the tool very quickly and it requires an inordinate amount of redressing. We would try to get the most out of a tool before we redressed, and that's where we ran into trouble.

The U.S. Mint's engravers, early in John Mercanti's career: Frank Gasparro, Matthew Peloso, Philip Fowler, Sherl Winter, Mercanti, Edgar Steever, and Michael Iacocca.

Periods when the staff had projects that required hand engraving were the few times that there was no levity in the department. This was serious business. No papers rattling, no music or eating. Just focusing on the job at hand. The office was as quiet as a tomb. We might be working for a half hour or so, feeling that we were getting through the program with no problems, when we'd hear "@#%&*!" Then tap, tap, tap, tap, as the perpetrator of the error tried desperately to correct his mistake. It might take longer to fix the problem than it took to carve the recipient's name. The quantity of medals was limited, especially if they were gold; only so many would be struck.

Every member of the staff made an error cut at one time or another. It was part of the job.

Then there's die cleaning. It took me about six months to really become proficient at die cleaning. It entailed using a sharp Arkansas stone and various paste abrasives to clean off all the concentric circles left on the artwork from the Janvier reduction process. It took a delicate touch not to obliterate fine detail. I must have gone through a hundred condemned practice dies before I began to pick it up.

Condemned dies are dies of all denominations and programs that are inspected and for some reason or another are not fit to go into production. Any number of things could be wrong with them: they might have gouges or scratches; there could be doubling. They're set aside and ultimately destroyed. I would regularly use them to practice on.

There was a gentleman who was in charge of the die shop during my formative years by the name of John Nicolardi—a man of medium build, and very powerful from years of moving heavy metal around. His voice would echo from one end of the die shop to another. You knew when John was upset. He was also a demanding taskmaster. Every production die went through his office to be checked and inspected.

One day John said to me that it was time I start cleaning production dies and stop playing around with condemned dies, which up to that time I had been practicing on. He reached into a box of obverse dime dies, took one out, handed it to me, and said, "Clean it and don't mess it up."

This was the moment I'd been training for up to that point.

I took the die back to my desk and inserted it in the engraver's vise, secured it, and with my hands shaking began to clean it with a stone and abrasives. When I reached a point that I thought it was cleaned I returned to John, who took it to an inspection station and looked at it under a microscope.

A Mint technician inspecting a die for quality.

He rotated the die around, tilted it for a different light source, looked up at me over the eyepieces, and bellowed, "Not good enough! Take it back and work on it some more."

This went on for I don't know how many times—and for how many dies—until my skills improved and I developed more confidence. What I was really trying to achieve was John's approval. I knew that if he was satisfied with my cleaning skills, I could clean anything that came across my desk. He taught me the proper methods and techniques used in die cleaning. He taught me what abrasives to use and how to use them. Under him I became proficient. He was one of my early mentors who I'll always be indebted to.

All the silver bullion dies that were cut on the Janvier had to be hand cleaned. This is the case even today, in the era of digital technology. All dies are hand cleaned but in today's world they don't need to be cleaned as extensively as in the past. Digital technology produces a far better reduction than we had in the era of the Janviers.

The American Silver Eagle obverse and reverse have an enormous amount of detail and required an extensive amount of cleaning.

Another problem with the Janvier machines was repeatability. In a program like the American Silver Eagle it was extremely hard to get multiple reductions that were exactly the same. Every time you set up the artwork it was a little different. Measurements always varied slightly. Sometimes there were considerable variations. Heights of relief might differ. Basin measurements might vary. This all had to do with the fact that every machine was unique. Each machine was an assemblage of levers and pulleys that had to be coordinated just right, and reduction ratios had to be established; consequently, the final product generated on every machine was slightly different to some degree, in every case.

Our transfer engravers (the men in charge of operating the Janvier machines and producing the steel reductions that ultimately would generate the tooling to create the product) were constantly performing maintenance and tweaking. It was a never-ending job. These men are the unsung heroes of numismatics. They're required to produce tooling that replicates all the detail the designer/sculptor has put into the master model—no easy task then or now, I assure you. It requires one of the highest skill levels in the process, especially today with computer technology and the complex programs that are required to generate cutter paths for the machines that make the final product. There is a great debt owed to every one of them.

Both sides of the American Silver Eagle are intricately detailed, which requires frequent and careful cleaning of the dies.

Digital Technology

As I begin this section I want to make clear that the events I describe may not have occurred exactly in the sequence I relate. To the best of my recollections this is what happened.

On or around the year 2003, under the directorship of Henrietta Holsman Fore, there suddenly appeared in the Mint a young engineer by the name of Steve Antonucci. I would go into the chief engraver's office and see Steve working on his laptop, not really knowing what his official capacity was. He was on board for weeks before I even had a proper introduction. Little did I know how he would ultimately change the face of numismatics in the Mint as far as die production, preparation, and Proof polishing were concerned.

Steve had been hired by headquarters as a private contractor to begin the transition from the standard drawing, modeling, and reduction process to digital technology. This was not going to be easy. There was a great amount of resistance—from older members of the staff and a few individuals who couldn't see the benefits of digital technology—but the decision had been made, and in spite of the pushback we were resolved to move forward.

My immediate supervisor gave me a mandate, in jest: "Those machines will go to the Smithsonian or you will." That pretty much sealed the fate of the Janviers as far as I was concerned.

They had to go.

As an organization, we were increasing our workload every year. Congress was approving more programs than ever. There was our normal circulation-coin workload that consisted of date changes for all denominations, and the ever-increasing commemorative and medal programs. To accomplish all of this we were still using nineteenth-century technology. We were modeling by hand on old plaster basins and still producing reductions on Janvier machines.

A major problem with the Janvier was that you were never guaranteed a good-quality reduction on the first go-round. There were times the transfer engravers had to make as many as 20 reductions before they had tooling that was good enough to forward to the engravers for cleaning. That certainly would not suffice in this new age.

Something had to be done.

One of our Mint engineers, Barry Claybrook, had been to a show on machine tooling and he saw milling machines that he thought could be used in the coining process. He returned to headquarters and pitched his idea, and this was the genesis that ultimately led us into the digital age.

We had an old Bostomatic milling machine in storage at our Denver mint, and we decided to bring it to Philadelphia for testing. The machine had been sitting in storage out in Denver for a number of years. It wasn't the newest technology and getting parts to refurbish it would be a problem. We had it shipped to Philadelphia and it was eventually brought online. Parts were obtained wherever possible or manufactured in-house.

In the early 2000's the U.S. Mint's workload was growing. The number of regular circulating coins, new State quarters, commemoratives, and medals added to the pressure to move to digital technology.

We determined that the Mint director's medal for Henrietta Holsman Fore would be a good project to move forward with digitally. An outside sculptor working in the toy industry was contracted to model the design in virtual reality. It was a slow, tedious process, but he eventually produced a decent digital model that we could move forward with. Our engineers took everything they learned from that process and built on it. The organization had jumped from the nineteenth century to the twenty-first and didn't look back.

The Mint director's medal for Henrietta Holsman Fore.

Once I saw what our engineers had accomplished with the Fore medal I wanted to do something with coinage dies. I asked Steve if, with his milling machine, he could cut in a mintmark on a master die. He looked at me from across my desk where he was sitting and said, "John, I could do this."

We went to the die vault, where I gave him a 50-cent master die. He did the programming and made all the necessary calculations, and the next day I had on my desk a master die with a digitally cut mintmark. I don't recall whether it was an S or a D. It doesn't matter. That small mintmark was the longest leap we had taken so far in digital coinage production. We had replicated something that we were using in production, and it was good enough to move forward with.

Up to that time all mintmarks had been struck by hand. As an example: If we were producing Denver dies, the die shop would bring me a soft master die without a mintmark. I would secure it in the engraver's vise and hand-punch a D into it. The mintmark could only be within a pre-established area of the die. It also had to be vertical with the date. Every engraver had a set of drawings with described tolerances that showed mintmark locations—and God forbid you struck the mintmark out of the specific locations.

The die would then be cleaned, sent to the furnaces for hardening, and re-cleaned, then a production hub would be struck. That in turn would be used to produce Denver production dies.

I was the only engraver on staff who had experience mintmarking dies, and until we moved into digital technology I would still be called on periodically to mintmark a die for production.

Making sure the punch was vertical and in the right location was not an easy task, especially if the task wasn't performed every day. I remember in the late 1970's, when we were still mintmarking dies by hand, it could take all morning to complete the process. Every morning the die shop would roll in to the engraving studio, carts piled high with boxes of dies, 25 dies in a box, all denominations, cents, nickels, dimes, quarters, and half dollars. On some mornings there might be as many as 50 boxes waiting to be mintmarked. These took priority over all other work. The die shop needed these dies mintmarked ASAP so that they could meet their production schedules.

After a number of months mintmark punches would wear or, in most cases, break. New ones had to be made, and they were all made by hand. We took the existing mintmark and made a matrix. A flat piece of soft steel about a half-inch thick with the mintmark P, D, or S punched into it was hardened. A bar of soft steel about a quarter of an inch square was cut to about a four-inch length. It was then ground to a point on one end. The pointed end was flattened slightly. The matrix was secured into an engraver's vise and the four-inch soft ground steel bar was positioned vertically over the secured matrix and the selected mintmark. The bar was then lightly punched, creating a soft

These photographs illustrate the potential variation in mintmark locations—within certain tolerances.

image of the mintmark on the tip. The bar was then placed into the vise and the image of the letter was gently nursed out using files, gravers, and abrasives. The bar might be punched into the matrix three or more times and reworked to obtain an image capable of meeting production standards. This process itself could take a week. When the new mintmark was completed, it was sent to heat treating to be hardened.

There were risks in the hardening process. Sometimes the bar would crack in the furnace and the whole process would have to start over. There were times we received a mintmark back from heat treating thinking it was hardened and it wasn't. We'd strike a die and it would collapse. After expending our anger, we'd start the whole process over.

That's why this little task of cutting the mintmark digitally into the die was so important. The engineers knew that if they could locate such a small element on a die and cut it, they could do much more.

This mintmark was an incredible leap forward for us.

Two D (for Denver) mintmarks on Kennedy half dollars—the 1999 made by hand, and the 2009 made digitally.

My supervisor at this time at our headquarters office in Washington, D.C., sent me a website related to digital sculpting. The name of the company was Freeform. They had developed a program and a device that enabled the user to sculpt in virtual reality. At the outset the program lent itself more to industrial design, but we saw the potential and purchased a seat (software access for one user) for about seven or eight thousand dollars. As it turned out, it was just what we needed, and ultimately we would buy almost ten seats.

The problem was the learning curve. We would have to isolate a sculptor and we couldn't at that time afford to take a person offline; our schedule was brutal. Steve confided to me that in order for us to make any headway we would either have to train someone on staff or find a digital sculptor. The decision was made to find one, and he did. He found a young sculptor by the name of Joseph Menna, who was working at the Johnson Atelier in Princeton, New Jersey. He joined the Mint's staff in 2005.

As it turned out, Joe was just what the doctor ordered. He was classically trained in sculpture here in America and studied for some years in Russia, where he met his wife. He had been working at the Johnson Atelier using the technology for some time. He became a teacher and a mentor to the Mint's staff in everything related to digital sculpting. I nicknamed him the "Yoda" of the new technology.

Freeform and the related programs we used for modeling are geometric modeling disciplines. Joe knew his way around them better than anyone. We isolated him and allowed him to experiment with various programs. Eventually he was modeling portraits in virtual reality. His knowledge, inquisitiveness, and ability to adapt and utilize multiple programs ultimately enabled us to move forward. He became the cornerstone of the sculpting department.

I remember one night watching the movie *Shrek* with my grandson and after the movie watching the special features. I saw how they constructed the images of the characters in the film and that they were using programs that Joe had been testing. It looked to me as though these programs could be used for modeling coins and medals.

A sampling of coins designed and sculpted by Joseph Menna.

The next day I called the West Coast, made some inquiries, established connections, and, some weeks later, had an artist who worked with these new sculpting programs come to Philadelphia to work with my staff. We were on our way.

It also became apparent that we couldn't move forward with the Bostomatic milling machine. Originals were not available anymore and parts had to be manufactured, so we started a worldwide search for new state-of-the-art machines.

Non-sensitive data was established by Steve Antonucci, Barry Claybrook, and their crew of technicians. We sent the data out around the world to various companies, who in turn supplied us samples. Our staff of sculptors, engineers, and technicians then evaluated the samples for quality and cleanability. Every sample we received was brought into my office for cleaning. The length of time it took to clean a die just off the milling machine was a major factor, along with the quality of the reduction. With the Janvier machines you had one tool to cut the die. The cutting tool started in the center of the hub and ran in a circular motion out to the edge, producing an image that had concentric circles running throughout. These circles had to be very carefully cleaned off the image using stones and abrasives, producing a final product that was clear, retained all necessary detail, and reflected the intent of the sculptor or designer. Believe me, this is no easy job. As I mentioned earlier, at the beginning of my career I went through hundreds of dies obliterating images and detail.

With digital milling machines a number of tools are used to produce a reduction. All the tool paths are calculated and written by the transfer engravers. Tool paths can be horizontal, vertical, or diagonal. There may be a roughing tool to rough out the artwork . . . a finer tool to cut the portrait . . . and a very fine tool to clean up all imperfections over the finished artwork. Because there are multiple tools, the quality of the final product is far superior to that of the Janvier machines, thereby requiring less cleaning time for the engraver.

We decided on a company by the name of Micron, out of Switzerland. They furnished the best sample that we knew we could improve and build on. Our standards were extremely high. We were fast becoming the world leaders in this technology. Ultimately we purchased six machines.

We proved we could manufacture a medal and in the following weeks produced a few prototype dies, multisided and round, but we now had to advance to the next level, which was to produce a coinage die as good as or better than our standard dies, enabling us to move into digital die production.

Which of our coins would serve as our prototype—the first in the new digital age? As it turned out, the coin selected was the American Silver Eagle.

I must pause here for a moment to describe another tool we obtained that is critical to the process: a digital scanner. It was one of the first components we purchased. The scanner enables the user to scan a product—in this case, plaster artwork—into virtual reality, where it can be manipulated. Elements can be added, subtracted, or altered. A scanner is a vital component in this new age because it enables members of the staff who don't feel comfortable modeling on screen in virtual reality, and who still prefer the tactile feeling of modeling in clay, to continue to model the old way. Once the model is completed it's finished in plaster. A final master cast is produced and then scanned into the computer. Once in the computer, cleanup, texturing, or minor modifications can be made.

Let me divert again for a brief second to explain something: I have grossly simplified the whole digital process in this section. It's not my intent to furnish the reader with a thesis on digital technology. I'm not qualified to do that; Steve Antonucci has already provided it. The same with laser Proof polishing: a gentleman by the name of Ron Collins has written that. Ron was brought in as a contractor and was our guru on laser technology. He worked extremely hard bringing laser Proof polishing online. Developing these processes took an extraordinary amount of time and labor, resulting in long days and late nights and great financial expense.

The programs for the milling machines, laser machines, and developing the artwork are extremely complicated. These are extremely bright and dedicated and talented individuals, and we wouldn't have made the strides we did without them at the helm. On a far simpler level, I'm describing what we're capable of doing with various elements of this new technology.

We scanned the American Silver Eagle plasters into the computer. All the elements were segregated. Separate files were created for the text and the artwork. A new basin was constructed and images adjusted to fit on the new virtual basin. At the time I modeled the original artwork I didn't use a standard alphabet; a font close to the original was used. Ultimately this caused a problem that resulted in the manufacture of an error coin (or, more accurately in numismatic language, a die variety). The letter U in the selected font had a bar on one side and didn't curve around like my original.

Once the new artwork was created in virtual reality, calculations were made for the reductions and they were cut. Eventually dies were struck from the digital reductions and sent to West Point for minting. The year was 2007, and the dies were dated 2008. Both Philadelphia and West Point were instructed to purge their inventory of Janvier-cut dies. Unfortunately, not all the 2007 reverse dies were purged out at West Point. Some still remained in their inventory. They were inadvertently put into the mix at the striking of the 2008 American Silver Eagles and resulted in a number of 2008 coins that had 2007 reverses—a variety that was a boon to the collecting fraternity.

The American Silver Eagle's reverse lettering style of 1986–2007. Note the lack of a spur or stem at the bottom right of the U in UNITED.

The reverse lettering style of 2008 to date. Note the spur at the bottom right of the U.

Laser Proof Polishing

For years Proof polishing has probably been the most labor-intensive element of coin production. Proof polishers would have to tape and cut around all elements of the production die to protect these concave areas from being polished as they worked on the surface of the dies. A good Proof polisher could only produce a small number of dies in a day.

I remember in 1984 attending a chief engravers' conference in Wales. Elizabeth Jones couldn't make it and sent me in her place. One of the stops on the tour of the British Royal Mint was the Proof polishing division. I was astounded to see that they were exclusively using wood tools to accomplish their task—it might take them a day to produce just two Proof polished production dies. True, their production numbers were far below those of the United States, but it was still an extremely long and labor-intensive process. At that time in the United States we used similar methods and techniques; the only difference was that we used electric polishers. Little did we know that there were new processes to come in the world of Proof polishing.

Barry Claybrook found a machine capable of polishing 25 dies at a time to a Proof gloss. It was called a Gerber polisher. A horsehair brush with the aid of abrasives was capable of polishing a box of 25 production dies in minutes. Barry, working together with Ron Collins, eventually developed a process of laser Proof polishing.

In the past, dies selected for Proof polishing were first sandblasted (with sand; later, ceramics were used). The goal of Barry and Ron was to texture the dies with a laser machine, producing a surface that mimicked sandblasting. No easy task, because the laser produced a discernible pattern, and no matter at what angle you viewed it, it still looked like a pattern. With Ron's dedication, hard work, and long hours of experimentation, things began to change and the laser pattern became less detectable. At my retirement at the end of 2010 they were well on their way to producing a scattered pattern that had more of the effect of sand.

American Silver Eagle dies.

The key element in laser Proof polishing is a mask. It is generated from the drawing and model and programmed into the laser. It tells the laser what areas are to be textured on the die and what areas are to be left polished.

Dies prepared for polishing.

A box of 25 dies is first put into the Gerber machine and the dies are polished. They are then taken to the laser, where a technician has a program related to that particular commemorative or denomination. The mask related to that coin is part of that program. The dies are then run through the laser and one by one the dies are textured. They're all exactly alike; repeatability is one of the major benefits of digital technology. The dies may then be touched up by hand if needed.

I hope what I have described in this chapter gives the reader a better understanding not only of the history of the American Silver Eagle, but also what's involved in their production. Also, I hope you will have a better appreciation not only of the beauty of the piece, but also the time and effort that went into creating it.

I had the honor for 36-plus years of working with the most talented and dedicated people in the history of numismatics. I also had the honor of apprenticing under one of the giants in the field, Frank Gasparro. He taught me how to engrave, how to model, and how to design. In my studio today there is a picture of two men who most influenced me in my life. It's Frank and my father standing side by side. I look at it often and think back on all those years, and wonder where the time went. I'll always be grateful to both: one for giving me life, and the other for giving me a career.

In my tenure, we at the Mint literally went from nineteenth-century to twenty-first-century technology. It was an incredible journey. There are no people like Mint people, and to have been a part of that family for all those years is something I will always cherish. I will always remember my first day and my last. They're branded in my soul—as are all the years in between. Someday I hope to tell the story of all those in-between years, the good and the bad. It is my hope, dear reader, that you will want to hear it.

The photograph John Mercanti keeps in his studio, showing his father, Samuel Mercanti (left), and his mentor, Chief Engraver Frank Gasparro.

3

Coin-by-Coin Study of American Silver Eagles

This chapter sets each American Silver Eagle within its historical context and gives collectors an insightful market overview. Each coin is identified by its date, mintmark (if any), and format (i.e., *bullion strike* for the coins produced for bullion sales; or *Proof, Reverse Proof, Burnished,* or *Enhanced Uncirculated* for those formats). Mintages are specified. The mint facilities that produced each coin are noted. Enlarged photographs of each coin are provided, along with relevant close-ups and other related images. The charts include data on how many coins have been certified by NGC in Mint State and Proof conditions up to 70; and values in several conditions.

A note about spotting: White spots have been known to occasionally appear on American Silver Eagles (as they do on other .999 silver coins)—sometimes shortly after minting, sometimes weeks or months later. Not every coin will develop such spots, but they do show up with some frequency, and buyers should be aware of the possibility.

A note about First Strike, Early Release, and similar designations: The U.S. Mint does not have a program or designation for the first or earliest coins struck by a set of dies, or for the coins produced first or earliest in a particular year or series. PCGS and NGC designate American Silver Eagles packaged and delivered by the Mint within 30 days of initial sales as *First Strike* or *Early Release*. The coins must be shipped by their owner to the grading firm postmarked within the cutoff date and in their original sealed packaging. Extra fees apply for certification with these designations. More details can be found online at www.PCGS.com and www.NGCcoin.com.

1986, Bullion Strike

Mintage: 5,393,005

GSID: 10644

Minted at San Francisco, without mintmark

Historical context: In the financial arena of the mid-1980's unwise lending strategies of some banks, and poor oversight of savings and loans institutions, led to turmoil and the closing of many banks.

The debut year of the American Silver Eagle, 1986, was also the year the Professional Coin Grading Service (PCGS) began operation as a third-party grading service. That summer the American Numismatic Association added numbers to its official grading standards (which previously consisted of text descriptions only), including 11 Mint State increments from low-end MS-60 to perfect MS-70. Hobby periodical *Coin World* boasted a circulation of 80,394 subscribers; *COINage* magazine, 60,367; *Numismatic News*, 35,923; and *The Numismatist* (official magazine of the ANA), 33,072. Gold as bullion was priced in the New York market at an average of $368.24 per ounce for the year.

1986 average silver price: $5.47/ounce.

Coin commentary: In its first year of issue a new coin will often be popular with collectors as well as curious members of the general public. The first American Silver Eagle was no exception. The coins were on sale only in the final weeks of 1986, in late November and December, and it took a mintage of more than 5 million to satisfy demand. San Francisco produced the entire coinage for 1986; this was revealed in 2020 (earlier, it was thought that the West Point and Denver mints had assisted with the first year of production). In *Coin World*, October 16, 2020, Paul Gilkes reported: "A United States Mint response to a Freedom of Information Act inquiry on American Eagle silver bullion coin output confirms that all 1986 and 1987 production was executed at the San Francisco Mint. . . . Lee Minshull from Lee Minshull Rare Coins Inc. in Palos Verdes, California, submitted the FOIA inquiry seeking clarification of the mintage information." Some coins have been authenticated as being from the "First Strike" ceremony at the San Francisco Assay Office presided over by Secretary of the Treasury James Baker (see chapter 1).

The popular 1986 bullion strike has remained affordable since its debut.

The coin was ranked no. 84 in the fifth edition of *100 Greatest U.S. Modern Coins* by Schechter and Garrett, who call it "the coin that started it all."

1986-S, Proof

Mintage: 1,446,778

GSID: 10657

Minted at San Francisco, with S mintmark

Coin commentary: The 1986 American Silver Eagle has the highest mintage among Proofs in the series, reflecting collector and investor demand for this first-year-of-issue coin. The 1986 Proof was sold by the Mint for $21. Aftermarket premiums have remained modest over the years. Although more than 1,000 examples have been certified at PF-68 and lower, the discerning collector will seek a higher-grade example.

1987, Bullion Strike

Mintage: 11,442,335

GSID: 10645

Minted at San Francisco, without mintmark

Historical context: 1987 was the first year American Silver Eagles were available for sale from January through December. (The debut issue of 1986 was on sale only in the closing weeks of that year.) The U.S. Mint had awarded a contract to Grey Advertising of New York City to assist in publicizing and marketing the bullion coins, globally as well as in the home market. These efforts were expanded in 1987. Numismatic Guaranty Corporation of America (NGC) was launched as a third-party grading firm this year.

Silver's bullion value peaked above $10 per ounce during 1987 and averaged out to about $7 by year's end. Like silver, gold also averaged higher than it did in 1986—about $80 per ounce higher, at $447.95.

1987 average silver price: $7.02/ounce.

Coin commentary: Demand for the 1987 bullion strike was high, and the coin's mintage surpassed 11.4 million—a record that would stand for more than 20 years.

In 2020 the Mint revealed that the entire production of 1987 bullion strikes was made at San Francisco, not at Philadelphia.

A so-called "monster box" (15 x 8.5 x 4.5 inches) containing 500 American Silver Eagles.

1987-S, Proof

Mintage: 904,732
GSID: 10659
Minted at San Francisco, with S mintmark

Coin commentary: While orders for bullion-strike 1987 American Silver Eagles more than doubled in the series' sophomore year, demand for Proof examples fell by one-third. Still, the 1987-S American Silver Eagle Proof has the second-highest mintage of all Proofs minted in the 1980's. The Mint sold the 1987 Proof for $23 (an increase of $2 over the preceding year). Premiums for the 1987-S Proof are typical for a type coin in the series, though the date has traditionally traded at $1,000 or more in PF-70. In recent years the population of PF-70 coins has doubled and doubled again (in the second edition of this book it was just over 500 coins, and in the third it was more than 1,400). While the 1988 Proof is scarcer, demand for these coins is such that the market remains strong at historic levels.

Collectors should seek spot-free specimens with thick and consistent cameo frosting and rich black mirrors, while avoiding coins that exhibit imperfections, such as haze or milk spots. Pieces with vivid toning can also be found.

1988, Bullion Strike

Mintage: 5,004,646

GSID: 10646

Minted at San Francisco and West Point, without mintmark

Historical context: The stock market crash of October 1987 did little to shake the fundamentals of the American economy, which continued to grow. Some investors looking to outperform the stock market turned their attention to rare coins. Some investment firms went so far as to establish rare-coin funds.

Grading, then as now, was an important part of coin collecting. In Chicago in May 1988 the American Numismatic Association scheduled a three-day seminar on how to grade rare coins. The emergence of third-party grading services and the promise of standardized grading helped fuel this growth segment within the hobby. However, many newcomers discovered that, buying and selling rare coins for profit requires highly technical knowledge and a nuanced understanding of numismatics.

Wealthy novice collectors sometimes found themselves the victims of unscrupulous dealers and telemarketers. To combat this, the American Numismatic Association and the Federal Trade Commission announced their intention to co-publish a brochure, "Consumer Alert: Investing in Rare Coins," designed to educate consumers interested in the investment side of the hobby.

By the beginning of 1988 nearly 17 million ounces of silver had been absorbed into the marketplace through the American Silver Eagle bullion program. The bullion value of gold was slightly down compared to 1987, averaging $438.31 per ounce for the year, while silver was off more than 7 percent from its position in 1987.

1988 average silver price: $6.52/ounce.

Coin commentary: Demand for the 1988 issue was less than half that of the previous year, with just over 5 million coins being sold.

In 2020 the Mint revealed that West Point and San Francisco were the production facilities for the 1988 bullion strikes. Earlier, it was thought that the Philadelphia Mint was their source. In an October 16, 2020, article in *Coin World*, Paul Gilkes reported that professional numismatist Lee Minshull had submitted a Freedom of Information Act inquiry seeking clarification of mintage information. The Mint provided mintages and production-facility information for American Silver Eagles struck from 1986 through July 17, 2017. For the 1988 bullion strikes, that included 755,000 coins minted at West Point, and 4,249,646 at San Francisco. (The year's reported total mintage quantity did not change.)

The 1988 bullion strike today enjoys a strong premium in the highest Mint State grade, MS-70.

1988-S, Proof

Mintage: 557,370

GSID: 10660

Minted at San Francisco, with S mintmark

Coin commentary: Demand declined for the 1988-S Proof, with some 347,362 fewer coins being purchased than in 1987. The Mint kept its price steady at $23 per coin.

Although several hundred have been certified at PF-68 and lower, savvy collectors will pursue a higher-level example for their collections.

The year 1988 was significant for the West Point Mint, which had been built in 1937 as the West Point Bullion Depository—a storage facility for silver bullion, nicknamed "The Fort Knox of Silver." According to the Mint's historical literature, "From 1973 to 1986, West Point produced cents, and in 1980 began striking gold medallions. Shortly afterward, approximately 20 billion dollars worth of gold was stored in its vaults, making it second only to Fort Knox for gold storage. Today, it is also the major producer of gold coins."

Continuing: "The red letter date for West Point was March 31, 1988, when it gained official status as a United States Mint."

The newly minted mint was called into service to produce 755,000 American Silver Eagle bullion strikes in 1988 (supplementing the more than 4 million struck in San Francisco that year). The facility's first Proof coin in the silver bullion series would be the famous 1995-W.

Today West Point continues as a storage facility, but as a branch mint it also manufactures, packages, and ships gold and silver commemorative coins, as well as American Eagle bullion coins in regular, Proof, and Burnished formats. It has also produced special circulating coins.

The 1988-S Proof American Silver Eagle is actually underrated at PF-70. It has also produced special circulating coins. Compare the number of 1998 Proofs certified at PF-70 to other Proof issues of the 1980's.

1989, Bullion Strike

Mintage: 5,203,327

GSID: 10647

Minted at San Francisco and West Point, without mintmark

Historical context: The big international news of 1989 was the fall of the Berlin Wall. News in the United States was dominated by the crash of the oil tanker *Exxon Valdez* and the spilling of its crude oil in Alaska's waters.

Investor money continued to flow into the hobby marketplace in 1989, with interest from Wall Street and fortune-seekers driving the prices of many popular coin series up beyond normal collector levels. Collectors didn't know it yet, but 1989 represented a peak in the market for silver dollars and other high-visibility coins (the kinds that attracted Wall Street attention). The excitement would cool off over the next several years, but for now the markets were flush with cash.

Coin collecting as a popular hobby made national headlines when some 1989 Washington quarters were discovered without mintmarks (normally a quarter struck for circulation would have either a P mintmark for the Philadelphia Mint, or a D for the Denver Mint).

The *Chicago Tribune* reported on the 1989 coin market in a January 21, 1990, article. "Investors in extremely rare coins enjoyed a profitable 1989, according to comprehensive price surveys compiled by the hobby's two largest newspapers," the *Tribune* noted. "*Coin World*'s Trends Index suggests that rarities in the 'choice uncirculated' category (MS-65) jumped 50.6 percent in value in the 12 months ending Nov. 30. The MS-65 index went up 26.2 percent in 1988 and 13.2 percent in 1987. Likewise, the *Numismatic News* coin index—which tracks prices in 17 areas of the market—went up 45.5 percent in 1989. Experts attribute the strong market . . . to the creation of limited partnerships that invest in rare coins in the top condition categories, and to other factors."

Silver's bullion value was down about $1 per ounce for the year, and gold dropped more than $50, averaging at $382.58.

1989 average silver price: $5.52/ounce.

Coin commentary: Demand for the 1989 bullion issue was slightly stronger than for the 1988, with just over 5.2 million coins sold.

In 2020, following a Freedom of Information Act inquiry, the Mint revealed that West Point and San Francisco—not Philadelphia—had been the production facilities for 1989 American Silver Eagle bullion strikes. Most of the coins in 1989 were produced at the West Point Mint. Of the year's 5,203,327 coins, 4,038,045 were minted at West Point, and 1,165,282 at San Francisco. This was a reversal of the two facility's productions of 1988, when San Francisco did the heavy lifting. 1989 (among other dates) "World Trade Center" American Silver Eagles have been graded and authenticated by PCGS. The coins were certified as being found in a vault pulled from the wreckage at Ground Zero, post-9/11.

1989-S, Proof

Mintage: 617,694
GSID: 10661
Minted at San Francisco, with S mintmark

Coin commentary: 1989 saw a slight uptick in the number of Proof American Silver Eagles purchased, reversing a two-year decline. Mintage stood at 617,694 pieces. The Mint sold the coins directly to the public for $23 each.

As one might expect, coin quality continued to be excellent out of the gate. However, age and improper storage have marred many specimens over the years. PF-69 is the "typical" grade for certified examples, with a much smaller number of certified coins grading PF-70. The term *typical* is misleading, however, since most American Silver Eagles submitted for grading are hand-selected for quality.

Expect hazy or discolored coins to grade lower, and avoid buying them as numismatic items.

Attractive toned examples exist, but collectors who prefer the original black-and-white cameo contrast should exercise some discernment. Cameo frosting varies from well frosted to extra thick.

1990, Bullion Strike

Mintage: 5,840,110

GSID: 10648

Minted at San Francisco and West Point, without mintmark

Historical context: Iraq's occupation of oil-rich Kuwait, and the subsequent Gulf War led by the United States, was one of the biggest news stories of 1990. The war's far-reaching impact on geopolitics and energy policy would play out over the course of the next couple decades. Another historic international event, the reunification of East and West Germany, signaled the beginning of the end of the Cold War.

1990 was a pivotal year for the numismatic market as well. The industry was forced to reinvent itself after the Wall Street investment bubble deflated. Easy-to-promote coins, such as high-end commemoratives and silver dollars, suffered the most during this bear market. Collectors' series suffered only minimally, as esoteric and scarce numismatic items, such as colonial tokens and early-1800's coins, retained their core group of buyers.

The American Numismatic Association and the Federal Trade Commission jointly continued to educate consumers about safety in the marketplace. The *Chicago Tribune* in its April 15, 1990, edition reported that nearly 100,000 copies of the ANA/FTC brochure on investing in rare coins had been distributed since 1988. The newspaper further noted that "Numismatic keepsakes outperformed most other types of investments—including stocks and Treasury bills—in the 12 months ending last June 1, according to a widely quoted survey by Salomon Brothers, Inc."

Bullion coins like the American Silver Eagle continued to operate in the market primarily as investment instruments. The spot price of silver was down about 70 cents per ounce on average for the year, while gold remained steady—a couple dollars up from 1989, averaging $384.93 per ounce.

1990 average silver price: $4.82/ounce.

Coin commentary: Demand for the 1990 bullion strike American Silver Eagle increased 12 percent over the prior year, marking the third consecutive year of increased demand. A majority of the certified population of 1990 American Silver Eagles grades MS-69. Coins designated "First Strike" are elusive for this date.

Answering a Freedom of Information Act inquiry in 2020, the United States Mint revealed that West Point and San Francisco—not Philadelphia, as was previously believed—produced 1990's bullion strikes. As with the previous year, West Point minted more than San Francisco (3,456,425 and 2,383,685 coins, respectively).

Like many dates in the series, the 1990 bullion strike features many exquisitely toned coins. These one-of-a-kind treasures can command significant premiums and are desirable for collectors in Mint State regardless of numerical grade.

1990-S, Proof

Mintage: 695,510

GSID: 10662

Minted at San Francisco, with S mintmark

Coin commentary: The fifth year of American Silver Eagle Proof production saw a noticeable spike over the past year, with 695,510 coins struck. This benchmark would go unmatched for more than ten years. The U.S. Mint continued to offer the coin to collectors for $23 each.

In PF-70 the 1990-S is the most common of the original run of 1986–1992 San Francisco Mint American Silver Eagles. Since the first edition of this book went to press, population totals for this coin in the ultimate grade have grown quadruple and beyond. Demand for this coin at the high end remains strong, with pieces trading for more than around $300 each. PF-69 coins are readily available and affordable. Attractively toned pieces in PF-68 or PF-69 can sell for as much as a perfect black-and-white example!

1991, Bullion Strike

Mintage: 7,191,066

GSID: 10649

Minted at San Francisco and West Point, without mintmark

Historical context: Many of the former Soviet states comprising the USSR became independent in 1991. The American economy was strong. In the numismatic market, formerly inflated investment-level prices continued to drop to more realistic levels.

The *Chicago Tribune* in its August 15, 1991, edition (in an article titled "A Penny Saved May Be Big Deal to Collectors") reported on the American Numismatic Association's summer show, held in Chicago because that's the city the ANA had been founded in 100 years earlier. "In everything from impressive leather bags to emptied cottage cheese containers, all kinds of coins and money-related material came through the center," the *Tribune* observed. "There was the 22-karat gold, 'sailor head, half-eagle' coin, part of the Ed Trompeter collection valued at $10 million. There were wooden coins, miniature coins, quarters the size of dimes, dimes the color of pennies, coins that circulated during biblical days, medals won during the civil war, U.S. Treasury documents signed by Abraham Lincoln and Richard Nixon. There was not, however, any sign of the 1909 and 1914 pennies that had earlier been secretly circulated near the expo center to present a challenge: Anyone who recognizes them and brings them to the convention during its five-day run will receive the $370 and $400 the coins are worth, respectively. But as longtime coin collector Chet Krause said, 'By now, those pennies might be anywhere, in a toll booth or a bubble gum machine.' But maybe not."

Silver bullion was down nearly $1 per ounce for the year. Gold, too, dipped, averaging about $21 less per ounce than 1990, at $363.29.

1991 average silver price: $4.06/ounce.

Coin commentary: The mintage of 1991 bullion strikes hit a post-1986 peak of nearly 7.2 million coins—a record that would hold until near the end of the decade. At the MS-70 level the 1991 has one of the strongest values in the marketplace.

In an October 16, 2020, article in *Coin World*, Paul Gilkes reported that professional numismatist Lee Minshull had submitted a Freedom of Information Act inquiry seeking clarification of mintage information for American Silver Eagles. In response, the Mint reported that West Point and San Francisco were the production facilities for the 1991 bullion strikes. The year's total mintage quantity didn't change with this report, but it clarified that 4,172,000 coins were made at West Point, and 3,019,066 at San Francisco.

1991-S, Proof

Mintage: 511,925
GSID: 10663
Minted at San Francisco, with S mintmark

Coin commentary: The Mint's issue price of $23 remained in place for 1991 Proofs but demand fell sharply, to about three-quarters the 1990 level. Even with the decreased sales, the 1991 mintage of 511,925 coins would be a high point until 1999.

With the majority of professionally certified 1991-S American Silver Eagles grading PF-69 and PF-70, a collector with an eye for quality will seek one of those higher levels. The U.S. Mint offers such high-quality collectible products that collectors risk becoming spoiled; any 1991-S Proof American Silver Eagle grading below PF-69 would be considered on the low end of the acceptable scale.

1992, Bullion Strike

Mintage: 5,540,068

GSID: 10650

Minted at San Francisco and West Point, without mintmark

Historical context: By 1992 the Wall Street hullaballoo in the coin market had quieted down, allowing collectors—as opposed to investors—to dominate the hobby once again. The American Numismatic Association held its annual springtime National Money Show in Dallas, Texas, and its summer World's Fair of Money in Orlando, Florida.

The price of silver continued to decline, as it had for several years. However, by mid-1992 analysts began to anticipate a rise in silver prices, up to $4.25 per ounce. In the end silver averaged just under the $4.00 mark for the year. Gold, too, proved to be a loser in 1992, shedding $20 an ounce to average $344.97 for the year.

1992 average silver price: $3.95/ounce.

Coin commentary: The lack of action in the silver market led to a 26 percent decline in the number of bullion American Silver Eagles struck in 1992. Currently, this issue commands a modest numismatic premium in MS-69.

PCGS and NGC certification data show distributions that significantly favor MS-69. This reflects a high percentage of coins hand-picked for quality before being submitted for grading. Very few MS-70 examples have been certified by the major grading firms—all the more reason for savvy collectors to keep an eye out for those elusive perfect coins.

A Freedom of Information Act inquiry by professional numismatist Lee Minshull led, in October 2020, to the Mint reporting details of the 1992 bullion-strike mintage (along with clarifying other mintages of 1986 to 2017). The Mint documented two production facilities for the year's silver bullion coinage: West Point (3,957,024 coins) and San Francisco (1,583,044 coins). West Point—popularly known as the "Fort Knox of Silver"—had already been minting more American Silver Eagles than San Francisco leading up to 1992, but this was the first year its production was more than double that of its West Coast counterpart.

1992-S, Proof

Mintage: 498,654
GSID: 10664
Minted at San Francisco, with S mintmark

Coin commentary: 1992 marks the end of the American Silver Eagle's initial seven-year Proof run at the San Francisco Mint. Starting in 1993 American Silver Eagle Proof coinage would be produced at the Philadelphia Mint. American Silver Eagle production didn't return to the "Granite Lady" until 2011.

1992 was also the first year since 1964 that the U.S. Mint struck 90 percent silver coinage in Proof sets. The 1992-S Silver Proof Set included three coins traditionally struck in 90 percent silver (the Kennedy half dollar, Washington quarter, and Roosevelt dime), along with the base-metal denominations of the nickel and cent. The set was offered for sale at $37.50. More than a million United States Silver Proof Sets were sold.

1993, Bullion Strike

Mintage: 6,763,762

GSID: 10651

Minted at San Francisco and West Point, without mintmark

Historical context: 1993 saw the rare-coin market begin the long road to recovery after the investment bubble burst. High-end coins began to rebound but still traded well below peak levels.

The American Numismatic Association polled its 28,000 members about current U.S. money, in a mail-in survey published in the June 1993 issue of its monthly magazine, *The Numismatist.* The general consensus was that the cent and the half dollar should be retained (so said nearly two-thirds of respondents); that a dollar coin should replace the $1 bill; that at least one side of each circulating coin should be modernized with a new design; and that more color should be used on the nation's paper currency (the latter three opinions voiced by more than half of respondents). The ANA board of governors endorsed a bill in Congress for a golden-colored dollar coin to replace the $1 note.

Two fantastic rarities set auction records this year: the Mickley-Hawn-Queller 1804 dollar sold for more than $475,000 at a Heritage auction and the Olsen-Hawn 1913 Liberty Head nickel (which PCGS has certified at PF-64) sold for $962,500 . . . a bargain by today's standards.

Meanwhile, gold and silver prices saw some long-overdue upward movement in 1993. Gold finished the year averaging $360.91 per ounce ($15 higher than 1992 levels), while silver crossed the $4 barrier for good. Bullion-strike American Silver Eagle production rose nearly 20 percent in 1993, thanks to climbing metals prices.

1993 average silver price: $4.31/ounce.

Coin commentary: MS-70 perfection continues to be elusive, with very few examples certified at that level. The crop of American Silver Eagles of 1993, like many others of that decade, offers fans of toned coins many pleasing examples. As most of these coins have been removed from original packaging and exposed to the elements, the typical grade dips between MS-66 and MS-68. Plenty of hand-selected MS-68 and MS-69 examples exist, trading for a slight premium over melt.

In 2020 the Mint clarified the details of American Silver Eagle mintages, in response to a Freedom of Information Act query. The bureau revealed that in 1993 West Point made 5,552,000 bullion strikes, and San Francisco made 1,211,762. This was a remarkable production year for West Point—its mintage alone equivalent to more than the entire production of 1992, including San Francisco's.

1993-P, Proof

Mintage: 405,913
GSID: 10665
Minted at Philadelphia, with P mintmark

Coin commentary: Proof production for the American Silver Eagle was moved from San Francisco to the Philadelphia Mint in 1993.

The 1993-P has one of the lowest mintages among regular-issue American Silver Eagle Proofs, at just over 400,000 pieces. Not surprisingly, it commands a premium over Proofs of the preceding years, especially at the PF-70 level.

The U.S. Mint's issue price for the 1993-P Proof was $23.

Some 1993-P Proof American Silver Eagles were issued in a special package of coins—the Philadelphia Mint Bicentennial Set (see next entry for more details). The Knight Ridder / Tribune syndicate publicized the set in an article entitled "Philadelphia Mint's 200 Years Are Honored": "The U.S. Mint is offering a set of coins to mark the 200th anniversary of the first coins struck at the Philadelphia Mint. The Philadelphia Set, created for collectors, contains three fractional gold Eagle proofs, the silver Eagle proof and a silver medal marking the mint's anniversary. All the proofs and medal bear the 'P' mint mark. The set will be sold only in 1993. It is the first year the Philadelphia Mint has struck the silver eagles, and the last year the Philadelphia Mint will strike fractional gold Eagles. The Philadelphia Set sells for $499." The coins in these sets accounted for nearly 13,000 of the year's Proof American Silver Eagle mintage (out of a total of 405,913).

"The resulting coloration can be dramatic and visually appealing," writes Dennis Tucker in *American Gold and Silver: U.S. Mint Collector and Investor Coins and Medals, Bicentennial to Date*, "of course with beauty being in the eye of the coin holder."

Eagles from the 1993 Philadelphia Set tend to tone in a unique, pastel-purple toning pattern that starts around the rim and proceeds toward the center of the coin. This is probably the result of exposure to chemicals from the set's packaging. Finding an example of this coin in the original white-and-black is very tough.

1993 Philadelphia Mint Bicentennial Set

Mintage: 12,869
GSID: 79849
Minted at Philadelphia, with P mintmarks

Set commentary: This set was issued to celebrate the 200th anniversary of the first official regular coins struck for general circulation by the U.S. Mint in Philadelphia. It includes three denominations of 1993 American Gold Eagles ($5, $10, and $25, from one-tenth ounce to one-half ounce), plus the 1993 American Silver Eagle. In addition the set includes a .76-ounce, .900 fine silver commemorative medal depicting the famous John Ward Dunsmore painting of Martha Washington inspecting the first U.S. coinage (see *The Secret History of the First U.S. Mint*, by Orosz and Augsburger) and various U.S. coin designs.

The coins and the medal are all in Proof format.

In *American Gold and Silver: U.S. Mint Collector and Investor Coins and Medals, Bicentennial to Date*, Dennis Tucker writes:

> Many of the silver medals (and the accompanying American Silver Eagle) have toned over the years from exposure to the heavy green cardboard of the set's packaging.

This set was packaged with a green velvet box and a certificate of authenticity. Its issue price was $499.

1994, Bullion Strike

Mintage: 4,227,319

GSID: 10674

Minted at San Francisco and West Point, without mintmark

Historical context: Political instability in Mexico and increased demand from India drove silver upward for the first quarter of 1994. Silver peaked in March at $5.75 per ounce. These gains quickly subsided, and silver was trading below $5.00 by November. While orders for bullion-strike American Silver Eagles were strong in the first half of the year, the decline in precious-metal prices led to weaker demand for the coins in the second half. As a result, sales of 1994 bullion strikes fell by nearly one-third in 1994. The issue's total mintage of 4,227,319 is the second lowest among American Silver Eagle bullion strikes.

The coin market, like the U.S. economy as a whole, continued to grow in strength in 1994. Classic American coin prices continued to recover, and the Mint released seven different commemorative designs. This made 1994 the busiest year for the U.S. commemorative program since 1936, when the Mint released an astonishing 21 different coins.

Gold climbed to an average price of $385.42 per ounce for the year, while silver ended 1994 with a yearly average of $5.29 per ounce.

1994 average silver price: $5.29/ounce.

Coin commentary: MS-70 remains the most elusive of grades for the 1994 bullion strike. More than half the coins submitted for professional grading (cherrypicked for quality by their submitters, of course) come close to perfection, grading MS-69. Series specialists observe that the 1994 bullion strike is one of the tougher dates to find in very nice quality. Usually some slight tick or surface mark keeps the issue from reaching higher grades, making the coin slightly underrated at MS-69.

The Mint in 2020 gave details on mintages and on the production facilities used to make American Silver Eagles from 1986 into July of 2017. This was in response to a Freedom of Information Act request from professional numismatist Lee Minshull. In its reply, the Mint spelled out that the West Point Mint created 3,436,010 of the 1994 bullion strikes, and San Francisco made 791,309. West Point had been the major producer of the bullion coins since 1989.

1994-P, Proof

Mintage: 372,168

GSID: 10682

Minted at Philadelphia, with P mintmark

Coin commentary: The 1994-P has the lowest mintage of any regular-issue American Silver Eagle Proof. (Only the 1995-W, sold by the Mint in special sets rather than individually, has a lower mintage.)

Collectors and investors had cooled on the desirability of Proof American Silver Eagles by 1994; with silver hovering around $5 an ounce as bullion, Proofs could be found on the secondary market for prices lower than the Mint's official issue price of $23 per coin. The Mint sold fewer and fewer of the Proofs each year from 1991 through 1994, until finally they bottomed out at less than 400,000 coins.

The 1994-P Proof was ranked number 64 in the *100 Greatest U.S. Modern Coins,* fifth edition, where it is noted that "the 1994 issue has emerged as a key date, often more difficult to locate than the 2006-W Reverse Proof issue, and therefore it can also be more expensive." The coin commands a premium at all collectible levels, with the examples graded at PF-70 being especially valuable.

1995, Bullion Strike

Mintage: 4,672,051

GSID: 10675

Minted at San Francisco and West Point, without mintmark

Historical context: In 1995 the federal government's budget was too small to meet expenses, and as the year ended there was the threat of some government services being shut down. Precious metals had their normal ups and downs but held steady. The price of silver surpassed $6 an ounce in May and then had a downward trend. Compared to 1994 the metal averaged a few cents weaker for the year. Gold, meanwhile, averaged out a few cents higher, at $385.50 compared to the previous year's $385.42.

Numismatics made national headlines early in the year when it was publicized that the Willis H. duPont family was donating two famous silver dollars to museums. The coins, dated 1804 but actually made years later from old unused dies, had been stolen from the duPonts in an armed robbery in 1967. One was a Class I specimen, one of only eight struck in the 1830's as official gifts of the United States to be presented to foreign rulers and dignitaries, including the king of Siam. This one was donated to the American Numismatic Association's Money Museum in Colorado Springs, Colorado. The other was a Class III restrike, one of 15 known to have been secretly made at the Mint in the 1850's, using the old dies, for back-door sale to wealthy and well-connected private collectors. This coin was donated to the Smithsonian Institution's National Numismatic Collection. (The story of these coins is told in *The Fantastic 1804 Dollar*, by Eric P. Newman and Kenneth E. Bressett.)

1995 average silver price: $5.19/ounce.

Coin commentary: Demand for the 1995 bullion strike was higher than for the 1994, resulting in 4,672,051 coins being sold.

In *Coin World*, October 16, 2020, Paul Gilkes reported that professional numismatist Lee Minshull had submitted a Freedom of Information Act inquiry seeking clarification of mintage information for American Silver Eagles. The Mint, in response, reported that 1995's bullion strikes had been coined at West Point and San Francisco. This report didn't change the year's total mintage quantity, but it clarified that 2,890,919 coins were made at West Point, and 1,781,132 at San Francisco.

The 1995 bullion strike offers a dramatic illustration of the fluidity of certification data. When the second edition of this book was published, a single example of the 1995 bullion strike had been graded MS-70 by PCGS. When the third edition went to press, 23 had been graded MS-70. This reality—the fact that today's uniquely perfect coin might have dozens of companions a week, a month, or a year later—acts as a governor on the market prices for MS-70 coins.

1995-P, Proof

Mintage: 438,511

GSID: 10683

Minted at Philadelphia, with P mintmark

Coin commentary: The American Silver Eagle entered its tenth year of production in 1995. The U.S. Mint offered two collectible versions of the coin to the public: the standard Philadelphia-minted Proof (issue price $23) and the considerably rarer 1995-W Proof (see next listing).

Mintage of the 1995-P Proof was capped at 500,000. The year's sales came under that limit, to just under 440,000 coins; this quantity was lower than most previous Proofs of the series. Today the 1995-P enjoys a modest secondary-market premium over most other American Silver Eagle Proofs. Thousands have been graded by PCGS and NGC at the highest level, PF-70.

A possible reason for the lower mintage than those seen in previous years was that many collectors did not welcome the 1995-W Proof American Silver Eagle, which was only available as part of a set costing $999. In a "Guest Commentary" column published in the June 26, 1995, issue of *Coin World*, Mint Director Philip N. Diehl wrote, "I acknowledge that the $999 purchase price for the 10th Anniversary set with the 1995-W Proof silver Eagle seems high and that not every collector of Proof silver Eagles can afford it. However, that price is more affordable than you might think. I've just finished scanning the 'buy prices' for 1994 American Eagle Proof gold coins in the coin market section of several numismatic publications. I see that collectors can, on average, sell unpackaged, individual Proof gold American Eagles in each of the four denominations to a dealer for $949. And that's an average resale price; by shopping around, you could do better than this." He added, "Using the $949 price as a guide, a single Proof silver Eagle from the 1995 10th Anniversary set has an effective price of $50 for collectors of silver Eagles who buy the five-coin set and immediately sell the four gold coins back to a dealer. Other things being equal, a $50 effective price seems like a reasonable, reachable, and even tempting price for one of the lowest mintage U.S. coins in this century."

In this remarkable statement, Diehl foreshadowed the speculation that would accompany later limited-release U.S. Mint products where some buyers would purchase coins not to add to their collections but with the hope of flipping them for a quick profit.

1995-W, Proof

Mintage: 30,125

GSID: 10684 / 70815 (set)

Minted at West Point, with W mintmark

Coin commentary: The tenth year of the United States' bullion coinage program was marked in 1995 by a special set of Proof coins issued by the U.S. Mint. The set included all four denominations of the 1995 American Gold Eagle—the tenth-ounce $5 coin, the quarter-ounce $10, the half-ounce $25, and the one-ounce $50. All were struck at West Point, with a W mintmark. The fifth coin in the set would become known as the "king of the Silver Eagles." Like its gold companions, the silver Proof was minted at West Point and bears that facility's W mark.

There was only one way for collectors to get the 1995-W Proof American Silver Eagle: by purchasing the complete tenth-anniversary set of coins. (The gold Proofs were available individually, but the silver West Point Proof was not.) At the issue price of $999, this was a prohibitively expensive option for most collectors, who instead chose the regular 1995-P Proof (available for a much more affordable $23). The set had a limit of 45,000, but not even that many were sold. By the time the sales period ended, only 30,125 sets had been purchased. In comparison, collectors bought nearly 440,000 of the 1995-P Proofs.

Hundreds of thousands of people collect Proof American Silver Eagles, and many desire to own a complete set—one coin of each date-and-mint combination. On the secondary market these collectors are forced to compete for a mere 30,125 available 1995-W coins. The law of supply and demand brings an inevitable result: even in raw (not professionally graded) form, these West Mint Proofs are worth a premium several times the issue price of $999 that originally paid for the entire set of tenth-anniversary coins.

The "king of American Silver Eagles" was ranked number 5 in the *100 Greatest U.S. Modern Coins*, fifth edition. Authors Schechter and Garrett describe the rare bird: "The mystique and desirability of this coin have only grown over time. To say that the 1995-W is the 'key' to the series is an understatement. Its small mintage of 30,125 is dwarfed by that of every other Proof silver eagle in the series. Its value is nearly equal to that of all the other coins in the series combined. By any measure, the Proof silver eagle program is more popular today than at any point in the past, which only continues to bolster demand for its king rarity, the 1995-W."

On March 31, 2013, a PCGS Proof-70 Deep Cameo example sold for an astounding $86,654.70 in an online auction by Great Collections. At that time, PCGS had only graded a handful of examples in that grade but since the sale, more have been certified in this grade and prices have dropped substantially.

1996, Bullion Strike

Mintage: 3,603,386

GSID: 10676

Minted at San Francisco and West Point, without mintmark

Historical context: In May 1996 a monumental barrier was broken in the numismatic market: for the first time, a coin sold for more than $1 million at auction. It was the famous 1913 Liberty Head nickel from the Eliasberg Collection, and it went for $1,485,000. This was also the year that Congress passed legislation authorizing the U.S. Mint's State quarter program, which would launch in 1999.

The bullion price of silver ranged from about $4.70 to $5.80 through the year. Averaged against 1995, silver, like gold, held fairly steady. Gold's average price per ounce for the year was $389.09, compared to $385.50 for 1995.

1996 average silver price: $5.20/ounce.

Coin commentary: Demand for the American Silver Eagle reached a low in 1996. Because the coins are produced in quantities to satisfy public consumption, this low demand resulted in 1996 having the lowest bullion-strike mintage for the entire series. Today the coin enjoys a premium because of its relative scarcity.

In 2020 the Mint, responding to a Freedom of Information Act inquiry, released clarifications on the coinage of American Silver Eagles from 1986 partway through 2017. For the 1996 bullion strikes, it was revealed that 2,831,649 coins were struck at West Point, and 771,737 at San Francisco.

A wise collector will carefully examine 1996 bullion strikes (especially those in unopened boxes) for small spots of white haze, called "milk spotting." This visually unpleasant effect is common enough on American Silver Eagles of the mid- to late 1990's that it pays to examine all specimens carefully: it will usually keep a coin from grading higher than MS-68.

The 1996 bullion strike was ranked number 88 in the *100 Greatest U.S. Modern Coins,* fifth edition. Authors Schechter and Garrett address the topic of milk spotting: "Concern regarding spotting dissuades dealers from bidding too aggressively on these issues and keeps their prices in check, despite their scarcity. This creates an opportunity for collectors who can take the extra time to search out a pristine example."

1996-P, Proof

Mintage: 500,000
GSID: 10685
Minted at Philadelphia, with P mintmark

Coin commentary: 1996 was the first year the ceiling for Proof American Silver Eagle production was reached. (Caps had been set, but never reached, for Proof mintages since 1990.) The maximum authorized mintage was 500,000 coins, and collectors and investors bought them up. Interestingly, demand for the bullion-strike American Silver Eagle reached an all-time low this same year.

The Proofs were sold by the Mint at an issue price of $23.

The Mint announced the sellout of the 1996-P Proof American Silver Eagle on May 13, 1997. "Sales of the half million Proof Silver Eagles mark the first sellout since the Mint established a maximum mintage for the coin in 1990," noted the press release, "and the highest Proof Silver Eagle sales since 1991's total sales of 511,950."

"The Proof Silver Eagle continues to be the world leader in silver coins," Mint Director Philip N. Diehl was quoted as saying. "Its classic design and affordability make this coin a unique value, both artistically and for collectors."

The press release continued as follows: "The Proof Silver Eagle obverse features Adolph A. Weinman's renowned 'Walking Liberty,' which originally appeared on the U.S. half dollar in 1916. Priced at $23, the Proof Silver Eagle went on sale on March 22, 1996."

1997, Bullion Strike

Mintage: 4,295,004

GSID: 10677

Minted at San Francisco and West Point, without mintmark

Historical context: The coin market continued to hum along in 1997, with its apex being the sale of the amazing John J. Pittman collection, which was auctioned off starting this year. Pittman, who spent the majority of his career working as an executive at the Eastman Kodak Company, Rochester, New York, had an amazing talent for recognizing high-quality coins and good deals. He famously bought an 1833 $5 gold piece for $605. He also assembled an 1859 Proof set for less than $2,000—a set that later realized $387,500 at auction. Numismatist David Akers, who oversaw the sale of Pittman's collection, observed that while Pittman "was way ahead of his time in terms of knowing which coins to buy," he did so on a "definite budget."

In the summer of 1997 the American Numismatic Association urged people to check their pocket change for rare coins: to promote the hobby, the Association released ten valuable coins, including four 1914-D Lincoln cents, into circulation in New York City.

For the most part, the precious-metals market was softer in 1997 than in 1996. Silver spiked in December to above $6 an ounce but ended the year with an average price of $4.91, nearly 30 cents lower than the preceding year. Gold, too, was down, finishing the year with an average price of $332.39 an ounce—a far cry from the $389.09 average price a year earlier.

A new bullion program went into production in 1997. Joining the American Silver and Gold Eagle programs was a four-coin Platinum Eagle program, featuring a tenth-ounce $10 coin, a quarter-ounce $25 coin, a half-ounce $50 coin, and a one-ounce $100 coin. John Mercanti designed the coins' obverse, which depicts a close-up shot of the Statue of Liberty. Engraver Thomas D. Rogers Sr. provided a lovely soaring eagle design for the reverse. 173,850 bullion-strike platinum coins were sold in this, the series' inaugural year.

1997 average silver price: $4.91/ounce.

Coin commentary: The 1997 has the third-lowest mintage of the bullion-strike American Silver Eagles; premiums, however, are only modestly greater than those of others in the series. Although thousands have been certified at MS-68 and lower, savvy collectors will seek a higher grade for their collections.

In 2020 the Mint, responding to a Freedom of Information Act inquiry, released clarifications on the coinage of American Silver Eagles from 1986 partway through 2017. For the 1996 bullion strikes, it was revealed that 2,831,649 coins were struck at West Point, and 771,737 at San Francisco.

1997-P, Proof

Mintage: 435,368
GSID: 10686
Minted at Philadelphia, with P mintmark

Coin commentary: Demand for the 1997-P Proof American Silver Eagle did not reach the authorized ceiling of 500,000 coins. Collectors purchased just over 435,000, giving this date the third-lowest mintage in the Proof series. In the secondary market the date commands a small premium over most others.

The Mint's issue price for a single Proof coin remained steady at $23, as it had since 1987.

The 1997-P Proof was also sold in the Mint's Impressions of Liberty set, which included the one-ounce gold bullion coin, the newly debuted one-ounce platinum coin, and the American Silver Eagle. Sales of the set reached the maximum authorized 5,000 sets (priced by the Mint at $1,499).

On January 15, 1998, the U.S. Mint announced that "approximately 7,000 of the 1997 Proof Silver American Eagle bullion coins remain in inventory from its 1997 production run of 435,000 coins, which ended December 31." The press release went on to quote Mint Director Philip N. Diehl as follows: "The mintage level for the 1997 Proof Silver Eagle will be the fourth lowest since the program began, so with only 7,000 remaining, we expect to sell all of these coins within the next month." The announcement concluded with a description of the coin: "Priced at $23, the Proof Silver Eagle obverse features Adolph A. Weinman's classic 'Walking Liberty,' which originally appeared on the U.S. half dollar in 1916."

The number of 1997-P Proofs graded PF-70 has skyrocketed in recent years—notably doubling between the publication of the second and third editions of this book (in 2013 and 2018). This is a good reminder that seemingly rare high grades can only become more common as time passes and more coins are submitted for professional grading and certification.

1997 Impressions of Liberty Set

Mintage: 5,000

GSID: 376892

Minted at Philadelphia, without mintmarks

Set commentary: The U.S. Mint issued the limited-edition Impressions of Liberty Set to celebrate the debut of platinum in its lineup of bullion coins. The set included a one-ounce Proof American Gold Eagle, a one-ounce Proof American Platinum Eagle, and the Proof American Silver Eagle. Maximum production was set at 5,000 sets, and the price was $1,499. The issue sold out.

Packaging included a hardwood box and a certificate signed and numbered by Philip N. Diehl, director of the U.S. Mint.

The Mint announced the sellout of the 1997 Impressions of Liberty Set on June 27, 1997, only a few weeks after its June 6 debut. In its press release, the Mint noted that it had set a limit of one set per customer, "to ensure a fair chance for the maximum number of collectors to purchase the set."

"The great response to this new coinage removes any doubt about numismatic platinum coinage," said Mint Director Philip N. Diehl, "and augurs well for the launch of the bullion platinum Eagle this fall."

"The Impressions of Liberty Set was the first numbered set offered by the Mint," the press release continued, "and features one-ounce proof platinum, proof gold and proof silver American Eagles in a luxurious display case, including a certificate of authenticity personally signed by the director of the Mint. The obverse design of the .9995 Proof platinum coin is Mint sculptor/engraver John Mercanti's 'Portrait of Liberty,' and the reverse design is Mint sculptor/engraver Thomas D. Rogers Sr.'s 'Eagle Soaring Above America,' which will only appear on the coins this year. The one-ounce carries a $100 face value; the half-ounce a $50 face value; the quarter-ounce a $25 face value, and the tenth-ounce a $10 face value."

1998, Bullion Strike

Mintage: 4,847,549

GSID: 10678

Minted at San Francisco and West Point, without mintmark

Historical context: The strength of the rare-coin market continued in 1998, with the sale of trophy rarities making headlines. The U.S. Mint issued various gold and silver commemorative coins, as it had in recent years. News made the rounds of the upcoming series of circulating commemorative coins (State quarters, to be issued through 2008) and a new dollar coin, the Sacagawea "golden dollar."

The year 1998 brought recognition to the U.S. Mint's commitment to customer service. On October 8, 1998, U.S. Senator Paul S. Sarbanes presented Mint Director Philip N. Diehl with a bronze Maryland Quality Award, honoring the work of the Mint's Customer Care Center. "This award is a testimony to the hard work and dedication of our staff at the Customer Care Center," said Diehl. "We have consistently demanded a higher and higher level of performance from our customer service team, and their commitment and results have been impressive." The award, presented at the 1998 Maryland Excellence Conference in Baltimore, recognized the Mint's significant gains toward achieving best-in-business customer service. A Mint press release noted that "The center now averages 90 percent of all orders delivered within three weeks, with overnight delivery provided on select items; 98 percent of orders requesting overnight delivery in 1997 were shipped within one day; and customer telephone inquiries are now answered within an average of six seconds, down from 50 seconds in 1996, and two minutes in 1995."

The average bullion price of silver rose by about 10 percent over the preceding year. Gold, meanwhile, was *down* at about the same rate, averaging $295.24 per ounce. Platinum fell about 6 percent, to $372.15.

1998 average silver price: $5.55/ounce.

Coin commentary: Consumer interest in silver increased in 1998 as the metal saw an early spike and ended the year about $0.65 higher than 1997. This interest translated into about 550,000 more bullion-strike American Silver Eagles being sold than the previous year.

A Freedom of Information Act query initiated by professional numismatist Lee Minshull led to a revelation in October 2020. The Mint released detailed mintage information on American Silver Eagles struck from 1986 partway through 2017. For the 1998 bullion strikes, the Mint's report noted that 3,050,115 coins had been produced at West Point, with San Francisco contributing the remaining 1,797,434 coins of the year's mintage, which neared 4.9 million total.

1998-P, Proof

Mintage: 450,000

GSID: 10687

Minted at Philadelphia, with P mintmark

Coin commentary: In 1998 the Mint raised its issue price for the Proof American Silver Eagle (the first increase since 1987), from $23 to $24 apiece. The coins went on sale March 27 and Mint Director Philip N. Diehl explained the upward price change, telling *Coin World* before the coins went on sale, ". . . . silver prices have risen in the past year, and given the fact we have not raised Proof silver Eagle prices in 12 years, we decided the time had come to do so." At the same time the maximum authorized mintage was lowered from 500,000 coins to 450,000. This resulted in a sellout despite the increased price.

As time goes by, collectors and dealers submit more and more American Silver Eagles to PCGS and NGC for grading. Thousands of 1998-P Proofs have been certified at the ultimate level of PF-70 (the quantity doubled between 2013 and 2018, when the second and third editions of this book were published). Today the 1998-P Proof is the least expensive date of the 1990's in that perfect grade.

1999, Bullion Strike

Mintage: 7,408,640

GSID: 10679

Minted at West Point, without mintmark

Historical context: The year 1999 saw renewed interest in coin collecting as the U.S. Mint launched the 50 State Quarters program. The program allowed states to choose their own designs, which were then adapted for coinage by skilled Mint engravers. States' designs were released at a rate of five per year by order of admission into the Union. The first five states (starting with Delaware) had begun the process of selecting their designs the previous year.

The release of each new quarter was cause for celebration in its home state, and untold millions of new collectors began to assemble sets of State quarters. The excitement generated by the program spilled over into several other areas of the hobby, including the sale of bullion-strike American Silver Eagles, which saw a significant increase in 1999.

In total, 7,408,640 bullion-strike American Silver Eagles were issued in 1999, a 2.5-million-coin increase over 1998, and the second-highest number of coins struck per release in the series up to this point, with only 1987's production run being higher.

Silver's bullion value decreased slightly in 1999, finishing the year at an average cost of $5.22 per ounce. Gold and platinum saw mixed results. Gold fell by $15, with an average price of $279.91 per ounce, and platinum was up $5 per ounce over its 1998 average, with an average price of $377.93.

1999 average silver price: $5.22/ounce.

Coin commentary: With such a substantial mintage, the 1999 bullion strike does not command significant premiums in raw (not professionally graded) form, or even in high Mint State grades up to MS-69. This issue is surprisingly rare certified in MS-70, with examples trading for substantial amounts at auction, e.g., one graded MS-70 by NGC sold for $17,625 at a June 2015 Heritage auction.

On grading this issue, Scott Schechter, coauthor of *100 Greatest U.S. Modern Coins*, wrote in his "Making Moderns" column in the March 10, 2014, issue of *Coin World*, "The main concern among all the coins is milk spots. The spots form as a result of detergents used to wash the planchets. If inadequately rinsed away, the detergent is struck into the coin. Not apparent at first, over time it causes the coin's metal to discolor into an irregular milky-white haze or spots that cannot be removed. Not every coin is affected, but many produced during the middle and late 1990's are."

1999 was the first year that an entire annual mintage of bullion-strike American Silver Eagles was accomplished at the West Point Mint. San Francisco had produced the program's first two years' total output (1986 and 1987), and from 1988 to 1998 the two mints had worked in tandem. From 1999 to 2011 West Point, the "Fort Knox of Silver," would be the bullion version's sole producer.

1999-P, Proof

Mintage: 549,769

GSID: 10688

Minted at Philadelphia, with P mintmark

Coin commentary: In 1999 the Mint continued with its issue price of $24 per coin for the Proof American Silver Eagle. The maximum authorized mintage was 550,000 and the issue sold out (the quantity of 549,769 accounts for record-keeping adjustments).

On April 21, 1999, the U.S. Mint announced the upcoming sale of the year's Proof Eagles, stating that it would begin sending out order forms on April 30.

Mint Director Philip N. Diehl was quoted as saying, "As the last Proof Eagles to be issued in the 1900's, we anticipate very high demand for these coins. To celebrate the coins' historical significance and to thank our customers for their loyalty, we're offering a specially commissioned Art Nouveau–style poster of the Augustus Saint-Gaudens 'Liberty' design free to those who place orders for $150 or more by June 15." The Mint's press release described the poster thus: "Renowned illustrator Oren Sherman has created a stunning Art Nouveau interpretation of the most cherished and enduring gold coin design on U.S. coinage, which originally graced the 1907 twenty-dollar gold piece. A nationally acclaimed artist and illustrator working in Boston's Fenway Studios, Sherman's award-winning poster designs have depicted the Tall Ships, the Kentucky Derby, the Brooklyn Bridge Centennial, the Ringling Brothers Barnum & Bailey Circus and numerous magazine covers, theatre productions, and movies."

With the vast majority of certified examples graded at PF-69 and PF-70, discerning collectors seek those higher grades rather than settling for a lower level. The number graded PF-70 doubled between 2013 and 2018, when the second and third editions of this book were published. The quantity has naturally increased since then, as more and more collectors and dealers submit more and more coins for certification.

2000, Bullion Strike

Mintage: 9,239,132

GSID: 10680 / 70996 (set)

Minted at West Point, without mintmark

Historical context: The nation's "dot-com" investment bubble burst early in 2000, with many Internet-based and technology companies collapsing, being sold, or losing large parts of their market capitalization. (An extreme example: software firm The Learning Company, which Mattel bought in 1999 for $3.5 billion and sold in 2000 for $27.3 million.) The nation's general economy was strong, however, and unemployment was low. On the numismatic scene, the Sacagawea dollar debuted, and gold coins and ingots rescued from the wreck of the SS *Central America* were enthusiastically promoted. Interest in silver continued to be strong, resulting in a new post-1987 record for the American Silver Eagle's mintage.

Silver's average price for the year was down about 25 cents compared to 1999. Gold held steady, with its average price ($280.10 per ounce) a few cents higher than the preceding year. Platinum, meanwhile, saw a dramatic leap of more than $150 per ounce, from $377.93 to $544.03.

2000 average silver price: $4.95/ounce.

Coin commentary: Production of the 2000 American Silver Eagle exceeded 9.2 million coins, a high up to that point surpassed only by the 11.4 million minted in 1987. Although millions of the 2000 coins were produced and hundreds of thousands have been professionally graded, those certified by PCGS and NGC as MS-70 number only in the hundreds. As a result, they enjoy significant premiums at that perfect level.

Separately from its normal bullion-strike production, the U.S. Mint offered collectors a special "Millennium Coinage and Currency Set" that included three 2000-dated pieces of American money with the $1 denomination. These were the newly debuted Sacagawea golden dollar, the $1 Federal Reserve Note, and the American Silver Eagle. The set sold out with an authorized production limit of 75,000. American Silver Eagles from these sets are graded and slabbed by the professional third-party services with a "Millennium Set" designation.

2000-P, Proof

Mintage: 600,000

GSID: 10667

Minted at Philadelphia, with P mintmark

Coin commentary: The maximum mintage of the Proof American Silver Eagle was raised from 550,000 to 600,000 for the 2000-dated coin. The Mint's issue price remained at $24 per. Marketed as a collectible souvenir of "Y2K" (the year 2000), the Proof attracted enough demand to reach the production limit, and it sold out.

On May 9, 2000, John P. Mitchell, acting director of the U.S. Mint, made this observation about the Proof series as the American Silver Eagle rolled into the new millennium: "The 2000 American Eagle gold and silver Proof coins are the perfect collector's items to commemorate the year 2000. Renowned as classics of American design, the Proof Eagles rank among the most admired and sought after coins in the world."

The Mint's press release announcing the availability of the 2000 Proofs was enthusiastic. "Because mintages of the 2000 American Eagle Proof coins are limited, place your order early. . . . American Eagle Silver Proof coins are available for sale while quantities last or until the 2001 coins are issued. The Mint reserves the right to limit quantities and may discontinue accepting orders at any time."

2001, Bullion Strike

Mintage: 9,001,711

GSID: 10681

Minted at West Point, without mintmark

Historical context: *Coin World*'s editor, Beth Deisher, on March 12, 2001, estimated that two million Americans were serious, active coin collectors, not including the millions of more casual collectors who were saving the Mint's popular new State quarters from circulation. Meanwhile the Sacagawea dollar, which had debuted in 2000, was rarely seen in pocket change; the coins were mainly stored in Treasury vaults, unwanted by the public. The U.S. Mint, after several years of increased coinage production, began to cut back and instigated a round of deep budget cuts and layoffs. The *Philadelphia Inquirer* described the situation in its December 2 edition ("Workers Suffer Following Production Frenzy at Philadelphia Mint; Excess Coinage Turns Into Job Cutbacks"): "It was only a year ago that the government was so frantic to make coins at the Philadelphia Mint it paid employees $100 weekly bonuses to work overtime. Workers practically needed a doctor's note to avoid putting in extra hours. . . . But now we're drowning in 2.4 billion pennies, 480 million nickels, 470 million dimes, 1.8 billion quarters, 62 million half-dollars, and 192 million Sacagawea golden dollars. That's the ocean of coinage—worth about $750 million—that has piled up in government vaults and armored-car coin terminals around the country since the summer of 2000. . . . [The] Mint curtailed production in April and has enacted deep employee and budget cutbacks in the last two months." The 2001 American Buffalo commemorative silver dollar sold out (500,000 coins total) and quickly commanded strong premiums on the secondary market. On the national scene, the September 11 terrorist attacks on American soil were the biggest news of the year.

Silver averaged down for the year, about 60 cents per ounce lower than 2000. Gold dropped about $8 per ounce, to $272.22. Platinum weakened but largely maintained its recent high level, averaging only $15 per ounce lower than the preceding year, at $529.04.

2001 average silver price: $4.38/ounce.

Coin commentary: Just over 9 million American Silver Eagles were minted in 2001—a small decline from the previous year but greater than any single year's mintage from the 1990's.

Tens of thousands of 2001 bullion strikes have been professionally graded, with several hundred certified as MS-70 by PCGS and NGC.

PCGS certified 400 of the coins (all MS-69) in slabs with inserts autographed by road-racing cyclist Lance Armstrong. It also graded and authenticated 979 coins (all MS-69) certified as being found in a vault pulled from the Ground Zero devastation wrought on September 11, 2001.

2001-W, Proof

Mintage: 746,398

GSID: 10668

Minted at West Point, with W mintmark

Coin commentary: In 2001 production of the U.S. Mint's Proof American Silver Eagles was moved from the Philadelphia Mint to the West Point facility. The coins bear a W mintmark. Their issue price was maintained at $24, with sales commencing in mid-April, and there was enough collector interest that the production limit of 750,000 was reached.

The Mint announced the transition of Proof American Silver Eagle production to West Point on April 6, 2001. "As part of the Mint's commitment to continuous improvement," said Mint Director Jay W. Johnson, "we felt it was time to integrate and consolidate production of all the Proof American Eagle Coins at one facility. The entire family of Eagles—gold, platinum, and silver—will now be manufactured at the West Point Mint, where we're renovating and expanding our production facilities."

Associate Director for Numismatics David Pickens said, "The modernization program we're pursuing will ensure continuous process improvement in the production of the highest-quality Proof precious-metals products. We're anticipating a great deal of interest in the 2001 W-mintmark Proof Silver Eagle, so we've raised the mintage level to 750,000 coins this year."

The Mint's press release noted the Mint's plans to continue striking Proof American Silver Eagles at West Point in the future. It went on to describe the coins: "Each 2001 American Eagle Proof coin is sealed in a protective capsule, comes in a presentation case, and is accompanied by an official certificate of authenticity, documenting the coin's place in history. The Mint will begin sending out order forms for the 2001 American Eagle Gold and Silver Proof Coins on April 18, 2001. Effective April 18, 9 a.m. (Eastern Time), these coins will be available for online orders at www.USMINT.gov."

The Proofs of 2001 are among the more affordable in perfect PF-70 condition.

The number of 2001-W Proofs graded PF-70 continues to rise (as is true for all American Silver Eagles, as collectors and dealers submit more and more for certification). The number doubled between the publication of the second and third editions of this book (2013 and 2018), and the upward trend is ongoing.

2002, Bullion Strike

Mintage: 10,539,026

GSID: 10652

Minted at West Point, without mintmark

Historical context: Numismatics once again entered the national spotlight with the record-setting sale of a 1933 double eagle ($20 gold coin) once owned by Egypt's King Farouk Al-Awwal. In order to allow for the sale of the coin, the U.S. government relented (but only slightly) on its stance that all 1933 double eagles were illegal to own since the coin was never monetized and released into circulation. Stack's and Sotheby's auctioned the coin. The winning bid came in at $7,590,000—plus $20 to cover its face value! It would be nearly 20 years before the coin entered the market again, at a June 2021 auction by Sotheby's. The coin was sold along with other treasures owned by renowned fashion designer and collector Stuart Weitzman.

The sale capped off another good year for the hobby: the wildly successful 50 State Quarters program entered its fourth year, and sales of the bullion-strike American Silver Eagle soared past 10 million coins, finishing the year with a total mintage of 10,539,026—the second-highest total to date during the program's 16-year run.

An editorial by Beth Deisher in *Coin World* quoted the U.S. Mint in stating that more than 139 million adults "have saved at least one of the 50 state quarters since the program was launched in January 1999." This led numismatic historian Q. David Bowers to observe, "Numismatics is expanding by leaps and bounds, with interest precipitated by television and shopping networks, Mint promotions, and more. Simply put, there are not enough old coins to go around. Recently when my fine friend David Sundman, CEO of Littleton Coin Company, visited, he stated that he would give an eyetooth to buy quantity lots of hundreds or thousands of large copper cents (1857 and earlier); these were once a commodity in the hobby, but now are usually seen only one at a time, even for common dates."

Silver prices saw a modest increase over 2001. Gold rose by nearly $40, averaging $311.33 per ounce. Platinum was up slightly, averaging $539.11 per ounce for the year. 2002 average silver price: $4.61/ounce.

Coin commentary: Increased demand for the American Silver Eagle led to a slight rise in the number of coins certified for collectors. Quality for this date is excellent, with nearly all pieces struck by the West Point Mint (uncredited on the coin) grading in the MS-68 to MS-69 range.

Since the third edition of this book was published in 2018, the number of 2002 bullion strikes graded by PCGS and NGC as perfect MS-70 has jumped from very low hundreds to many thousands. This illustrates the reality of third-party certification of modern coins with mintages in the millions: a "top pop" unique MS-70 or PF-70 specimen won't be unique for long. Although perfection will always command a premium value, *Caveat emptor*.

2002-W, Proof

Mintage: 647,342

GSID: 10669

Minted at West Point, with W mintmark

Coin commentary: In 2002, as in 2001, production of Proof American Silver Eagles was at the U.S. Mint's West Point facility, instead of Philadelphia or San Francisco, where nearly all pre-2001 Proofs had been struck. The coins bear West Point's W mintmark. Their official issue price was kept at $24. Sales began mid-year, on June 5, and a mintage limit of 750,000 was set. Collector demand was not sufficient for a sellout, although the 2002 sale of nearly 648,000 coins exceeded the mintages of most preceding years.

The Mint announced the upcoming sale of the 2002-W Proofs on May 22, 2002. Mint Director Henrietta Holsman Fore noted that the American Silver Eagle features one of the most popular obverse coin designs in history, "recalling the golden era of coinage during which the design was first produced. . . . The American Eagle Silver Proof coin features sculptor Adolph A. Weinman's 'Walking Liberty' design, depicting Liberty striding confidently toward a rising sun, first issued as the obverse of the half dollar in 1916." The Mint noted that "Each 2002 American Eagle Proof coin is sealed in a protective capsule, comes in a presentation case, and is accompanied by an official certificate of authenticity, documenting the coin's place in history."

2003, Bullion Strike

Mintage: 8,495,008

GSID: 10653

Minted at West Point, without mintmark

Historical context: In March 2003 the United States and its allies launched an invasion of the nation of Iraq. Coalition forces, using an overwhelming complement of air and ground power, toppled the regime of Saddam Hussein within weeks. The war opened up a second theater of operations for the United States, with American involvement in Afghanistan continuing.

The wars, tax cuts, and general economic weakness pushed the federal budget deficit to a record $374 billion. On Wall Street, all three major indexes finished higher at the end of the year than they'd begun. The bull market took off after the market hit bottom in March. Bullion-strike American Silver Eagle sales, which started the year very strong, weakened in the bull market, finishing the year at a healthy but slightly disappointing mintage of 8,495,008.

The American Numismatic Association's spring National Money Show brought thousands of coin dealers and collectors to Charlotte, North Carolina, and the association's summer World's Fair of Money was held in Baltimore.

In 2003 Congress authorized the creation of the Citizens Coinage Advisory Committee, a public group tasked with advising the secretary of the Treasury on designs, themes, and other matters involving U.S. coins and medals.

Silver's bullion price climbed through 2003, nearing the $6 per ounce mark in the fourth quarter and averaging slightly under $5 for the year—an increase of nearly 30 cents over 2002. Gold was more than $50 per ounce stronger, averaging $364.80 for the year; and platinum jumped more than $150 per ounce, to $691.31.

2003 average silver price: $4.87/ounce.

Coin commentary: The quality of the bullion-strike American Silver Eagles produced at West Point remained strong. A substantial percentage of the coins submitted to PCGS and NGC for certification grade MS-69 or finer. This coin can be readily owned at the perfect level of MS-70.

PCGS has graded thousands of "First Strike" 2003 American Silver Eagles, about three-fourths of which were given an MS-69 grade. Dozens of examples earned an MS-70, with one such piece selling for $1,600 in a September 2012 online auction. Since then, prices for perfect "First Strikes" have softened.

Collectors also had the opportunity to buy PCGS-certified bullion-strike American Silver Eagles in limited-edition holders featuring the signatures of such notable individuals as Private First Class Jessica Lynch (the first American POW successfully rescued since World War II), who signed 1,432 labels, and cycling legend Lance Armstrong, who signed 204. General Tommy Franks signed one.

2003-W, Proof

Mintage: 747,831

GSID: 10670

Minted at West Point, with W mintmark

Coin commentary: Proof sales were on a steady course in 2003: the Mint's issue price stayed at $24 per coin, and the mintage cap was 750,000 coins, as in previous years. Collector interest was up by about 100,000 coins—a general trend that would continue for several years—and the mintage neared but did not break the authorized limit.

On March 19, 2003, the U.S. Mint announced that the 2003-W Proofs would go on sale April 2. "For 17 years, the American Eagle Silver Proof coin has had special appeal to collectors," said Mint Director Henrietta Holsman Fore. "With almost 10 million coins sold since 1986, this classic American design has proven to be one of the most popular coins in our nation's history." The Mint's press release noted that the Proof coin would have a limited mintage of 750,000, would be minted at the West Point facility, and would bear the W mintmark. As in years past, the Mint's marketing materials extolled the beauty of the coin's artistry. "The American Eagle Silver coin's obverse (heads) design is Adolph A. Weinman's full-length figure of Liberty in full stride, enveloped in folds of the flag, with her right hand extended and branches of laurel and oak in her left. The reverse (tails) design, by United States Mint sculptor/engraver John Mercanti, features the heraldic eagle with shield, an olive branch in the right talon and arrows in the left." The Mint also emphasized the coin's attractive packaging: "Each 2003 American Eagle Silver Proof coin is sealed in a protective capsule, mounted in a handsome, satin-lined velvet presentation case, and accompanied by an official certificate of authenticity, documenting the coin's place in history." Finally, making sure consumers understood the importance of the program's urgency, the Mint advised: "Because mintages of the 2003 American Eagle Silver Proof coins are limited, orders should be placed early. American Eagle Silver Proof coins are available for sale while quantities last or until the 2004 coins are issued. The United States Mint reserves the right to limit quantities and may discontinue accepting orders at any time."

Collectors and dealers have submitted tens of thousands of the 2003-W Proof to PCGS and NGC for certification. Many thousands have been graded at the perfect PF-70 level. Among the special labels and slabs that some collectors find desirable, PCGS encapsulated 103 coins (all PF-69) in "American Heroes Edition" packaging autographed by Jessica Lynch, an Army private rescued in Iraq (the first American POW rescued since World War II).

2004, Bullion Strike

Mintage: 8,882,754

GSID: 10654

Minted at West Point, without mintmark

Historical context: In 2004 silver began a four-year increase in average annual price of $2 or more per ounce. Of course, 2004's average silver price of $6.67 an ounce doesn't tell the whole story: the metal started the year off strong before peaking in April at $8.29 per ounce. It took a dive in May (touching $5.50) but ended the year on a high note.

The resulting bull market saw mintages of bullion-strike American Silver Eagles rise to record levels. The mintage of the 2004 bullion strike rose to 8,882,754. Early sales of the coin were very strong, with production exceeding the one-million mark in January and February before finishing the year with more than 2.6 million coins struck.

The American Numismatic Association held its spring 2004 National Money Show in Portland, Oregon, and its larger annual summer show, the World's Fair of Money, in Pittsburgh. Also in 2004 the American Numismatic Society relocated its headquarters (including the Harry W. Bass Jr. Library, the ANS Museum and Library, and other facilities) to its own office building at 140 William Street in lower Manhattan, not far from where the Society was founded in 1858. The ANS would relocate again several years later to 75 Varick Street in lower Manhattan, where it remains today. In Maryland, in December, the annual Baltimore coin show was a huge success, with coordinators impressed by the convention's traffic of thousands of attendees.

By 2004 interest in the 50 State Quarters program had started to wane. The Wisconsin quarter caused a frenzy among variety collectors as several die-related varieties were discovered in coins minted in Denver.

2004 average silver price: $6.66/ounce.

Coin commentary: The typical coin submitted for professional grading is MS-69, which is indicative of the overall quality of coins struck this year by the West Point Mint. A number of beautifully toned coins have been certified, with grades ranging from MS-67 to MS-69. The purity of the .999 fine silver can bring forth a captivating array of jewel-tone colors, and collectors pay strong premiums based on the pleasing nature and rich coloration of these naturally occurring toned coins.

Between 2013 and 2018 (when the second and third editions of this book were published), the number of 2004 bullion strikes certified by PCGS and NGC at MS-70 more than tripled. Since then, it has more than tripled again. For modern coins, "rare" grades don't stay rare forever. This gives collectors an opportunity to buy perfect-quality coins at affordable prices.

2004-W, Proof

Mintage: 801,602

GSID: 10672

Minted at West Point, with W mintmark

Coin commentary: The Mint raised the maximum mintage for the 2004 American Silver Eagle Proof to 850,000 (up from a limit of 750,000 in 2003). At the same time it instituted a higher issue price—the first such increase since 1998. The price was raised from $24.00 to $27.95.

The Mint announced the upcoming sale of the 2004-W Proofs on April 20, 2004. "The American Eagle Silver Proof coin's obverse (heads) design is Adolph A. Weinman's full-length figure of Liberty in full stride with her right hand extended and branches of laurel and oak in her left," the press materials noted. "The reverse (tails) design, by United States Mint sculptor/engraver John Mercanti, features the heraldic eagle with shield, an olive branch in the right talon, and arrows in the left. Each 2004 American Eagle Silver Proof coin is sealed in a protective capsule; mounted in a handsome, satin-lined velvet presentation case; and accompanied by a certificate of authenticity documenting the coin's place in history. Because mintages of the 2004 American Eagle Silver Proof coins are limited, orders should be placed early. American Eagle Silver Proof coins are available for sale while quantities last or until the 2005 coins are issued. The United States Mint reserves the right to limit quantities and may discontinue accepting orders at any time."

The third-party grading services have certified thousands of Proofs of 2004, most of them at the PF-69 level, but many in PF-70. Between 2013 and 2018, when the second and third editions of this book were published, the number of 2004-W American Silver Eagles certified by NGC and PCGS as PF-70 more than doubled. Since then the population has doubled again. The coin is affordable even in the perfect grade—among the least expensive of the entire series.

2005, Bullion Strike

Mintage: 8,891,025

GSID: 15388

Minted at West Point, without mintmark

Historical context: The first year of President George W. Bush's second term proved to be a time of great challenge for the American people. Hurricane Katrina struck the Gulf Coast in late August, wreaking devastation on an epic scale. The federal government famously mishandled the disaster, and fuel prices soared. Stocks finished the year slightly higher than they had started. In numismatics, 2005 was a record year for the sale of ultra-rarities, with 14 coins bringing $1 million or more each (a mark first surpassed only nine years earlier). Notable pieces include a 1787 Brasher doubloon (Punch on Breast variety) and a 1907 Ultra High Relief, Lettered Edge, 1907 Saint-Gaudens double eagle. Both sold for $2.99 million.

The Colorado-based American Numismatic Association boasted membership of more than 32,000 hobby enthusiasts in 2005. The Association held its spring National Money Show in Kansas City, and, in the summer, the ANA World's Fair of Money attracted coin collectors, investors, and dealers to San Francisco. That December the ANA named its museum after hobby legend Edward C. Rochette—a former ANA president, executive director, and editor of *The Numismatist.* Rochette had also been instrumental in the founding of the ANA's annual Summer Seminars, held at Association headquarters in Colorado Springs.

Silver continued its rise. Gold, too, had a good year, with an average price of $446, which was an increase of $40 over 2004's average price. Platinum rose in price by $50, finishing at an average price per ounce of $896.87. 2005 average silver price: $8.82/ounce.

Coin commentary: 2005 marked the debut of PCGS's "First Strike" program, a designation called "Early Release" by NGC. Coins submitted for these designations from preceding years had to be submitted in their original government-shipping packaging, unopened, with a postmark from within 30 days of their release. This accounts for the low numbers of pre-2004 "First Strike" and "Early Release" coins compared to the population of such coins of 2005.

There is a market for First Strike and Early Release coins, and coins encapsulated with special labels, though many professional numismatists such as Q. David Bowers advise collectors to "buy the coin and not the slab." In *American Gold and Silver: U.S. Mint Collector and Investor Coins and Medals, Bicentennial to Date*, this advice is summarized in the appendix on investing: "This kind of special packaging has limited premium value over the long run, in the secondary marketplace. A slab autographed by a coin designer or other famous person might have personal sentimental value, but ask yourself if other collectors will pay a premium for it in the future, and let your own buying be guided by the answer. Usually coin collectors consider only the alphanumeric certified grade (MS-69, PF-70, and the like) and pay little or no premium for extra adjectives."

2005-W, Proof

Mintage: 816,663

GSID: 15391

Minted at West Point, with W mintmark

Coin commentary: In 2005 the U.S. Mint started selling its Proof American Silver Eagles earlier in the year than normal (March 15, compared to April or even as late as May or June in recent years). The Mint kept the issue price at $27.95 after having raised it the year before. It also abolished the Proof coins' mintage limit, which had already been raised several times. Proof sales for 2005 were the highest since 1986 and 1987, the first two years of the bullion program. Collectors purchased more than 816,000 of the 2005-W coins.

On March 10, 2005, the U.S. Mint announced that the 2005-W American Silver Eagle Proof coins "will be available for sale on March 15, 2005, at 12:00 noon (ET). The release date for this product is six weeks earlier than in 2004, as part of the United States Mint's commitment to make many of its 2005 products available earlier in the year." The official press release went on to describe the issue: "Priced at $27.95 each, the 2005 American Eagle Silver Proof coins have an unlimited mintage and are minted at the United States Mint at West Point. The coins bear the 'W' mintmark. The popularity of the Silver Eagle Proof program has been increasing steadily over the past few years, and the United States Mint is committed to meeting the collecting needs of its longtime customers, as well as accommodating the requirements of the many new coin collectors joining the ranks of this growing hobby." The Mint's special care in packaging the Proofs was emphasized in its announcement: "Each 2005 American Eagle Silver Proof coin is sealed in a protective capsule; mounted in a handsome, satin-lined velvet presentation case; and accompanied by a certificate of authenticity documenting the coin's place in history." The Mint also noted a service for coin collectors: "As an added convenience, customers can participate in a subscription-ordering program in which American Eagle Silver Proof coins can be charged and shipped to the customer automatically as each new coin is released."

PCGS and NGC have certified tens of thousands of Proofs of 2005, most of them at the PF-69 level, but considerable thousands in PF-70. The 2005-W is affordable even in the latter perfect grade—among the least expensive of the entire series.

2006, Bullion Strike

Mintage: 10,676,522

GSID: 68740

Minted at West Point, without mintmark

Historical context: The price of silver jumped from an average of $8.82 an ounce to $11.54 in 2006. For the second time in five years, mintages of bullion-strike American Silver Eagles eclipsed the 10 million mark. Stocks continued to perform well, despite a slowing real-estate market. Housing prices peaked in 2006, while the number of foreclosures exceeded 1.2 million for the first time in United States history.

The U.S. coin market was strong through the middle of the year, when the weakening economy began to affect it. The U.S. Mint expanded the American Silver Eagle program for the first time in its 20-year history, offering not just bullion-strike and Proof versions of the coin but also a specially prepared burnished version bearing the W mintmark for West Point. Not only that, but a Reverse Proof featuring frosted fields and mirrored devices was produced for the first time ever in the Mint's history.

The numismatic press updated the hobby community on John Mercanti's elevation to chief engraver at the U.S. Mint in 2006. *Numismatic News* reported on June 13: "Mercanti's responsibilities will include overseeing the artistic design of all new products; the complete development of master tooling (including the reduction hub, master die and work hubs), from approved designs through approved trial strikes; supervision of tool makers, engravers, and other craft and trades personnel involved in the development of master tooling; and the timely delivery of reduction hubs/master dies for all recurring and new products to the die shops at the mints in Denver and Philadelphia." *Coin World* in a June 12 article reported that "The demands on the engraving staff today include projects that in the early stages of Mercanti's career would have been granted many months of preparation time, but now have deadlines of just weeks after inception. The workload has nearly tripled over the past few years, and is only expected to increase." 2006 average silver price: $11.54/ounce.

Coin commentary: West Point again had the honor of minting the American Silver Eagle bullion strikes in 2006. Consistent with their typical production quality, coins of this date were beautifully struck on high-quality planchets. The typical coin is virtually flawless with an attractive lightly-satin finish.

As general demand for the American Silver Eagle increased, so did collector demand for certified examples. PCGS and NGC have graded hundreds of thousands of the 2006 bullion strike, including many tens of thousands designated as First Strike or Early Release. The vast majority grade MS-69.

Collectors seeking slabbed perfect-grade MS-70 coins have ample opportunity to take their pick from among thousands that have earned that grade from PCGS and NGC, including many hundreds labeled as First Strike or Early Release.

2006-W, Burnished

Mintage: 468,020

GSID: 70901

Minted at West Point, with W mintmark

Coin commentary: The Burnished (called *Uncirculated* by the Mint) 2006-W American Silver Eagle was released late in the year. In celebration of the 20th anniversary of the Mint's bullion coinage program, the W mintmark was used on these special bullion coins made at West Point. The coins were struck on what the Mint called "burnished" planchets. Some of these 2006-W Burnished American Silver Eagles were packaged for collectors in three-coin 20th Anniversary sets (along with a Proof and Reverse Proof coin; see following for more on those sets). In addition to being available in sets, these American Silver Eagles were offered individually, with an issue price of $19.95 per coin (a price between that of the regular bullion-strike coin and the Proof version).

The finish of the Burnished coin is nearly indistinguishable from that of the regular bullion issue. It's the W mintmark, for West Point, that makes this version easily identifiable.

The 2006-W Burnished American Silver Eagle is ranked number 68 among the *100 Greatest U.S. Modern Coins,* fifth edition.

Also see the separate entry in this chapter for more information on a 20th Anniversary gold-and-silver two-coin set (which included a Burnished 2006-W American Silver Eagle) issued in 2006.

2006-P, Reverse Proof

Mintage: 248,875

GSID: 68427

Minted at Philadelphia, with P mintmark

Coin commentary: The 2006-P Reverse Proof American Silver Eagle was sold by the U.S. Mint in a special three-coin 20th Anniversary Silver Eagle set. This set, announced on August 21 of that year and available for purchase on August 30, was the only way of acquiring the Reverse Proof coin. Mintage was capped at 250,000 sets, with a limit of 10 sets per household. The issue price for the set was $100.

This was the first time the Mint used a Reverse Proof format on the American Silver Eagle. Mint literature described the effect as "a unique finish which results in a frosted field, or background, and a brilliant, mirror-like finish on the raised elements of the coin, including the design and inscriptions."

Collector interest was high from the first hour of sales, and the anniversary sets sold out in a little more than two months. Weeks out of the gate they were being traded on the secondary market at twice their issue price.

The coin is ranked number 33 among the *100 Greatest U.S. Modern Coins*, fifth edition. "Its look is so distinctive within the series that the Reverse Proof will always be a curious standout among silver eagles," write Schechter and Garrett.

The 2006-P Reverse Proof American Silver Eagle, like many of the series' recent special-finish collectibles, has been discussed in the trade papers. Market observer Eric Jordan noted in an August 2012 commentary in *Numismatic News* that the 2006-P is no longer the only Reverse Proof in the series, but it still holds appeal for collectors. "The distinction of being the only one is gone," wrote Jordan, "but something else is taking its place and what that will be is largely dependent on how these sets are going to be put together. . . . [If collectors] start working on sets of Reverse Proofs as a cost-effective way to get around buying an expensive 1995-W, then this 2006-P and by extension its Reverse Proof siblings may get a life of their own" (*Numismatic News*, "Silver Eagle: The Modern Morgan," August 21, 2012). Since then, of course, other Reverse Proofs have joined the lineup, giving collectors a nice set to assemble.

2006-W, Proof

Mintage: 1,092,477
GSID: 65333
Minted at West Point, with W mintmark

Coin commentary: The 2006-W Proof was issued by the Mint early in the year. There was no production limit established for the mintage of this collectible coin. It was released at an issue price of $27.95 per coin (the same price as in recent years). Collector demand for this year's Proof coin exceeded 1 million for the first time since the American Silver Eagle debuted in 1986.

Sales of the 2006-W Proof were boosted by the coin's inclusion in the 20th Anniversary Silver Eagle Set, which went on sale August 30, 2006, and which ultimately accounted for nearly 250,000 of the total Proof coins sold. For more information on the anniversary set, see its separate entry in this chapter.

The U.S. Mint announced on April 5, 2006, that the year's Proof American Silver Eagles would be available at the Mint's booth at the American Numismatic Association's National Money Show, April 7 through 9. The show was held at the Cobb Galleria Centre in Atlanta, Georgia.

In *Coin World*, Steve Roach used the 2006-W Proof as an example in an article about First Strike coins. "By virtue of population numbers alone, early release coins generally are not scarcer than their later-issued brethren," he noted. "Take for example the Proof 2006-W American Eagle silver dollar. As of mid-June, PCGS graded 7,285 examples under its normal program and 7,716 pieces under its First Strike program. The early release programs take into account only when a coin was shipped from the U.S. Mint, not when it was minted. The programs were first developed by the grading services in 2005. The 'First Strikes' are visually imperceptible from their later-released counterparts" (*Coin World*, "First Strikes, Early Releases: Buyers Should Do Homework," August 1, 2011).

PCGS and NGC have graded tens of thousands of the 2006-W Proof, most in PF-69 but a significant percentage of them in PF-70, making even the most "perfect" coins affordable.

2006 American Eagle 20th Anniversary Silver Coin Set

Mintage: 248,875

GSID: 70815

Minted at Philadelphia and West Point, with P and W mintmarks

Set commentary: This set of coins marked the 20th anniversary of the United States' bullion program with three American Silver Eagles, each produced with a different finish. One had the Mint's new Burnished (*Uncirculated*, in Mint jargon) finish; another had the standard brilliant mirror-like Proof finish; and another had the Reverse Proof finish (used on the American Silver Eagle for the first time).

The set went on sale August 30, 2006, at the issue price of $100, and with a production limit of 250,000 sets. The Mint sought to curb speculation and hoarding by limiting each household to ten sets. Collectors and investors were excited about the set, its innovative finish formats, its historical significance, and its limited mintage. The issue sold out in about ten weeks, and by that time prices were rising on the secondary market. The set was selling for six times its issue price by mid-2007, after which its value sloped down and leveled out.

See each coin's separate listing for more information.

2006-W American Eagle 20th Anniversary Gold & Silver Coin Set

Mintage: 20,000

GSID: 65332

Minted at West Point, with W mintmarks

Set commentary: The U.S. Mint in 2006 issued a 20th Anniversary Gold and Silver Set, marking this milestone in the nation's bullion coinage program. Each set contains a one-ounce American Gold Eagle and an American Silver Eagle. The coins bear the W mintmark of the West Point facility and were struck in the Burnished or "Uncirculated" finish.

Production of the two-coin set was limited to 20,000. It was packaged with an informative booklet outlining the international history of gold and silver coins. The issue price was $850, with a limit of ten sets per household, and there was enough collector and investor interest to cause a sellout.

2007, Bullion Strike

Mintage: 9,028,036

GSID: 68989

Minted at West Point, without mintmark

Historical context: The Dow-Jones Industrial Average surpassed 14,000 for the first time in July 2007. Interest rates were high and the real-estate market was weakening. In the numismatic market, higher interest rates and slow sales translated into a scarcity of ready cash for many coin dealers. A strong market existed for classic collector coins—key dates in popular series—as well as for higher-grade silver and gold coins. Exonumia (medals and tokens) and paper currency also enjoyed robust markets.

In an attempt to reinvigorate the "golden" dollar coin program, Congress authorized the release of a new series of dollars featuring the likenesses of the presidents of the United States. The program also called for the continued production of a Native American dollar coin featuring a modified Sacagawea obverse and new reverses celebrating Native American heritage.

The new dollar coins were eagerly awaited by collectors. Production errors unintentionally left the congressionally mandated edge lettering off of some coins. These coins became the first U.S. coins struck in more than a hundred years to omit the motto IN GOD WE TRUST. These accidental varieties became known as "Godless dollars."

The *Philadelphia Inquirer* described the new small-size dollars as "cool" and "edgy" (playing off their innovative edge lettering). "Hold up one of the new dollar coins, which debuted two days ago, and you'll see letters and numbers around the rim," the *Inquirer* reported ("New Dollar Coins Rolled Out," February 17, 2007). "The P, of course, is for the Philadelphia Mint, the world's biggest. Other features to inspire interest and acceptance: a big '$1' on the back (other coins spell out amounts). Presidents on the front, a new one every three months. The Statue of Liberty on the back. . . . Time will tell whether the coins become common in pockets and cash registers. The Mint has dreams: 'I even suspect the tooth fairy will love leaving these beautiful coins under pillows,' Washington-based director Edmund C. Moy stated."

Silver as bullion continued on the rise, its average increasing by about $1.75 per ounce over 2006. Gold's average rose as well, climbing nearly $100 per ounce, to $699.00, and platinum saw another healthy increase of $160, averaging at $1,303.05 for the year.

2007 average silver price: $13.32/ounce.

Coin commentary: Demand dropped slightly for the American Silver Eagle in 2007, compared to 2006. They remain among the series' most affordable.

2007-W, Burnished

Mintage: 621,333

GSID: 68986

Minted at West Point, with W mintmark

Coin commentary: In 2007 the U.S. Mint released its second Burnished (or *Uncirculated*) American Silver Eagle. Like the Burnished issue of the previous year, the 2007-W was produced at West Point and bears that facility's unique mintmark. Sold directly to the public, its issue price was $21.95 per coin—an increase of $2 over 2006—and no mintage limit was mandated. Collector interest pushed the mintage to more than 150,000 coins over the quantity sold in 2006.

In addition to being offered individually, the 2007-W Burnished American Silver Eagle was packaged in the 2007 U.S. Mint Annual Uncirculated Dollar Coin Set (along with Satin finish strikes of the year's Sacagawea dollar and four Presidential dollars). The set's issue price was $31.95.

PCGS and NGC have graded tens of thousands of the 2007-W Burnished American Silver Eagles. Most of these are MS-69, but a significant quantity of thousands are MS-70. Collectors seeking perfection do not have to pay a large premium.

2007-W, Proof

Mintage: 821,759
GSID: 68606
Minted at West Point, with W mintmark

Coin commentary: The 2007-W Proof American Silver Eagle was issued by the Mint on March 27 of that year. There was no maximum mandated for the production of this collectible release. It was issued at $29.95 per coin—an increase of $2 over the 2006 price. Perhaps as a result, collector demand declined compared to the previous year by more than 270,000 coins.

The Mint announced the upcoming sale of the 2007 Proof coins in a press release dated March 12, 2007. "Priced at $29.95 each, the 2007 American Eagle Silver Proof coins will not have a pre-determined mintage," the letter stated, "as the United States Mint will produce these coins to meet demand. The American Eagle Silver Coins are minted at the United States Mint at West Point, with the 'W' mintmark."

Describing the coin, the Mint's promotional materials noted that "The American Eagle Silver Proof coin's obverse (heads) design is Adolph A. Weinman's full-length figure of Liberty in full stride with her right hand extended and branches of laurel and oak in her left. The reverse (tails) design, by United States Mint Sculptor-Engraver John Mercanti, features the heraldic eagle with shield, an olive branch in the right talon and arrows in the left."

The Mint lavished praise on the coins' attractive packaging: "Each 2007 American Eagle Silver Proof coin is sealed in a protective capsule; mounted in a handsome, satin-lined velvet presentation case; and accompanied by a certificate of authenticity documenting the coin's place in history."

Tens of thousands of 2007-W Proofs have been professionally graded by NGC and PCGS. Historically some 25 percent of this quantity has graded at the PF-70 level, with the bulk of the remainder being PF-69. This reflects the high quality that characterizes modern U.S. Mint production. Anything below PF-69 is, ironically, a "condition rarity"—not that collectors would pay a premium for that rare distinction.

2008, Bullion Strike

Mintage: 20,583,000
GSID: 68913
Minted at West Point, without mintmark

Historical context: Three stories dominated the news in 2008: the nation's worsening financial crisis (in particular the collapse of the housing market); the presidential campaign of Republican John McCain vs. Democrat Barack Obama; and Obama's election that November. In numismatics, the market for high-quality coins maintained its strength, although collector spending was slowing down slightly.

Demand for silver surged worldwide in the first half of the year, with its price spiking upward of $20 per ounce but settling back in the second half; its yearly average increased over 2007 by more than $1.50 per ounce. Gold saw a dramatic bump, from $699 per ounce in 2007 to an average of $900 in 2008. Platinum also climbed, up $270 per ounce to $1,573.53.

2008 average silver price: $14.99/ounce.

Coin commentary: Demand for the American Silver Eagle exploded in 2008, with production more than doubling the previous year's output. The mintage of 20.6 million coins was far greater than the previous record, set in 1987, of 11.4 million. The Mint struggled to keep up with production and had to temporarily suspend (and then ration) orders for the coin. It even stopped orders for the Proof version, diverting all silver blanks to production of the regular bullion strikes.

The Mint issued a statement (reported in the June 5, 2008, issue of *Numismatic News*): "Since the introduction of the 2008 American Eagle Silver Bullion Coin Program, the United States Mint has issued a record number of coins (about 9.65 million), as demand for them has increased exponentially. That number is almost as high as . . . production for the entire year of 2007 (about 9.8 million). By law, the . . . bullion coins must meet exacting specifications and must be composed of newly mined silver acquired from domestic sources. The United States Mint will continue to make every effort to increase its acquisition of silver bullion blanks that meet these specifications and requirements to address continuing high demand in the silver bullion coin market." Production did continue, with millions more of the coins being minted through the year.

With so many 2008 bullion strikes in existence, the coin is one of the most affordable of the series.

2008-W, Burnished, Reverse of 2007

Mintage: *47,000 (estimated)*

GSID: 197930

Minted at West Point, with W mintmark

Coin commentary: The 2008-W, Reverse of 2007, Burnished American Silver Eagle is the only significant die variety in the series. Since its discovery in mid-April 2008 it has excited collectors and has been avidly sought as a required coin in the set.

The variety is the result of rehubbing (creation of a new hub, which is used to make coinage dies) during the Mint's transition to digital engraving methods. Minor changes for the new 2008 coins were made to the design of the reverse, most notably in the font used in the legends. The font difference is most noticeable in the U of UNITED. In the lettering style of 1986–2007, the U has a smooth curve at the bottom right. In the new lettering style adopted for 2008, the U has a spur or foot at the bottom right.

The Reverse of 2007 variety is ranked number 14 in the book *100 Greatest U.S. Modern Coins*, fifth edition, which describes the Mint's reaction to the coin's discovery. "The Mint responded quickly, acknowledging that during three production shifts for the 2008 coins, dies originally crafted for 2007-W silver eagle production were used inadvertently. Approximately 47,000 silver eagles had been struck with the reverse style of 2007. This type of variety is called *transitional* because it is a hybrid that combines the styles of coins used in two consecutive years."

This interesting and very collectible coin is also featured in the *Cherrypickers' Guide to Rare Die Varieties*.

2008-W, Burnished, Reverse of 2008

Mintage: 533,757

GSID: 68999

Minted at West Point, with W mintmark

Coin commentary: In 2008 the U.S. Mint produced its third Burnished (or *Uncirculated*) American Silver Eagle. Like the Burnished issue of previous years, the coin was struck at West Point and bears that facility's W mintmark. Sold directly to the public, its issue price was $25.95 per coin and no mintage limit was set. Collector interest was down by about 90,000 coins compared to 2007.

The Mint waxed poetic in its March 10, 2008, announcement of the coin's release. "'She walks in beauty, like the night / Of cloudless climes and starry skies.' Although Lord Byron wrote those words almost two centuries ago, they can serve to describe the classic beauty of Adolph Weinman's image of Liberty. That image—featured on United States Mint American Eagle bullion and Proof coins since 1986—graces the 2008 American Eagle Silver Uncirculated coin, scheduled for release on March 17 at noon." The Mint's promotional materials went on to further describe the coin's design and its packaging: "The 2008 American Eagle Silver Uncirculated coin, offered at $25.95, contains one troy ounce of .999 silver. The obverse features Liberty in full stride enveloped in the folds of the American flag, with her right hand extended and branches of laurel and oak in her left. Featured on the coin's reverse is the image of a heraldic eagle with shield, an olive branch in the right talon and arrows in the left. Struck on specially burnished blanks, the American Eagle Uncirculated coins feature a finish similar to their bullion counterparts, but carry the 'W' mintmark, indicating their production at the United States mint at West Point. Each coin is encapsulated in protective plastic and placed in a blue presentation case accompanied by a certificate of authenticity signed by the director of the United States Mint, Edmund C. Moy."

In addition to being offered individually, the 2008-W Burnished American Silver Eagle was packaged in the 2008 U.S. Mint Annual Uncirculated Dollar Coin Set (along with Satin finish strikes of the year's Sacagawea dollar and four Presidential dollars). The set's issue price was $37.95.

Substantial quantities have been graded MS-70.

2008-W, Proof

Mintage: 700,979
GSID: 68914
Minted at West Point, with W mintmark

Coin commentary: The hyperactive silver market of 2008 adversely affected production of the year's Proof American Silver Eagle. As in recent years, no maximum mintage limit was established for the Proof coins; however, by August of 2008 the Mint was forced to suspend sales of the Proofs because of a shortage of silver blanks. All available and incoming silver planchets were being diverted from the Proof coinage to continue production of regular bullion strikes. (The American Silver Eagle's authorizing legislation mandates that the bullion coins be minted "in quantities sufficient to meet public demand," while the Treasury Department has discretion over how many collector-format coins, such as Proofs, are struck.)

Sale of the Proof coins was suspended in mid-August, and the coin was listed as "Not Available" in the Mint's online catalog. The "temporary" suspension was not lifted, so production of 2008-W Proofs effectively ended after about 700,000 of the coins were sold. The suspension of Proof coinage continued through 2009, and it wasn't until 2010 that the collector-format coins were produced again.

The 2008-W Proof had an issue price of $31.95.

Historically the thousands of 2008-W Proofs professionally graded by NGC and PCGS have yielded about 25 percent in PF-70, making perfect coins readily available and affordable.

2009, Bullion Strike

Mintage: 30,459,000

GSID: 69445

Minted at West Point, without mintmark

Historical context: The American economy, in turmoil for most of 2009, hit rock bottom but by the end of the year began to show some signs of improvement. In numismatics, retail prices held steady for most series. However, overall retail and auction sales volume was slightly less than in recent years.

This year marked the bicentennial of the birth of Abraham Lincoln, commemorated by the U.S. Mint in four new reverse designs for the Lincoln cent. The first, Birth and Early Childhood in Kentucky, depicts a small log cabin like the one in which Lincoln was born. The second, Formative Years in Indiana, shows a youthful Abe Lincoln taking a break from rail-splitting to read a book. On the third coin, Professional Life in Illinois, Lincoln stands in front of the state capitol of Illinois (the design commemorates his pre-presidential career in law and politics). Finally, Presidency in Washington depicts the partially completed U.S. Capitol dome as it appeared when Lincoln held office. The state of the Capitol building represents "the unfinished business of a nation torn apart by slavery and the Civil War."

Silver saw swings in its bullion value, ranging from $10.51 to just over $19 per ounce. Its average for the year was about 30 cents lower than 2008's. Interest in gold was intense, with its price peaking at $1,215 per ounce in December, but its overall average for the year was up a mere 1 percent (compared to 2008), to $910 per ounce. Platinum tumbled $370, to $1,203.49.

2009 average silver price: $14.66/ounce.

Coin commentary: In a repeat of 2008, in 2009 demand for the American Silver Eagle made the coin's mintage skyrocket. The supply of silver continued to be a production challenge for the Mint. As in the previous year, the Mint rationed purchase of the bullion coins, with its authorized distributors limited to preset quantities. To further assist production, all silver blanks in 2009 were reserved for standard bullion-strike coins, with none allocated for Proofs or Burnished pieces. The distributor rationing was lifted on June 15 after the Mint's silver-planchet suppliers were able to meet demand, but by late November it had to temporarily *suspend* sales and then re-establish the rationing system.

Even with these challenges, the Mint produced more than 30 million American Silver Eagles by year's end, setting another record for the series.

Of the hundreds of thousands of 2009 bullion strikes professionally graded by NGC and PCGS, nearly half were granted the Early Release or First Strike designation.

2010, Bullion Strike

Mintage: 34,764,500

GSID: 71049

Minted at West Point, without mintmark

Historical context: The year 2010 started with a catastrophic earthquake in Haiti; then a massive British Petroleum oil spill dominated the news for much of the spring and summer. Domestically the U.S. economy continued in its slump, with high unemployment.

In numismatics, rarities and $100,000-plus coins were not as active in 2010 as in preceding years, although there were exceptions. In January one of five known examples of the 1913 Liberty Head nickel sold at auction for $3,737,500. Throughout the year several individual coins sold for $1 million or more. Meanwhile, popular collector coins and paper money continued to enjoy solid footing in the marketplace. The Mint introduced its new program of circulating America the Beautiful quarter dollars (popularly known as "National Park quarters") and companion five-ounce silver bullion coins.

The silver market was active, with per-ounce prices ranging from $15 to more than $30. In late summer the price hit $20 and climbed steadily. Silver averaged for the year more than $5 per ounce higher than 2009. Gold rose as well, more than $200 per ounce, to $1,124.53; and platinum saw a $400 jump to an average of $1,608.98 for the year.

2010 average silver price: $20.19/ounce.

Coin commentary: The 2010 American Silver Eagle was available for purchase later in the year than previous dates. Under a normal production schedule the Mint would have started striking 2010-dated coins in late 2009, for distribution starting in the first week of January 2010. The immense demand for American Silver Eagles in 2009 kept Mint presses running through to the end of December. Production of 2010 bullion strikes was delayed; the coins finally were made available on January 19.

The Mint once again followed a rationing program, as it had in 2009, allocating quantities of the bullion coins to its distributors. For most of the year the Mint also delayed production of collector versions (Proof and Burnished) of the 2010 coins, and the hobby community was uncertain whether any would be forthcoming. These steps were necessary because of the ongoing shortage of silver blanks and the Mint's congressional mandate to produce sufficient bullion-strike coins to satisfy public demand. Finally, on September 2, the rationing was lifted. (Proofs would in fact be produced in 2010, but the Burnished collector coins would be further postponed until 2011.)

Tens of thousands of professionally graded 2010 bullion strikes have been certified as MS-70.

2010-W, Proof

Mintage: 849,861
GSID: 71050
Minted at West Point, with W mintmark

Coin commentary: Production of Proof 2010 American Silver Eagles was far from guaranteed until well into autumn that year. The Mint's situation was similar to that of 2009: a shortage of silver blanks forced all production to be focused on bullion-strike coins. (The legislation that authorized the bullion program mandated that the bullion coins be produced in quantities sufficient to satisfy public demand. When demand was greater than the supply of silver planchets, collector-quality Proofs had to take a back seat to the standard-quality bullion coins.)

Finally, in early October Mint officials were able to announce that 2010 Proofs would indeed be made available for collectors. Order-taking would start on November 19, and coins would begin shipping on December 1.

The issue price was set at $45.95 per coin—a $14 increase over the last available Proof, the 2008-W. Customers were at first limited to 100 coins per household (that limit was later removed), and no maximum mintage was established. Initial demand was high, with the Mint selling more than 700,000 Proofs in two weeks. Ultimately nearly 850,000 coins were bought by collectors.

No Burnished American Silver Eagles were issued in 2010.

Late in 2010 legislation was passed allowing the Mint to produce collectible (Proof and Burnished) American Silver Eagles even if public demand for the regular bullion coin is not met in a given year.

A large percentage of the 2010-W Proofs that have been professionally certified, graded, and encapsulated are at the PF-70 level.

2011, Bullion Strike

Mintage: 40,020,000

GSID: 84266 (San Francisco) / 84267 (West Point)

Minted at San Francisco and West Point, without mintmark

Historical context: Major news stories of 2011 included the death of terrorist Osama bin Laden and unrest and civil war in the Arab world, including the overthrow and killing of Moammar Gadhafi in Libya. In the United States, the continuing economic hard times dominated the news.

The coin market maintained its overall strength of recent years. Most collector items offered for retail sale or put up for bid enjoyed ready demand. A significant numismatic court case reached a milestone in July 2011. A jury decided unanimously in favor of the federal government regarding a family's inheritance of ten super-rare 1933 double eagles. The jury concluded that the coins had been illegally obtained from the U.S. government and therefore still were government property, subject to forfeiture. The decision would be affirmed a year later. The family appealed the decision, but the U.S. Third Circuit Court of Appeals affirmed it in 2016 and the U.S. Supreme Court declined to review the case in 2017.

Silver was robust in 2011, with its yearly average bullion value topping \$35 per ounce—a 75 percent increase over 2010. Gold was strong, as well, increasing by nearly \$450 per ounce, to \$1,571.52. Platinum, while not as dramatic, increased by more than \$100 per ounce, to a yearly average of \$1,721.86.

2011 average silver price: \$35.12/ounce.

Coin commentary: Demand for the American Silver Eagle was strong right out of the gate in 2011. Sales of 2011-dated bullion strikes commenced early in January, and more than 6 million of the coins were sold in that month alone. To meet the public demand for the silver coins, which had exploded in 2008 and had been increasing since, the U.S. Mint fired up its presses at the San Francisco Mint to assist West Point with production. It fine-tuned the production processes at the latter facility to boost output. Meanwhile, the Mint was also able to secure additional suppliers for the silver blanks used to make the coins.

In early 2013 the numismatic press reported that fake 2011 American Silver Eagles had come to light in Canada. Paul Gilkes noted that "A counterfeit 2011 American Eagle silver bullion coin recently passed as genuine at a coin shop in Toronto contains no silver, but does contain a trace amount of gold in its composition. . . ." (*Coin World*, "Fake American Eagle Silver Coins Surface," February 4, 2013).

The 2011 bullion strikes bear no mintmarks to distinguish which were struck at West Point and which at San Francisco. However, PCGS and NGC differentiate between the two when a San Francisco "monster box" with appropriate markings is submitted for grading. In October 2020 the Mint released detailed mintage information on American Silver Eagles struck from 1986 partway through 2017. Included was a breakdown of the 2011 bullion-strike production: 34,984,500 coins at West Mint; 5,035,500 at San Francisco.

2011-S, Burnished

Mintage: 99,882
GSID: 74464
Minted at San Francisco, with S mintmark

Coin commentary: The 2011-S Burnished (*Uncirculated*, in Mint terminology) American Silver Eagle was issued as part of the Mint's special five-coin 25th Anniversary Silver Eagle Set. The coin was unique to the set—that is, not available for sale individually. Production was limited to 100,000 sets, which sold out in a matter of hours on October 27, 2011.

For more information on the five-coin set, see its separate entry.

The 2011-S has been eagerly followed by collectors and commented upon in the numismatic press. Eric Jordan, writing in *Numismatic News* in August 2012, observed that "Sometimes a mintage listing is worth a thousand words and that is certainly the case with the 2011-S silver dollar" (*Numismatic News*, "Silver Eagle: The Modern Morgan," August 21, 2012). In the third edition of *100 Greatest U.S. Modern Coins*, published in 2014, coauthors Scott Schechter and Jeff Garrett comment on the Mint's reasoning behind this particular American Silver Eagle: "Even with so much enthusiasm about this coin, to many it seemed odd or somewhat arbitrary that a San Francisco–made silver eagle was included in the set at all. Why San Francisco? There are two reasons. First, to Mint personnel, the San Francisco Mint is closely associated with the early history of the silver eagle. In 1986, the first silver eagles were struck there. Proof silver eagles, the only silver eagles sold directly to collectors, were made at San Francisco exclusively from 1986 to 1992. Second, starting again in 2011, San Francisco joined West Point in the production of bullion silver eagles." Describing the 2011-S, Schechter and Garrett write, "Everything else in this set had been seen before, but this coin was truly a first: the first-ever Uncirculated silver eagle with an S mintmark." They sum up the hobby community's excitement at the time of release: "Wow! This was the coin that really got everyone talking." In the fourth edition of the Schechter/Garrett book, published in 2017, the 2011-S Burnished American Silver Eagle is ranked number 49 among the 100 Greatest U.S. Modern Coins.

2011-W, Burnished

Mintage: 409,927

GSID: 71303

Minted at West Point, with W mintmark

Coin commentary: In 2011 the Mint issued another Burnished American Silver Eagle—its fourth since 2006—for collectors. (Production of the Burnished collector coins was cancelled in 2009 and 2010 so the Mint could focus all its efforts on the regular bullion strike.) The issue price was established at $60.45 and later lowered to $50.95. The coins have yet to attain a significant premium on the secondary market. In addition to being sold individually, the 2011-W Burnished American Silver Eagle was available as part of the five-coin 25th Anniversary Silver Eagle Set.

The Mint announced the coins' release on September 8, 2011. "The United States Mint will offer 2011 American Eagle Silver Uncirculated coins beginning at noon Eastern Time (ET) on September 15, 2011," its press release stated. "The one-ounce .999 silver coin is currently priced at $60.45. As with all products sold by the United States Mint containing precious metals, pricing is subject to change." It then described the coins' production and packaging: "Struck on specially burnished blanks, American Eagle Silver Uncirculated coins feature a finish similar to their bullion counterparts but carry the 'W' mintmark, indicating production at the United States mint at West Point. Each coin is encapsulated in protective plastic and placed in a blue presentation case accompanied by a certificate of authenticity."

PCGS and NGC grade the individually sold coins as well as those issued in the Anniversary set (identified as such on their slab labels), including First Strikes and Early Releases for both types of coins. In order to certify individual coins as coming from the 25th Anniversary Set, the third-party grading firms require the entire set to be submitted in its original, sealed Mint shipping box.

2011-P, Reverse Proof

Mintage: 99,882

GSID: 71375

Minted at Philadelphia, with P mintmark

Coin commentary: The 2011-P Proof American Silver Eagle was issued as part of the Mint's special five-coin 25th Anniversary Silver Eagle Set. The coin was unique to the set—not available for sale individually. Production was limited to 100,000 sets, which sold out in a matter of hours on October 27, 2011.

The Reverse Proof has mirrored design elements and frosted fields—rather than frosted elements and a mirror field, as has a normal Proof.

The Mint announced the sale of the special set on October 20, 2011. "The United States Mint is pleased to announce the opening of sales for the limited-edition American Eagle 25th Anniversary Silver Coin Set at noon Eastern Time on October 27, 2011," it stated in a press release. "Orders will be limited to five (5) sets per household for the first week of sales. At the end of this period, the United States Mint will re-evaluate this limit and extend, adjust, or remove it. The current price is $299.95 per set, but as with all products containing precious metals, it is subject to change."

Commenting on the sales trend of collectible coins like the 2011-P Reverse Proof American Silver Eagle, market observer Eric Jordan wrote, "Hotly anticipated coins have a sales curve much like movie tickets. Each succeeding week's sales are about half that of the previous week and between 60 and 75 percent of an unlimited annual sales run will show up in the first four weeks" (*Numismatic News*, "Silver Eagle: The Modern Morgan," August 21, 2012). The 2017 fourth edition of *100 Greatest U.S. Modern Coins* (Schechter/Garrett) describes the enthusiasm within the hobby community: "Collectors could not resist the allure of the coins that were unique to this set, including the Reverse Proof. With only 100,000 minted, the 2011-P Reverse Proof is by far the scarcest of all Reverse Proof silver eagles yet issued and is among the most highly sought-after of all recent U.S. Mint releases." These factors have ranked the 2011-P Reverse Proof as number 20 among the 100 Greatest U.S. Modern Coins.

For more information on the set, see its individual entry in this chapter.

2011-W, Proof

Mintage: 947,355
GSID: 71046
Minted at West Point, with W mintmark

Coin commentary: The 2011-W Proof American Silver Eagle was made available June 30 of that year, with an issue price of $59.95 per coin. (The Mint's price for the coin was increased in September to $68.45 and later decreased to $58.95, to accommodate the changing bullion price of silver.) Collectors bought nearly 370,000 of the Proofs in the first six days of sales, before sales slowed down and leveled off. An established limit of 100 coins per household was lifted after two weeks of sales. No maximum mintage was set.

The 2011-W Proof was available individually and was also packaged in the Mint's 25th Anniversary Silver Eagle Set (see its separate entry in this chapter), which accounted for 100,000 of the coins.

PCGS and NGC grade the individually sold coins as well as those issued in the Anniversary set (identified as such on their slab labels), including First Strikes and Early Releases for coins from both sources. In order to certify individual coins as coming from the 25th Anniversary Set, the third-party grading firms require the entire set to be submitted in its original, sealed Mint shipping box.

Steve Roach commented on Proof American Silver Eagle values in the September 19, 2011, issue of *Coin World*. "Bullion continues to drive the market, and the U.S. Mint's recent repricing of many of its precious metal coins directly and quickly impacted the secondary market," he wrote. "For Proof American Eagle silver bullion coins, the Mint's price increase from the June 30 issue price of $59.95 to $68.45 on Aug. 29 sent secondary wholesale market prices for 1986 to 2011 Proof American Eagle silver coins soaring from $56 to $66 over just 48 hours" (*Coin World*, "Bullion Keeps Driving Market: Mint Raises Prices on Proof Silver," September 19, 2011).

2011 25th Anniversary Silver Coin Set

Mintage: 99,882

GSID: 71571

Minted at Philadelphia, San Francisco, and West Point, with P, S, and W mintmarks

Set commentary: In August 2011 the U.S. Mint announced an upcoming commemorative set of five American Silver Eagles that would mark the 25th anniversary of the start of the nation's bullion program. The production limit of 100,000 sets—and the fact that the set would contain two coins not available elsewhere—piqued collector interest. Sales started on October 27 . . . and ended on October 27. The 25th Anniversary Silver Eagle Set sold out in less than five hours of frantic, eager buying.

Each coin in the set has a different finish and/or mintmark:

> *2011, bullion strike, regular finish, no mintmark.* The 100,000 bullion strikes packaged in the 25th Anniversary Set were all made at the San Francisco Mint, although they bear no mintmark. Bullion-strike coins of 2011 (minted at both West Point and San Francisco, without mintmarks) were also available individually and in bulk.
>
> *2011-W, Burnished.* This West Point–minted coin (in what the Mint calls Uncirculated finish) was also available for individual purchase from the Mint.
>
> *2011-W, Proof.* The standard mirror-field Proof (with frosted design elements) could also be purchased individually from the Mint.
>
> *2011-S, Burnished.* This coin was unique to the 25th Anniversary Set (not offered for sale individually). So far it is the only Burnished American Silver Eagle not struck at West Point. It bears the mintmark of its source, the San Francisco Mint.
>
> *2011-P, Reverse Proof.* This coin was unique to the 25th Anniversary Set—not available for individual purchase. Struck at the Philadelphia Mint, it bears that facility's P mintmark. The Reverse Proof features mirrored design elements (e.g., the striding figure of Miss Liberty) and frosted fields—the reverse of the traditional Proof format.

The Mint limited purchasers to five sets per household, and the issue price was $299.95 per set. Sales began at 12:00 noon Eastern Time on October 27, and the Mint's phone lines and website were flooded with orders, with most customers ordering the maximum of five sets. In a matter of weeks the sets were selling on the secondary market for double their issue price. Values have risen since then.

In order to certify the individual coins as coming from the 25th Anniversary Set, PCGS and NGC require the entire set to be submitted in its original, sealed Mint shipping box. See the individual coins' listings for certified populations.

2012, Bullion Strike

Mintage: 33,121,500

GSID: 71114 (San Francisco) / 84272 (West Point)

Minted at San Francisco and West Point, without mintmark

Historical context: In the first half of 2012 silver was down \$3.50 per ounce compared to its average bullion price in 2011. Gold was up about \$100 (to \$1,660) and platinum was down \$150 (at \$1,572).

2012 average silver price: \$31.15/ounce.

Coin commentary: In a January 2012 article in *Coin World*, Paul Gilkes noted that the year's new American Silver Eagle was among the factors encouraging attendance at the annual Florida United Numismatists convention in Orlando. "An active buying public, strong coin and paper money auction sessions and the first public appearance of 2012 American Eagle silver bullion coins for sale helped bolster the 2012 Florida United Numismatists convention Jan. 4 to 8 in Orlando," wrote Gilkes (*Coin World*, "About 11,000 Attend 2012 FUN Convention," January 30, 2012). "The newest products of the U.S. Mint made a late arrival at the convention but still sold briskly. Shortly after 4 p.m. Jan. 7, two carts—each loaded with 20,000 2012 American Eagle 1-ounce silver bullion coins—were wheeled to SilverTowne's booth on the bourse floor. The Winchester, Ind., numismatic firm was the only company to receive the silver American Eagles at the show. The silver bullion coins, all struck at the West Point Mint, were contained in 80 plastic-strapped, 500-coin boxes. Each box contained 25 nylon-plastic tubes with 20 coins in each tube. . . . Although SilverTowne offered some of the 40,000 coins received as singles directly to customers, most were acquired by customers in multiple rolls and boxes. Abel said it took the firm less than two hours from the time of receiving the coins Jan. 7 to sell all 40,000 coins. The coins were from among 3,197,000 that the U.S. Mint's authorized purchasers placed orders for on Jan. 3 for distribution to secondary market dealers and the public, and were made available for pick up by the authorized purchasers Jan. 6."

American Silver Eagle bullion sales were down in the first half of 2012 benchmarked against 2011. *Coin World* reported that cumulative sales of 14,409,000 coins from January through May of 2012 were 23.7 percent lower than the same five-month period in 2011 (18,901,000 coins). (*Coin World*, "American Eagle Bullion Sales Rise During May: Mint Sales Show Increase After Declining in April," Paul Gilkes, June 18, 2012.)

As was the case in 2011, the bullion strikes of 2012 bear no mintmarks to distinguish which were struck at West Point and which at San Francisco. PCGS and NGC differentiate between the two when a "monster box" with appropriate mint markings is submitted for grading.

In October 2020 the U.S. Mint released production details: 29,575,000 of the 2012 bullion strikes were minted at West Point, and 8,421,000 at San Francisco.

2012-W, Burnished

Mintage: 226,120
GSID: 71116
Minted at West Point, with W mintmark

Coin commentary: The U.S. Mint began selling the 2012-W Burnished (called *Uncirculated* by the Mint) American Silver Eagle on August 2, 2012. The issue price was $45.95, with the Mint noting that, "as with all products sold by the Mint containing precious metals, pricing is subject to change." The coins were struck on specially prepared blanks, giving them a finish similar to their bullion counterparts, but distinguished by a W mintmark. The Burnished coins are sold in a blue presentation case accompanied by a certificate of authenticity.

2012-S, PROOF

Mintage: 285,184

GSID: 71644

Minted at San Francisco, with S mintmark

Coin commentary: The Proof 2012-S American Silver Eagle was at first made available by the Mint only in its two-coin 2012 San Francisco Proof Set. On July 19, 2012, the Mint announced that the 2012-S Proof would be available in another set, as well. The coin would be packaged in a "Making American History Coin and Currency Set" along with a $5 Federal Reserve note. The set was promoted as a commemorative of the 150th anniversary of the Bureau of Engraving and Printing and the 220th anniversary of the U.S. Mint.

The numismatic press kept the hobby community apprised on the changing situation. "Surprisingly," wrote *Coin World* editor Steve Roach in a late-August 2012 market analysis, "the U.S. Mint's recent announcement that it would be producing more Proof 2012-S American Eagle silver coins has not taken the pressure off of the 2012-S San Francisco Two-Coin Anniversary set."

The Mint released a statement on July 25, 2012. "The United States Mint is proud to bring to market this year two specially designed sets—the 2012 American Eagle San Francisco Two-Coin Silver Proof Set and the Making American History Coin and Currency Set. The 2012 American Eagle San Francisco Two-Coin Silver Proof Set contains an American Silver Eagle Proof coin and an American Eagle Reverse Proof coin, both with the 'S' mintmark. We provided our customers a four-week window to order the set and indicated that we would mint to the demands that our customers expressed during that period. Sales totals reached more than 251,000 sets. . . . Actual product development for the [Making American History set] was under way prior to the American Eagle San Francisco Two-Coin Silver Proof Set on May 2. The United States Mint, in developing these products, was responding to customers who have indicated an attraction to products produced in San Francisco and having the 'S' mintmark. In retrospect, it may have been appropriate to announce our intentions to produce the coin and currency set earlier in the year or perhaps simultaneously with the two-coin set."

2012-S, Reverse Proof

Mintage: 224,981
GSID: 71592
Minted at San Francisco, with S mintmark

Coin commentary: The Reverse Proof 2012-S American Silver Eagle was made available by the Mint only in its two-coin 2012 San Francisco Proof Set.

The hobby community eagerly followed news of the release of 2012 American Silver Eagles. At first collectors assumed the 2012-S Proof and Reverse Proof coins would both be issued only in the year's special two-coin San Francisco set. When the U.S. Mint announced that a second 2012 set would also include the 2012-S Proof, some collectors complained. "The good news," noted one front-page article, "is there are no plans to sell more 2012-S Reverse Proof silver American Eagle coins" (*Numismatic News*, "More 2012-S Proof Eagles," August 14, 2012).

The Mint's intentions for the 2012-S Reverse Proof were affirmed in a statement released on July 25, 2012: "The 2012 American Eagle Silver Reverse Proof coin will only be offered in the 2012 American Eagle San Francisco Two-Coin Silver Proof Set."

To avoid the disappointment felt by many collectors who weren't able to order the 2011 25th Anniversary set before its lightning-fast sellout, the Mint organized a new ordering process for the 2012 San Francisco set. Sale of the set started at noon on June 7, 2012, and was scheduled to last until 5:00 p.m. July 5. No household order limit was set. The Mint posted sales figures daily on its website, to keep collectors and investors informed. "A final and unexpected announcement came on December 6, 2012, that buoyed the spirits of those who had purchased the two-coin Proof set," Scott Schechter and Jeff Garrett write in *100 Greatest U.S. Modern Coins*, fifth edition. "After the processing of returns and order cancellations, net orders slid back to 224,998, pushing the rarity of this coin ahead of the 2006 Reverse Proof." The 2012-S Reverse Proof is ranked number 87 among the 100 Greatest U.S. Modern Coins.

2012-W, Proof

Mintage: 869,386

GSID: 71492

Minted at West Point, with W mintmark

Coin commentary: The U.S. Mint's original issue price for the 2012-W Proof American Silver Eagle was $59.95, with no maximum mintage established. In an April 9, 2012, *Coin World* article, Paul Gilkes noted, "The U.S. Mint has set a price of $59.95 for the Proof 2012-W American Eagle silver dollar for the coin's initial offering at noon Eastern Daylight Time April 12. The price was posted in the *Federal Register* on March 15. Pricing for the Proof silver American Eagle is subject to change weekly depending on the spot price of silver according to the London PM fix."

The original issue price of $59.95 was later lowered to $54.95 as an adjustment to prevailing silver prices.

Coin World editor Steve Roach commented on the price adjustment in an August 2012 article. "The Mint's recent price decrease for Proof 2012-W American Eagle silver coins—dropping $5, to $54.95—took pressure off of the existing stock of 1986 to 2010 issues and wholesale prices for nearly all Proof issues also dropped by $5," he observed. "The Mint can raise or lower the price of its bullion products to adjust for the price of gold and silver. Perhaps collectors will take advantage of the recent price drop and purchase additional examples to nudge sales for the 'normal' Proof 2012-W issues well past the 500,000 mark?" (*Coin World*, "Proof American Eagle Coins: 2012 Anniversary Sets Still Hot," August 20, 2012)

A Mint press release described the 2012-W Proof: "The obverse (heads side) design of the 2012 American Eagle Silver Proof Coin features Adolph A. Weinman's full-length figure of Lady Liberty in full stride, with her right hand extended and branches of laurel and oak in her left. The reverse (tails side) design, by former United States Mint Chief Engraver John Mercanti, features a heraldic eagle with shield, an olive branch in the right talon and arrows in the left. The American Eagle Silver Proof coin contains .999 silver. The one-ounce coin is struck on specially burnished blanks and carries the 'W' mintmark, indicating its production at the United States mint at West Point. Each coin is sealed in protective plastic and mounted in a satin-lined presentation case. A certificate of authenticity is included."

In November 2012 the Mint announced a new product: the eight-coin 2012 Limited Edition Silver Proof Set, which would include a 2012-W Proof American Silver Eagle. Mintage was limited to 50,000 sets (the original limit of two per household was lifted December 18, 2012), with a release date of November 27 and an issue price of $149.95. At the time of the set's release the 2012-W Proof American Silver Eagle was listed as sold out on the Mint's website. The new Proof set gave collectors another chance to purchase the coin.

2012 American Eagle San Francisco Two-Coin Silver Proof Set

Mintage: 224,981

GSID: 71491

Minted at San Francisco, with S mintmarks

Set commentary: In 2012 the U.S. Mint announced that it would offer a special two-coin set of American Silver Eagles, available for sale for four weeks, from June 7 to July 5. No cap was set on the mintage, with production instead being limited to the quantity ordered within that four-week window. The number of sets that each household could order was likewise not capped. The issue price was established at $149.95.

Each of the two coins in the set has a different finish. Struck at the San Francisco Mint, they bear that facility's S mintmark. When the set was first issued, neither coin was available for individual purchase, although the 2012-S Proof was later made available in another special set (discussed on the following page).

> *2012-S, Proof.* This coin features the standard mirror-field Proof format, with frosted design elements. It was available in the 2012 San Francisco American Eagle Two-Coin Silver Proof Set and (later) in the 2012 Making American History Coin and Currency Set.
>
> *2012-S, Reverse Proof.* The Reverse Proof features mirrored design elements (e.g., the striding figure of Miss Liberty) and frosted fields—the reverse of the traditional Proof format. This coin was available only in the 2012 San Francisco American Eagle Two-Coin Silver Proof Set.

"The 2012 American Eagle San Francisco Two-Coin Silver Proof Set is an exquisite collection that captures the essence and beauty of these cherished coins," the Mint said in its promotional literature. "This set—one American Eagle Silver Proof Coin and one American Eagle Silver Reverse Proof Coin minted at the United States Mint at San Francisco—is a testament to the fine, exacting craftsmanship that has been a United States Mint hallmark since 1792."

The Mint updated its website with daily sales numbers throughout the four-week ordering period. This allowed collectors and investors to watch the market and gauge when—and how many sets—they purchased. The first day tallied an impressive 85,000 sets sold. Sales dropped off dramatically after that, as collectors waited and watched, but then they spiked again as the July 5 deadline neared. At the end of sales the Mint announced that 251,302 sets had been ordered. That number was adjusted in December, after returns were processed and order cancellations were counted. The final net number of 2012 San Francisco American Eagle Two-Coin Silver Proof Sets sold was 224,981. This made the 2012-S Reverse Proof rarer than the 2006-P Reverse Proof (with its mintage of 248,875 coins), although not as rare as the 2011-P (at 100,000 coins).

2012 Making American History Coin and Currency Set

Mintage: 56,857

GSID: 393505

Minted at San Francisco, with S mintmark

Set commentary: This special set was announced by the U.S. Mint on July 26, 2012—several weeks after the July 5 sales deadline for the 2012 American Eagle San Francisco Two-Coin Silver Proof Set.

The 2012 Making American History Coin and Currency Set went on sale at noon Eastern Time, August 7. It was a joint production of the Mint and the Bureau of Engraving and Printing, marking their 220th and 150th anniversaries, respectively. The set consists of a 2012-S Proof American Silver Eagle and a Series 2009 $5 Federal Reserve Note with the seal of the Federal Reserve Bank of San Francisco. The serial number of each note starts with the numbers 150. The set debuted at the American Numismatic Association's annual summer convention, called the World's Fair of Money, in Philadelphia. The issue price was $72.95 per set, with no per-household ordering limits. Initial production was 50,000 sets and maximum production was capped at 100,000 sets.

Describing the 2012-S Proof coin, the Mint's promotional literature noted that "This 2012 American Eagle Silver Proof Coin not only honors the artistry and design of our Nation's coins, but also honors the heritage of coin production at the United States Mint at San Francisco." It went on to describe the commemorative banknote: "The Series 2009 $5 note commemorates the Bureau of Engraving and Printing's 150 years of service with a serial number beginning with '150' and bears the signature of Treasurer of the United States Rosie Rios and the San Francisco Federal Reserve Bank designation." And furthermore: "This Making American History Coin and Currency Set commemorates the history and achievements of these institutions and reflects the hard work of thousands of Americans in manufacturing our coins and currency. The beauty and quality of their craftsmanship showcase America's cutting-edge design and manufacturing processes. United States coins and currency exhibit the strength, security, confidence and excellence that are the hallmarks of our Nation."

2013, Bullion Strike

Mintage: 42,675,000

GSID: 71551 (San Francisco) / 71554 (West Point)

Minted at San Francisco and West Point, without mintmark

Historical context: Silver started strong in 2013 with a January average of $31.11 per ounce. It would fall gradually for the first half of the year before a particularly volatile July when it ranged from $19.10 to $26.40 per ounce. It would end the year relatively stable, hovering around $20 per ounce.

The American economy continued its slow recovery in 2013. Household debt was down, and corporate profits were up. Home prices nationwide had stopped falling and started to rise, although many families were still recovering from the market's collapse of earlier years. Many banks, wary of repeating the mistakes that led to the Great Recession, remained cautious in lending. Private-sector employment had been improving since 2010, and this trend continued, while nationwide the *public* sector (from the local up to the federal level) continued its cost-cutting layoffs and budget reductions. Many corporations continued to sit on cash reserves, reluctant to make large investments while future tax and budget policies were uncertain, although increased spending in corporate infrastructure such as information technology implied an anticipation of future growth.

2013 average silver price (first quarter): $23.79/ounce.

Coin commentary: In mid-January 2013 the U.S. Mint informed its authorized purchasers that it had temporarily sold out of 2013 American Silver Eagle bullion coins. "As a result," the Mint announced, "sales are suspended until we can build up an inventory of these coins. Sales will resume on or about the week of January 28, 2013, via the allocation process." Some 6,700,000 ounces of the bullion coins had been sold between January 7, when they first went on sale, and January 15. Business resumed later in the month, and January eventually saw sales of 7,498,000 coins—the single-month record for the series. First-quarter sales continued in that vein, with February (3,368,500 coins) and March (3,356,500 coins) both entering the top-20 tier for monthly sales. Sales for the quarter (14,223,000 coins) beat the previous record (first-quarter 2011) by 1,794,000 coins.

The strong sales seen in the first quarter of 2013 would continue throughout the year. Officially, on November 12 weekly sales pushed the calendar-year 2013 cumulative total to 40,175,000 coins sold, establishing a record for yearly sales (though the record would be short-lived and would be surpassed in 2014.

The bullion strikes of 2013 bear no mintmarks to indicate which were struck at the San Francisco Mint and which at West Point. PCGS and NGC differentiate between the two when a "monster box" (with appropriate mint markings) of 500 coins is submitted for grading. In October 2020 the Mint reported that West Point produced 36,775,000 of the 2013 bullion strikes, and San Francisco 13,100,000.

2013-W, Burnished

Mintage: 222,091

GSID: 71493

Minted at West Point, with W mintmark

Coin commentary: The U.S. Mint initiated sales of the 2013-W Burnished American Silver Eagle on May 28 at an issue price of $48.95 each, with no household ordering limits and the price being subject to change based on bullion markets. Later in the year the price dropped to $43.95 as silver declined in value. Although it sold out individually, the coin was available through early 2014 as part of the 2013 Annual Uncirculated Dollar Coin Set, along with the four 2013 Presidential dollars and the 2013 Native American dollar.

All examples were struck at the West Point Mint on the same blanks that the Mint receives from outside vendors that are also used to strike bullion and Proof examples. What characterizes the Burnished examples from the bullion examples—beyond the W mintmark on the reverse—is that the planchets are specially burnished and they are hand-fed into the coining press. The Mint describes it on its website as "a process similar to that used to create the magnificent American Eagle Proof coins," although the Burnished (or *Uncirculated*, in the Mint's wording) examples lack the deep mirrored fields and cameo contrasted devices, having instead a uniform satiny, matte finish.

2013-W, Enhanced Uncirculated

Mintage: 235,689
GSID: 71533
Minted at West Point, with W mintmark

Coin commentary: "It's not your daddy's U.S. Mint anymore," remarked *Numismatic News* in an April 9, 2013, front-page commentary. The Mint had announced that it would release a new product later in the year: an Uncirculated American Silver Eagle with an "enhanced" finish made possible by new technology. It would debut in a special two-coin set (packaged along with a 2013-W Reverse Proof American Silver Eagle) and would not be sold separately.

The new format features three visually distinct finishes on the same coin. A *brilliant mirrored finish* is used on the obverse in the date, the blue-field and red-stripe areas of the U.S. flag, the lines on Miss Liberty's dress, and the mountains in the background; and on the reverse in the devices held by the eagle (the arrows and branch, the banner, and parts of the shield). A *light frosted finish* is used on the fields of both the obverse and the reverse. A *heavy frosted finish* is used, both obverse and reverse, on the other portions of design elements and on the legends.

The enhanced Uncirculated coins are made from planchets specially burnished by stainless-steel shot, water, and soap. The planchets are fed into the coining press by hand. Each planchet is struck three times using specially prepared dies; the dies are auto-polished with a horsehair brush (to achieve the brilliant finish) and then have their heavy and light frosting applied by laser. The dies are coated (through physical vapor deposition) with chrome to increase their life cycle. After striking, the coins are inspected by the press operator before being released for packaging and sale.

Some parts of the process of making these enhanced Uncirculated coins are similar to steps used to produce *Proof* American Silver Eagles. However, there are notable differences, and the Mint does not consider the coins to be Proofs. Mint technician Steve Antonucci (head of digital process and development at the Philadelphia Mint) remarked in an April 3, 2013, media conference that the automated horsehair polishing of the dies imparts a finish less brilliant than does Proof polishing. Also, the planchets are processed differently and for a shorter time than are the polished planchets used to strike Proof American Silver Eagles.

Coin World reported that the 2013 enhanced Uncirculated American Silver Eagles are not the first U.S. Mint products to feature more than one finish. Multiple finishes were used on the Uncirculated 2012-P Hawai'i Volcanoes National Park five-ounce bullion coin, and also on the one-ounce .999 fine silver September 11 medals produced in 2011 and 2012 (*Coin World*, "Mint to Introduce New American Eagle Finish," Paul Gilkes, March 25, 2013).

2013-W, Proof

Mintages: 934,812

GSID: 71505

Minted at West Point, with W mintmark

Coin commentary: The U.S. Mint began accepting orders for the 2013 Proof American Silver Eagle at 12 noon Eastern Time on January 24, 2013. The coin was priced at $62.95. "There is no household order limit for this product," the Mint's media release announced. "Customer demand will determine the number of coins minted." Furthermore, "To ensure that all members of the public have fair and equal access to United States Mint products, orders placed prior to the official on-sale date and time January 24, 2013, at noon ET, shall not be deemed accepted by the United States Mint and will not be honored."

As would be expected, in its promotions the Mint publicized the historic and artistic aspects of the coins. "The obverse (heads side) design of the American Eagle Silver Proof Coin features Adolph A. Weinman's full-length figure of Liberty in full stride, enveloped in folds of the flag, with her right hand extended and branches of laurel and oak in her left. The reverse (tails side) design features former United States Mint Sculptor-Engraver John Mercanti's heraldic eagle with shield, an olive branch in the right talon and arrows in the left."

The Mint also promoted the exceptional quality of these coins and the attractiveness of their packaging: "The American Eagle Silver Proof Coins are struck using .999 fine silver blanks that are specially treated and cleaned to ensure high-quality strikes. Each coin carries the 'W' mint mark, indicating its production at the United States Mint at West Point. The coins are encapsulated in plastic, mounted in a satin-lined presentation case, and accompanied by a Certificate of Authenticity."

As in recent years, orders were accepted online through the Mint's web catalog (at www.usmint.gov), by phone, and through teletypewriter ordering for hearing- and speech-impaired customers. A fee of $4.95 was added to all domestic orders for shipping and handling.

The Mint sold 258,860 of the Proof coins in the first five days of ordering. Demand for the bullion strikes and a need for planchets for the bullion strikes led the Mint to declare a sellout of Proof 2013-W American Silver Eagles on November 11, 2013. However, because of an inaccurate sales report, on February 20, 2014, the Mint announced that it would offer almost 4,200 2013-W Proofs in its inventory to approximately 780 buyers (who had had their orders cancelled) on a "first-in, first-served" basis.

2013-W, Reverse Proof

Mintage: 235,689

GSID: 74465

Minted at West Point, with W mintmark

Coin commentary: The U.S. Mint announced on January 15, 2013, that it would issue a West Point Reverse Proof American Silver Eagle later in the year. The Reverse Proof would be part of "a special two-coin set of American Eagle Silver Coins, both of which will be struck at its facility at West Point, N.Y. The 2013 American Eagle West Point Two-Coin Silver Set (final product name subject to change) will include one American Eagle Silver Reverse Proof Coin and one American Eagle Silver Uncirculated Coin with an 'enhanced' finish. (A 'reverse proof' coin reverses the mirror-like background finish of a traditional proof coin and applies it to the design elements, creating a magnificent contrast.) These two coins will only be available in this special set. The bureau expects to begin accepting orders for the set in the spring. Pricing and other information will be available prior to its release."

As noted in the Mint's announcement, the 2013-W Reverse Proof was not sold separately; it was only available as part of the West Point two-coin set.

To avoid disappointing customers, the Mint had a limited four-week sales window with a sales odometer on its website that recorded daily sales. Sales opened at noon Eastern Daylight Time May 9 and ended at 5 p.m. EDT June 6, with the sets offered at $139.95 each. The first sales reported by the Mint on May 10 totaled 138,514 sets. Sales gradually climbed to 182,773 for the May 13 odometer reading; 187,541 for the May 14 count; 191,726 for the May 15 total; and 193,652 for the May 16 total.

Collectors lucky enough to place their orders within the first few hours of release were able to sell their sets at the $180 to $190 level via online auctions on sites such as eBay. At the close of the ordering window, on June 7, the unaudited sales figure for the sets was 281,310. With order cancellations—a result of consumers changing their minds after prices settled down on the secondary market and expired credit cards (since cards aren't charged until the items are ready for shipping)—the final mintage was substantially lower. Later in the year the Mint would lower the unaudited sales number to 235,689.

2013 American Eagle West Point Two-Coin Silver Set

Mintage: 235,689

GSID: 76851

Minted at West Point, with W mintmarks

Set commentary: "Later this year," the Treasury announced in January 2013, "the United States Mint will . . . offer a special two-coin set of American Eagle Silver Coins, both of which will be struck at its facility at West Point, N.Y. The 2013 American Eagle West Point Two-Coin Silver Set (final product name subject to change) will include one American Eagle Silver Reverse Proof Coin and one American Eagle Silver Uncirculated Coin with an 'enhanced' finish. (A 'reverse proof' coin reverses the mirror-like background finish of a traditional proof coin and applies it to the design elements, creating a magnificent contrast.) These two coins will only be available in this special set. The bureau expects to begin accepting orders for the set in the spring. Pricing and other information will be available prior to its release."

The two-coin set honors the 75th anniversary of the 1938 opening of the West Point depository as a federal storage place for silver bullion (similar to Fort Knox for gold). In the early 1970's the U.S. Mint installed equipment at West Point in order to meet increased demand for coinage. The facility produced cents for circulation from 1973 to 1986. No mintmark was used to distinguish these coins from those struck at the Philadelphia Mint (none of which bore a mintmark). In the early 1980's West Point was the producer of the Treasury's half-ounce and one-ounce American Arts Commemorative Series gold-bullion medallions (see *American Gold and Silver: U.S. Mint Collector and Investor Coins and Medals, Bicentennial to Date*) and some $20 billion worth of gold was moved into its storage. In 1988 it was elevated to the full status of a branch mint, equivalent to Denver and San Francisco (the latter of which returned from "assay office" status to full mint status at the same time). Today West Point is used to produce some of the U.S. Mint's commemorative coins as well as silver, gold, and platinum bullion pieces, as well as occasional quarter dollars and other coins. With gold reserves second only to Fort Knox, West Point—unlike other mint facilities—does not offer public tours.

2014, Bullion Strike

Mintage: 44,006,000

GSID: 84273 (San Francisco) / 84274 (West Point)

Minted at San Francisco and West Point, without mintmark

Historical context: 2014 was a relatively stable year for silver. Stability combined with affordability led to unprecedented demand for physical silver from investors and collectors alike. As a result, 2014 saw record-setting American Silver Eagle bullion sales of just over 54 million coins. The Mint was particularly busy producing the National Baseball Hall of Fame clad half dollars, silver dollars, gold $5 half eagles, and a gold Kennedy half dollar. These new coins kept the Mint occupied and no special sets of American Silver Eagles were offered. This gave collectors a break from the proliferation of sets in 2011, 2012, and 2013.

In a March 11, 2014, meeting of the Citizens Coinage Advisory Committee, Chairman Gary Marks announced an initiative to change the American Silver Eagle's reverse design. At an April 8 CCAC meeting 44 possible designs were considered and the CCAC selected number 41, featuring a side view of an eagle in flight with an olive branch in its talons. U.S. Mint officials informed CCAC members that it would not pursue the recommendation for changing the design. The proposed design would later be used on the 2015 high-relief American Liberty gold bullion coin (see *American Gold and Silver: U.S. Mint Collector and Investor Coins and Medals, Bicentennial to Date*). It would be another seven years before the Mint changed the reverse design, in 2021.

2014 average silver price: $19.08/ounce.

Coin commentary: Although 2014 would end up being a record-setting year, exceeding the 2013 sales total of 49,875,000 coins, the Mint sold just 4,775,000 2014 American Silver Eagle bullion coins in January. This was far from the record established the previous year when the Mint sold 7,498,000 of the 2013-dated bullion coins, setting a monthly sales record. This was because Authorized Purchasers were unable to place orders for the 2014 bullion coins until January 13, 2014. The late start was a result of the Mint's continued struggle to secure quantities of silver planchets to meet demand. Sales to Authorized Purchasers were suspended on November 5. Sales resumed on November 17.

Authorized Purchasers acquire the coins from the U.S. Mint based on the London PM closing spot price for one troy ounce of pure silver on a given day, plus a premium of $2 per silver coin to cover minting, distribution, and marketing costs. They have a minimum ordering requirement of 25,000 coins for each order placed with the Mint and are responsible for arranging their own pickup and delivery of the bullion coins. The Authorized Purchasers then sell the American Silver Eagles to secondary retailers, who in turn sell the coins, described by the Mint as "a convenient and cost-effective way to invest in precious metals," directly to the public. In October 2020 the Mint reported production details for the 2014 bullion strikes: West Point minted 46,920,500 coins, and San Francisco 7,231,000.

2014-W, Burnished

Mintage: 253,169

GSID: 74223

Minted at West Point, with W mintmark

Coin commentary: Sales for the 2014-W Burnished (called *Uncirculated* by the Mint) American Silver Eagle started on April 10, 2014, at $43.95. It unexpectedly sold out in December, although it remained available in the 2014 Annual Uncirculated Dollar Coin Set that was still for sale in 2015.

In light of the Citizens Coinage Advisory Committee's recommendation to change the reverse of some or all of the American Silver Eagles, some commentators suggested that the design change be used to revive the Burnished Silver Eagles. In a May 26, 2014, editorial in *Coin World*, editor Steve Roach wrote that although a design change was not needed for the bullion coins ("consistency has given the silver American Eagle a reliable, credible brand worldwide with collectors and investors"), he thought "a new reverse design could be transformative for the Uncirculated American Eagle silver coin," before concluding, "The U.S. Mint has no problem selling the bullion and Proof versions of the silver American Eagle (in fact, it often can't keep up with demand) but a new reverse could make the burnished Uncirculated American Eagle a coin at the forefront of collecting, rather than just another U.S. Mint offering."

Eventually the entire American Silver Eagle program (bullion strikes and numismatic products alike) would be given a new reverse design with a flying eagle motif. . . . but in 2014 that change was still several years in the future.

2014-W, PROOF

Mintages: 944,770
GSID: 74074
Minted at West Point, with W mintmark

Coin commentary: The single-option Proof 2014 American Silver Eagle went on sale January 23 and, as with its bullion counterpart, the Mint saw strong sales in the first weeks of issue. Within the first three months of 2014, total sales of the Proof American Eagle reached 446,373, or more than half of the sales of the 2013 Proof. Through mid-2014 more than 600,000 were sold individually.

The annual Proof American Silver Eagle was also included in a special Congratulations set, first introduced in 2010, as well as the Limited Edition Silver Proof set, which was first introduced as a packaging option in November 2012. The final mintage figure includes the total sales of all Proof American Silver Eagles in all of the product options for the year.

In any given year the U.S. Mint may offer products from previous calendar years for sale, as long as inventory is available. For example, in mid-2014 collectors could purchase 2013 and 2014 Proof American Silver Eagles as part of the Congratulations set, while only the 2014 Proof American Silver Eagle was available individually.

Not all of the 2014 Proofs were offered that year. The Mint offered the eight-coin 2014 United States Mint Limited Edition Silver Proof set—with a 2014 Proof American Silver Eagle—beginning at noon Eastern Time March 17, 2015. That set had a production limit of 50,000 and was priced at $139.95. Mint spokesman Michael White said the 2014 set's release was delayed into 2015 because of packaging issues, and the Mint had made improvements in the packaging based on collectors returning 2013-dated sets.

In a March 6, 2014, blog titled "Mint Stats: Proof silver Eagles move backwards," *Numismatic News* editor Dave Harper observed that sales for the 2014-W Proof American Silver Eagle dropped 9,420 coins to 365,188. He questioned, "Did buyers of that many coins suddenly get cold feet? Without any dramatic swings in the price of bullion, it seems odd. It could be a correction of a previous error in the total. That is one reason why numbers are issued each week." The Mint makes weekly sales figures available on its website and through reports that are analyzed by hobby news outlets, and through these collectors and dealers can see the ebbs and flows of the Mint's sales figures.

2015, Bullion Strike

Mintage: 47,000,000

GSID: 213361 (San Francisco) / 84275 (West Point)

Minted at San Francisco and West Point, without mintmark

Historical context: In 2015 silver started the year at $15.71 per ounce, jumping to $18.23 in late January. That would represent the high price for silver through October, with the metal dipping as low as $14.27 per ounce in September. Despite the relatively stable price of silver in recent years, due to a surge in global demand for silver bullion coins, the Mint has sought to identify additional suppliers for planchets. Through late 2015 the majority of the Mint's raw-material silver blanks came from two suppliers: Sunshine Minting and Stern Leach.

2015 average silver price: $15.68/ounce.

Coin commentary: In 2015 bullion strikes were produced at the West Point Mint and, for the first time, at Philadelphia. Adam Stump, deputy director for the U.S. Mint's Office of Corporate Communications, said on February 6 that the Philadelphia Mint conducted a "process validation run" of 2015-dated silver American Eagles late in 2014 totaling 70,000 coins. Later, in 2020, the Mint would update this information: 79,500 coins were released from Philadelphia, and the bulk of the 2015 bullion strikes were made at West Point. They were all mixed together before being shipped to Authorized Purchasers, making it impossible to discern the source of any given coin.

Grading services subsequently confirmed that they would not be encapsulating 2015 American Silver Eagle bullion coins as Philadelphia Mint strikes without concrete evidence that the coins were actually struck there. Since the Philadelphia Mint strikes were shipped to Authorized Purchasers in boxes with West Point Mint strap labels, these Philadelphia strikes are likely to be forever commingled with the West Point examples. (For more on the "kerfuffle" over 2015 American Silver Eagles, see below.)

On July 7 the Mint suspended sales of 2015 American Silver Eagle bullion coins to replenish inventory as sales exceeded the ability to strike coins to meet demand. Sales resumed on July 27. In a September 14 article in *Coin World*, Stump was quoted as stating, "The demand for American Eagle silver bullion coins has continued to increase throughout calendar year 2015 and remains on a record-setting pace," adding, "This demand is a global one and all mints are trying to meet the demand for this precious metal" (*Coin World*, "Silver American Eagles remain on allocation," September 14, 2015).

The monthly sales-figure report that January saw 5,530,000 coins sold, a record quantity. Sales for July reached another 5,529,000. For the year, West Point matched its record-high 2014 production, but because San Francisco minted no American Silver Eagles in 2015 and Philadelphia's production was limited to a small test run, 2015 didn't quite reach 2014's dizzying mintage heights.

The 2015 Kerfuffle: Data released by the Mint on March 20, 2017, showed that just 79,640 bullion-strike American Silver Eagles were produced at the Philadelphia Mint in 2015, the smallest mintage of the series. (This quantity was fine-tuned later; see below.) The Mint also shared information about the serial numbers on the boxes and the color of the bands used to secure the 500-coins "monster boxes" that could be used to identify the Mint of origin. Third-party grading services began certifying 2015 American Silver Eagles struck at Philadelphia based on these criteria.

The 2015-dated coins certified as Philadelphia Mint products by third-party grading services almost immediately began selling for 10 to 20 times their issue price, given their small mintage. Steve Roach of *Coin World* shared (June 5, 2017, issue) that examples certified MS-69 were regularly selling for $450 to $500, while some examples in MS-70 sold for more than $5,000.

In late May the Mint unnerved many hobbyists by announcing that some of the information it had provided on March 20 was incorrect and, in the words of Mint's announcement, "resulted in a mistaken belief that some of these coins are rarities."

On June 30 the Mint released additional information. Some of the tracking numbers on boxes of 2015 American Silver Eagles attributed to the Philadelphia Mint were actually applied to boxes from West Point. All coins struck at Philadelphia were packaged manually.

"Because of duplication of box tracking numbers at Philadelphia and West Point, as well as any mistakes in labelling or the possibility that labels on the boxes could have been removed or altered at any point after shipping," the Mint would "make no effort" to "'verify' the origin" of 2015 American Silver Eagles. The Mint said that the mintage shared in March was correct, though 140 of the coins had been condemned and never shipped, meaning the total number of coins that left the Mint was 79,500.

ANACS was unfazed by the revelations, claiming that its criteria for certifying 2015(P) bullion strike American Silver Eagles were consistent with the information the Mint put out on June 30.

Arnold Tescher, a *Coin World* reader from Medford, New York, expressed "bemusement" with the "kerfuffle" in a letter to the editor published in the July 24, 2017, edition. He elaborated: "The grading services, who saw a cash cow and, along with deep pocketed collectors/speculators, have unwittingly colluded to legitimize yet another new 'collectible.'" Another *Coin World* reader, Robert Savage, didn't understand the hype surrounding the 2015(P) American Silver Eagles, writing "there is nothing special about them," comparing the coins unfavorably to the 2011-S Burnished issue.

Coin World managing editor William T. Gibbs reflected on the "deeper philosophical undercurrents" relating to "the merits of modern slabbed coin market and the concepts of condition rarity and special slab labels" in an editorial opinion published on June 19, 2017. He shared that the trends and concepts "disturb a lot of longtime numismatists," who worry about "the prices charged (and paid) for some coins that would be judged common if removed from the context of the label on their slab."

2015-W, Burnished

Mintage: 201,188

GSID: 74224

Minted at West Point, with W mintmark

Coin commentary: The 2015-W Burnished (or *Uncirculated*) American Silver Eagle went on sale March 26 at an initial price of $39.95 with no household or product ordering limits.

In contrast to the distribution of bullion issues, the U.S. Mint sells Proof and "Burnished Uncirculated" coins to the public through its direct-sales channels. While the Mint calls the collectible American Silver Eagles "Uncirculated," collectors most often call them "Burnished Uncirculated"—a descriptive phrase not used by the Mint. However, it serves to distinguish these issues, which look similar to the bullion issues, with the key difference being the W mintmark on the reverse.

Scott Schechter, coauthor of *100 Greatest U.S. Modern Coins*, wrote in his "Making Moderns" column in the March 10, 2014, issue of *Coin World* that the burnishing process "does not affect the appearance of the coin in any way."

Sales were considerably softer than those of other Burnished American Silver Eagles of recent years. Collector demand dropped about 20 percent compared to sales of the 2014-W Burnished.

2015-W, Proof

Mintages: 707,518
GSID: 74075
Minted at West Point, with W mintmark

Coin commentary: Sales for the 2015 Proof American Silver Eagle began on January 2 at $48.95 each, with no household ordering limits or mintage limits. It was the first coin available in the Mint's 2015 numismatic program, which by the year's end would include more than 130 different products—individual coins, annual sets, special sets, new medals, and the like.

Collectors could buy examples online, or in person at the Philadelphia and Denver mints and the sales center at Mint headquarters in Washington. Examples were also made available for purchase directly from the U.S. Mint at the Florida United Numismatists convention in Orlando, January 8 to 11.

Officials from the Mint worked with several major dealers to make sure that collectors had an opportunity to purchase examples—the only 2015-dated coins then available for purchase—at the FUN show. In a statement released on December 29, 2014, the Mint wrote, "In order to ensure that we have adequate product available for the broadest range of customers possible for the duration of the FUN Show, we reached out to three of our bulk dealers who we know typically attend these events and tend to clear us out of available product stock in short order."

Sales followed the soft downward trend that Proof American Silver Eagles had experienced in recent years, though they topped out higher than 700,000 coins.

2016, Bullion Strike

Mintage: 37,701,500

GSID: 213171 (Philadelphia) / 84276 (San Francisco) / 84277 (West Point)

Minted at Philadelphia, San Francisco, and West Point, without mintmark

Historical context: Sales of American Silver Eagles increased consistently in the years leading up to the thirtieth anniversary of the series in 2016. A December 16, 2015, Mint press release examined and touted the increasing sales: "Since 2007, sales have increased nearly five-fold, from 9,887,000 in 2007 to more than 44 million last year." 2015 marked the third consecutive record-breaking year.

Some observers thought that sales in 2016 might continue the trend, especially in light of the thirtieth anniversary, but they did not. Bullion-strike American Silver Eagles finished significantly below their 2015 high for 2016, beginning a three-year decline.

Silver values started 2016 around $14 per ounce.[1] The Mint made the bullion coins available to its Authorized Purchasers on January 11, 2016, for $2 over the spot price of an ounce of silver. In the first four days of sales, all 4 million allocated coins (quadruple the usual allocation) were purchased, which some observers linked to the previous year's strong sales.[2] In mid-June, sales stood 35.16 percent higher than the same period in 2015.[3]

The strong initial showing proved an aberration for the year. Sales of the American Eagles declined as silver prices increased.

The first quarter of 2016 saw a 12 percent increase in the price of silver; *CNN Business* reported an 11-month high in April, and by summer silver would hit a two-year peak.[4] By July 6 the price for an ounce of silver stood at $20.43,[5] and it peaked on August 2 at $20.71, after consistent increases in value.[6]

American Silver Eagle sales languished in the summer, and Paul Gilkes reported in *Coin World* on the growing inventory of unsold 2016 bullion coins.[7] On July 18 the Mint removed the weekly allocation, implemented in response to limited planchet supply and increasing demand, that it had set for its Authorized Purchasers.[8]

After August, silver prices cooled, finishing the year around $16 per ounce. Bullion coin sales began to pick up again in the fall, with October's sales double those of September.[9] Production stopped on November 30.[10] The Mint recorded 37,701,500 coins sold for the year, the lowest number since 2012 and a 19.8 percent decrease from 2015.

2016 average silver price: $17.14/ounce.

Coin commentary: Production of bullion-strike American Silver Eagles was shifted partly to San Francisco and Philadelphia in 2016 “so that the West Point Mint could finish the development and production of the Proof 2016-W American Eagle bearing the special 30th anniversary edge inscriptions.”[11] For the year, West Point minted 31,900,000 coins, San Francisco 4,650,000, and Philadelphia 1,151,500.

The American Silver Eagles’ thirtieth anniversary coincided with the same anniversary of the establishment of Professional Coin Grading Service, a situation that PCGS capitalized on with special programs.[12]

The American Numismatic Association marked its 125th anniversary the same year and gave 2016 bullion-strike American Silver Eagles to new members. Coins certified MS-69 with special anniversary labels from Numismatic Guarantee Corporation were membership premiums at the Platinum level. Those who purchased a life membership received a coin certified MS-70. The ANA issued 2,500 of the former and 250 of the latter, aiming to “entice new collectors to discover what the ANA has to offer, and serve as a gesture of appreciation to our loyal members,” according to its president at the time, Jeff Garrett.

2016 bullion-strike coins retained the usual reeded edge of the series, while numismatic versions sported edge lettering reading 30TH ANNIVERSARY.

The Mint’s American Liberty silver medals were struck in 2016 on the same planchets as American Silver Eagles.

2016-W, Burnished

Mintage: 216,501

GSID: 74225

Minted at West Point, with W mintmark

Coin commentary: Like their Proof counterparts, the 2016-W Burnished (or Uncirculated) American Silver Eagles sported edge lettering celebrating the thirtieth anniversary of the series. Striking and release were delayed by the retooling process required to apply the edge lettering; the coins went into production on August 30 and were struck until the end of the calendar year.[13] They were released on December 1, priced at $44.95 without mintage or household ordering limits.

The 2016-W Burnished American Silver Eagles were included in the 2016 Uncirculated Dollar Coin set, which went on sale December 14 at noon Eastern Time, also without mintage or household ordering restrictions. The set included Uncirculated versions of 2016's Native American dollar, struck in Denver, and the Presidential dollars honoring Richard Nixon, Gerald Ford, and Ronald Reagan, all struck in Philadelphia. The set was priced at $49.95, only $5.00 higher than the single 2016-W Burnished American Silver Eagle and $3.00 higher than 2015's Uncirculated Dollar Coin Set. The 2016 sets, the last products the U.S. Mint released in 2016, remained on sale into 2017, like the individual 2016-W Burnished American Silver Eagles.

Both products' first-day sales included orders placed through the U.S. Mint's Enrollment Program.

There were 216,501 2016-W Burnished American Silver Eagles sold as of March 4, 2018, according to the Mint's cumulative sales figures.

The coins did not go on sale in fiscal year 2016 and were not included in the Mint's product sales for that fiscal year, which ran from October 1, 2015 to September 30, 2016; the 2016-W Proof American Silver Eagle was released two weeks before the end of FY2016. Silver coin product sales in FY2016 were a fraction of FY2015's sales, in large part because of the delayed release of the Burnished and Proof American Silver Eagles; 1,436,000 silver products were sold in 2015, while 656,000 were sold in FY2016.[14] This precipitous decline in silver product sales contributed to a 22.6 percent overall decline in numismatic product sales in FY2016 from FY2015.[15]

2016-W, Proof

Mintages: 651,453
GSID: 74076
Minted at West Point, with W mintmark

Coin commentary: To mark the thirtieth anniversary of the series, the Mint applied lettering to the edge of all Proof and Burnished American Silver Eagles struck in 2016. Reading 30TH ANNIVERSARY, the lettering was the series' first and only departure from the regular reeded edge. The rest of the edge of the 2016 collector editions was smooth.

Some collectors anticipated commemoration of the anniversary. A letter to the editor from numismatist Ross Johnson published in the January 18 issue of *Coin World* surmised: "The Mint has more discretionary latitude with its bullion coins, so I'm guessing these are likely candidates."

An editor's note published with Johnson's letter noted the edge inscription, describing the coins as "prime candidates for stealth collector products in 2016."

The application of edge lettering was approved on December 4, 2015, when President Barack Obama signed the Fixing America's Surface Transportation (FAST) Act (Public Law 114-94), to which a provision for the lettering was included, "one of several freestanding bills to be incorporated into" the law, according to managing editor William T. Gibbs's reporting in *Coin World*.[16]

An unintended consequence of the legislation was its effect on the 2015 Limited Edition Silver Proof Set. The law stipulated "all collector versions of the silver American Eagles released in 2016 to have a distinctive edge in recognition of the 30th anniversary of the series," which "Mint officials interpreted . . . as applying to any collector version of silver American Eagle sold in 2016 regardless of date," Paul Gilkes explained in *Coin World*.[17] Since sales of the Limited Edition Silver Proof Set had not yet gotten underway as a result of packaging issues (the coins were scheduled to go on sale November 23, 2015), sales of the 2015 set were cancelled.[18]

The edge lettering was applied using a three-part segmented collar, resulting in three vertical lines imparted by "the miniscule gap between the collar segments."[19] Gilkes explained the process in a *Coin World* article published on August 22: "The letter is raised in the collar die, making it incuse on the coin. The inscription is imparted on the plain edge during the striking process, from one section of a tripartite, or three-piece, segmented collar. The three pieces of the collar engage together at the same time that the obverse and reverse dies come together with a blank planchet already fed between. The metal flows from the strike pressure into the edge collar, when the edge of the coin receives the imprint of the edge design, before the dies and the edge collar retract." The incuse lettering appeared at the six o'clock position, relative to the obverse. The coins were struck three times on a Gräbener GMP 360 press, which applied 225 tons of pressure per strike.

The life span of the collar dies was quite a bit longer than the dies used to impart Weinman's Liberty Walking and Mercanti's Heraldic Eagle. Where the obverse/reverse dies could strike 2,000 coins, the collar die would last for 19,000.[20]

Striking and issuance of American Silver Eagles at the West Point Mint was delayed in 2016, owing to the "necessary tooling for the collar die that imparts the edge inscription ..."[21] Tests also had to be performed and "all that testing took time to complete."

The Proof coins were initially priced at $53.95 and went on sale at noon Eastern Time on September 16, months after Proofs usually are made available.

Some collectors were not satisfied with the execution of the edge lettering. *Coin World* dedicated a front-page story in its October 17, 2016, edition, documenting negative collector comments directed at the Mint from collector forums and subscriber messages.

Counterfeit 2016-W Proof coins began appearing within weeks of their release; *Coin World* reported on a counterfeit Proof example found at a flea market in Lynchburg, Virginia, on October 1.[22] The counterfeiter neglected to apply the edge lettering, which allowed it to be quickly identified. Also, the counterfeit's die orientation was medal turn, unlike the coin-turn orientation of genuine examples.

The 2016-W Proof American Silver Eagle was offered in three products: the Congratulations Set, the Coin and Chronicles Set honoring Ronald Reagan, and the Limited Edition Silver Proof set.

The Ronald Reagan Coins and Chronicles Set went on sale at noon Eastern Time on October 11 for $68.95, with a household ordering limit of three sets. A limit of 150,000 sets was imposed. The sets sold poorly, with only 21,511 purchased on the first day of sale; by October 16 the total stood at 24,893.[23] By the time the Mint removed household ordering limits on October 27, only 29,166 had sold.[24]

In addition to the 2016-W Proof American Silver Eagle, the set included a 2016-S Reverse Proof Ronald Reagan Presidential Dollar, a 1.5-inch bronze duplicate of the Congressional Gold Medal authorized for Ronald and Nancy Reagan in 2000, an engraved presidential portrait produced by the Bureau of Engraving and Printing, and a Coin and Chronicles booklet detailing Reagan's life and presidency.

The 2016 Limited Edition Silver Proof Set was released at noon Eastern Time on November 25, priced at $139.95. The Mint authorized 50,000 sets.

According to the U.S. Mint's cumulative sales figures, 595,840 of the coins were sold by January 27, 2019. In 2019 the Mint sold 183,781 to four bulk buyers at a discount by sealed bid rather than melt them.[25]

2017, Bullion Strike

Mintage: 18,065,500

GSID: 198090 (Philadelphia) / 84278 (San Francisco) / 84279 (West Point)

Minted at Philadelphia, San Francisco, and West Point, without mintmark

Historical context: Though they got off to a promising start, sales of American Silver Eagles dropped sharply in 2017 from 2016. Cumulative sales were less than 50 percent of their 2016 level.

Silver started 2017 at $15.95 per ounce on January 3. Its high point came on April 13 at $18.56, and its lowest, $15.22, on July 10. The year ended with a small net increase.

Silver prices behaved erratically in 2017 and some wondered if bullion coin sales would further decline from their 2015 highs, as they had in 2016. Louis Golino demurred in *Coin World*'s "Modern Numismatics" column, pointing to "greatly heightened geopolitical tension around the world and . . . the domestic political situation in the U.S. that some already call a constitutional crisis. . . ." as drivers of silver's price fluctuations and potential demand for American Silver Eagles.[26] He also contended that "world trade could be jeopardized by some of the proposals being floated by the U.S. administration," which could drive demand for American Silver Eagles. James Wyckoff of *Kitco News*, publishing in *Forbes*, too highlighted "heightened geopolitical risks" as a driver of silver prices in April 2017, though he noted President Donald Trump's comments about the dollar being too strong as another factor driving prices up.[27]

Almost six and a half years after his retirement, John Mercanti received the David Rittenhouse Award "for his contributions to America's artistic legacy" on May 17, 2017.[28] Paul Gilkes in *Coin World* reported that Mercanti is "perhaps most recognized for his Heraldic Eagle reverse that has graced the American Eagle silver dollar since its introduction in 1986."[29]

2017 average silver price: $17.04/ounce.

Coin commentary: The 2017 bullion-strike American Silver Eagles went on sale January 9, and first-day sales topped 2016's first-day sales by 35 percent.[30] That sales started after the Florida United Numismatists (FUN) coin show irked some dealers, who felt that they would have been able to sell a large number of the coins, had they been available.[31] Professional numismatist Scott Schechter described that time of the year as "Silver Eagle Season": "the period starting each year in mid-January when the new year's American Eagle silver bullion coins are released. During this time, dealers and the grading services are intensely focused on meeting the demands of collectors of silver American Eagles."[32]

The Industry Council for Tangible Assets (ICTA, today known as the National Coin & Bullion Association) distributed bullion American Silver Eagles certified Gem Uncirculated with a special NGC label to new "consumer patron" members as part of a membership drive in 2017.[33]

Strong demand for bullion-strike American Silver Eagles never materialized. "Bullion Sales Free Fall," declared a *Coin World* headline in late May, above a story detailing a 48 percent decrease in sales in April 2017 compared to March.[34] By the end of the year 18,065,500 of the silver bullion coins were sold, a decrease of more than 50 percent from 2016, when 37,701,500 were sold.

In October Dave Harper, writing for *Numismatic News*, declared 2017 a "bad year for silver Eagles."[35]

It proved to be a revelatory year for those interested in the minting process for American Silver Eagle bullion coins.

Officials of Numismatic Guarantee Corporation (NGC) noticed patterns in coin quality and box serial numbers with 2017 bullion strikes that they were grading and encapsulating. This raised suspicions that more than one facility struck the coins.[36] After Mint officials "balked" at the prospect of providing the information when asked by *Coin World*, the magazine and NGC filed Freedom of Information Act (FOIA) requests. *Coin World* filed its request on February 6, 2017.[37]

On March 20, in response to the FOIA requests, the U.S. Mint released mintage information about "nearly 17 million" bullion-strike American Silver Eagles, dated 2014 to 2017, struck at the Philadelphia and San Francisco Mints. These Mint facilities produced American Silver Eagles to help the West Point Mint build inventory ahead of the rush at the beginning of the year.[38]

"Until fairly recently," Paul Gilkes wrote in an article published by *Coin World* on April 17, 2017, "the U.S. Mint used either bands color-coded for each facility or, for coins from the West Point Mint, bands bearing the facility's name. During the last 12 months, the U.S. Mint switched to using generic straps to secure the lids on the 500-coin boxes without differentiating the origin of the coins, other than by the serial number system.

"Coins struck at the Philadelphia and San Francisco Mints were shipped in the generic strapped boxes to West Point and mixed in with boxes of West Point–struck coins for eventual pick-up by authorized purchasers."[39]

For information on how the hobby community reacted to this FOIA news and its understanding of 2015-dated American Silver Eagles, see the "2015, Bullion Strike" entry.

One million American Silver Eagles dated 2017 were struck at the Philadelphia Mint and 3,000,000 were struck at San Francisco, according to the Mint's data from March 20.[40]

2017-W, Burnished

Mintage: 176,739
GSID: 74226
Minted at West Point, with W mintmark

Coin commentary: Burnished (or Uncirculated) 2017-W American Silver Eagles were released without mintage or household order limits at noon Eastern Time on June 29, 2017, priced at $44.95.

The year saw the traditional reeded edge restored to numismatic/collector versions of the American Silver Eagle, replacing 2016's edge lettering honoring the thirtieth anniversary of the series. The 2017 Burnished American Silver Eagle was released much earlier in the year than its 2016 predecessor, which was delayed by the retooling process applying the edge lettering.[41] For a description of the process by which the reeded edge was applied, see the 2017-W Proof entry.

Visually quite similar to the bullion strike but struck on specially treated planchets and emblazoned with West Point's W mintmark, the Burnished American Silver Eagles are sold directly to Mint customers as a numismatic product for a substantial markup above their bullion value. This distribution method further distinguishes them from the bullion strikes, which are sold through a network of Authorized Purchasers at a small markup above the spot price of silver.

2017-S, Proof

Mintage: 123,799

GSID: 84294

Minted at San Francisco, with S mintmark

Coin commentary: Proof American Silver Eagles were struck at the San Francisco Mint in 2017, having last been struck there in 2012, and before that in 1992. Offered in only two sets, the Congratulations and Limited Edition Silver Proof sets, and not sold individually, the Proof coins drove sales for both products.

Congratulations Sets including the Proof 2017-S American Silver Eagles "for the first time ever" were offered for sale on April 4 at noon for $54.95. The number of sets was limited to 75,000, the first time such a limit was imposed since the product was introduced in 2012.

Priced only $1 above the less remarkable individual 2017-W Proof, the Congratulations Sets did not have household ordering limits imposed by the Mint. They sold out in about two minutes.[42] The sets were bringing prices higher than $200 on the secondary market within weeks of their release, frustrating customers who wanted the 2017-S American Silver Eagle but did not want to buy the Limited Edition Silver Proof set.[43]

In an editorial published in *Coin World*'s April 24, 2017, edition, Managing Editor William T. Gibbs drew a connection between the Mint's "bad marketing decision" with the 2017 Congratulations Set and the decision in 1995 that made a modern rarity of the 1995-W Proof American Silver Eagles. He argued that the American Silver Eagles' low initial cost is an integral component of their appeal: "It was the incredibly bad decision to impose no household limits on purchases of the set that angered collectors, because that choice allowed commercial sellers to buy large numbers of the set and caused it to sell out in two minutes!" He concluded: "If they [the Mint] keep making decisions like this latest one, they will see their customer base shrink . . . as once-loyal customers stop buying from the Mint in disgust at their anti-collector actions."

The Limited Edition Silver Proof Set offered collectors another opportunity to own the 2017-S Proof American Silver Eagle, and expectations for sales were high in light of the quick sellout and high secondary-market prices for the Congratulations Set. Sales began on October 5, 2017, at noon.

Initial sales underperformed relative to the rapid sellout of the Congratulations Set. Priced at $139.95 and limited to two sets per household, fewer than two-thirds of the 50,000 authorized sets, 29,164, sold in the first 22 hours of sale.[44] By March 2018 the Mint reported 48,906 sold. Some hobbyists thought that the underperformance was a result of the sets' price. Secondary market prices for the 2017 Congratulations Set remained strong for years after their issuance; *CoinWeek* reported in April 2019 that the sets were consistently selling for nearly double their issue price on eBay.[45]

Proof American Silver Eagles struck at the San Francisco Mint would be included in all Limited Edition Silver Proof Sets after 2017.

2017-W, Proof

Mintage: 440,596
GSID: 74077
Minted at West Point, with W mintmark

Coin commentary: The Mint put the 2017-W Proof American Eagle silver dollars on sale March 23, 2017, for $53.95, with no product or household limits.

Reeded edges returned to the numismatic American Silver Eagles in 2017, applied with a close collar die.

"The close collar, bearing the reeded edge design," Paul Gilkes wrote in *Coin World*'s coverage announcing the release of the West Point Mint's Proof American Silver Eagle, "rises from the platform and surrounds the obverse hammer and reverse anvil dies during the striking process, acting to contain the flow of the metal in the planchet and apply the reeding as the planchet is struck."[46]

The first day saw sales of 226,173 Proof American Silver Eagles, through orders taken "on the opening days of sales to the public as well as orders placed by Mint customers through the Mint's Enrollment program for annual products."[47]

The Mint reported on September 10 that 306,808 2017-W Proof American Eagle silver dollars had been sold; by the end of year, sales stood at 372,173 coins. Dave Harper described "a worrisome downtrend in Proof silver American Eagle demand" in *Numismatic News* shortly after the 2017-W Proof's release, commenting on its lackluster first-day sales compared to the previous year.[48]

West Point Mint Proofs were sold individually and in bulk, unlike 2017 Proofs struck at San Francisco, which were only offered in two limited-edition products. The Mint's January 27, 2019, sales report recorded 390,816 coins sold. Later audits fine-tuned the sales to more than 440,000. The Mint also sold 240 bulk packages.

2018, Bullion Strike

Mintage: 15,700,000

GSID: 81693

Minted at West Point, without mintmark

Historical context: Silver prices in 2018 spent most of the year between about $14 and $18 per ounce, gradually declining over the course of the year. January 25 saw the year's highest silver price, at $17.52, while the lowest price was reached on November 14, at $13.97.[49] According to *Forbes*, industrial use of silver increased significantly in 2018, mainly for "photovoltaic solar panels, brazing alloys and solders, electronics and ethylene oxide" but a strong dollar, particularly in the fourth quarter, held silver prices down.[50] American Silver Eagle sales declined over the course of the year alongside silver prices.

2018 average silver price: $15.71/ounce.

Coin commentary: Sales of bullion American Silver Eagles were dismal in 2018. The first two months saw sales down 34 percent compared to the first two months of 2017 and they never recovered, despite a brief spike toward the end of the summer.[51] In September sales rallied unexpectedly to almost double their August level, and the Mint announced on September 6 that its stocks were temporarily depleted. The West Point Mint, the only facility to strike bullion American Silver Eagles in 2018, increased production. Despite the increase in demand toward the end of the year, 2018 marked an 11-year low for American Silver Eagle bullion sales. According to the Mint's December 20, 2018, sales report, 15,560,000 coins had sold, a decline of more than two and a half million from 2017, itself a slow year for American Silver Eagle sales.

"Investors deciding to place their money in higher-yielding vehicles than precious metals translated into decreased U.S. Mint gold and silver bullion sales in 2018," Paul Gilkes wrote in the January 14, 2019, edition of *Coin World*.

The American Silver Eagle received a dubious distinction in 2018, identified as "the counterfeit bullion coin most widely encountered by U.S. dealers" in a survey conducted in June 2018 by the Industry Council on Tangible Assets (ICTA, now the National Coin & Bullion Association). There were 363 dealers surveyed, including members of ICTA, the Professional Numismatists Guild, and the American Numismatic Association. The survey found 43.3 percent of respondents reported customers seeking to sell counterfeit American Silver Eagles, while more than 80 percent observed an increase in the number of counterfeit coins and bars entering the marketplace during the last five years. American Gold Eagle bullion coins were a close runner-up, with 41.2 percent of survey respondents reporting customers attempting to sell counterfeit examples. Morgan dollars were the most commonly forged non-bullion collector coins; 71.7 percent of dealers claimed to have encountered them.

Coin World's managing editor, William T. Gibbs, expressed hope at the beginning of the year that Mint officials would "get serious about the problem" of counterfeiting bullion coins in 2018.[52]

2018-W, Burnished

Mintage: 138,947

GSID: 84269

Minted at West Point, with W mintmark

Coin commentary: The 2018-W Burnished American Silver Eagles went on sale at noon Eastern Time, May 24, 2018, priced at $46.95, a $2 increase in price from 2017. Burnished American Silver Eagles are by the Mint sold directly to customers, in contrast to the bullion coins, which are sold through a network of Authorized Purchasers for a premium over their precious-metal value.

The coins were still available for sale a year after their release. According to a Mint sales report, 138,891 had been sold by April 14, 2019. By May 29, 138,925 of the Burnished American Silver Eagles had sold. By January 26, 2020, the Mint reported 138,947 had been sold.

Paul Gilkes described the treatment of planchets used for Burnished American Silver Eagles in *Coin World*: "The Uncirculated [Burnished] finish results from planchets being subjected to a pre-strike burnishing, in which the raw planchets are tumbled with steel media in a solution of cleansing and brightening agents."[53]

2018-S, Proof

Mintage: 208,258

GSID: 81462

Minted at San Francisco, with S mintmark

Coin commentary: The San Francisco Mint struck Proof American Silver Eagles in 2018, the second Proof offering of the series that year. Released on August 14, the 2018-S Proof coins were sold individually, unlike their 2017-S Proof predecessors, which were only offered in two limited-edition products. This marked the second consecutive year that Proof American Silver Eagles were struck at the San Francisco Mint; before 2017, Proof American Silver Eagles had been produced at that facility from 1986 to 1992 and in 2012.

Proofs would continue to be struck in San Francisco after 2018, augmenting the Proof output of the West Point Mint.

There were 52,494 coins sold on the first day of issue for $55.95, the same price as the 2018-S coin's counterpart struck at the West Point Mint. No mintage limit was applied to either coin.

Proof 2018-S American Silver Eagles were included in the Limited Edition Silver Proof Set, which went on sale without household ordering limits on October 18 at noon Eastern Time, priced at $144.95. Between its release and December 3, a total of 34,423 of the 50,000 authorized sets had sold. As of January 27, 2019, according to the U.S. Mint's cumulative sales data, 158,785 2018-S Proof American Silver Eagles had sold. The number would later be updated to 208,258, with a final audit to be determined.

2018-W, Proof

Mintage: 411,397

GSID: 74078

Minted at West Point, with W mintmark

Coin commentary: Three of the first four products released by the Mint in 2018 featured a 2018-W Proof American Silver Eagle. Individual Proof coins, Congratulations Sets, and 210-coin bulk packs all went on sale in January 2018. Some of the news surrounding their issuance was not positive.

Steve Roach wrote *Coin World*'s January 2018 cover feature about distinct numismatic markets, with a subsection devoted to Proof American Silver Eagles titled "When a Market Disappears: Proof Silver American Eagles."[54] He explained that Proof American Silver Eagles had for years "enjoyed an active secondary market" but that demand declined in 2017. Brokers who sold the coins as investments for inclusion in individual retirement accounts (IRAs) made "substantial commissions," the *Wall Street Journal* reported, and supplies of the coins were being liquidated around the time the Mint announced that 2017-W Proofs coins would be released earlier than expected. The 210-coin bulk packs further increased supply. The 2016-W and 2017-W Proof American Silver Eagles remained available from the Mint at the time of the 2018-W Proofs' release.

"With such bad publicity for Proof American Eagles," Roach anticipated decreased demand and a sluggish market for the coins in advance of the January 4 release of 2018-W American Silver Eagles. Priced at $55.95 (a $2 price hike from 2017), 226,506 individual 2018-W Proofs sold by February 5, nearly 150,000 coins short of 2017's sales in the same period. Prices for Congratulations Sets, which included the Proof 2018-W American Silver Eagle (unlike 2017, when the set contained a Proof American Silver Eagle struck at San Francisco), were released on January 11 and also had a $2 price increase, to $56.95. By early February, 9,015 of the sets had sold.

The 210-coin bulk packs of Proof American Silver Eagles saw their prices increase as well, by $420 each. The Mint sold 166 bulk packs in the first month of the 2018-W Proof American Silver Eagle's availability.

2019, Bullion Strike

Mintage: 14,863,500

GSID: 81694

Minted at West Point, without mintmark

Historical context: Overall sales of bullion-strike American Silver Eagles in 2019 continued the downward trend that had defined the previous three years, and marked the nadir of the drop in sales.

Silver prices increased gradually over the course of 2019, from their lowest point, $14.37, on May 29 to their peak on September 4 at $19.30. The year marked a roughly $2.60 per ounce net increase in silver price.[55]

2019 average silver price: $16.21/ounce.

Coin commentary: The year's bullion-strike American Silver Eagles went on sale January 7 and got off to a strong start. In the first two months of 2019 American Silver Eagle sales were 45 percent higher than the first two months of 2018.[56] By February 21 the Mint ran out of inventory and had to suspend the sale of silver bullion coins. Sales resumed, under allocation, on April 1; 550,000 of the coins had been sold by April 24.[57]

In May 866,000 bullion-strike American Silver Eagles were sold, 27.6 percent fewer than the 1,196,000 coins sold in April.[58]

"2019 sales of the coin are well above those for the same period in 2018," Paul Gilkes reported in *Coin World*'s June 24, 2019, edition.

At the end of July American Silver Eagles sales stood 46 percent higher than sales from the same period of 2018, totaling 11,262,000 coins sold in seven months.

By the end of the year that momentum faded, and sales failed to top 2018's totals.

There were 14,863,500 American Silver Eagles recorded sold in 2019, compared to 15,700,000 in 2018. *Coin World* Managing Editor William T. Gibbs described 2019 as a "rough year for bullion coin sales for the U.S. Mint."

Sales totals for 2019 would be eclipsed in 2020.

Numismatic Guarantee Corporation (NGC) certified its ten millionth American Silver Eagle in 2019, the first third-party grading service to reach that milestone. *Numismatic News* reported that the American Silver Eagle was the most popular category in the NGC Registry in 2019.[59]

2019-W, Burnished

Mintage: 140,779

GSID: 84270

Minted at West Point, with W mintmark

Coin commentary: The 2019-W Burnished American Silver Eagles were released on May 29, 2019, at noon Eastern Time. No product limit or household order restrictions were placed on the coins, which were priced at $46.95, the same price as 2018-W Burnished American Silver Eagles.

Planchets used to strike Burnished American Silver Eagles are "subjected to a pre-strike burnishing, in which the raw planchets are tumbled with steel media in a solution of cleansing and brightening agents."[60] The production process for Burnished American Silver Eagles is different than the process for Proof planchets, which are highly polished and then rubbed with lubricating oil to keep them from sticking to the Proof dies (which are themselves specially prepared) during the high-pressure striking process.

Unlike bullion-strike American Silver Eagles, which are sold by the Mint through a network of Authorized Purchasers, Burnished coins are sold directly to the public.

The Mint reported selling the coins individually as well as in bulk packs sold at a discount to authorized coin dealers and similar businesses.

2019-S, Proof

Mintage: 192,811

GSID: 81737

Minted at San Francisco, with S mintmark

Coin commentary: The 2019-S Proof American Silver Eagles went on sale August 6, 2019, at noon Eastern Time. The coins were priced at $55.95 and struck to order, and no product or household order limits were applied. Like their predecessors in 2017 and 2018, the 2019 Proof American Silver Eagles struck at the San Francisco Mint were included in the Limited Edition Silver Proof Set.

The sets were released on October 17 with a product limit of 50,000, priced at $149.95 per set. All of the coins in the Limited Edition Silver Proof Set were .999 fine, the first time the composition was used for the entire set. The Fixing America's Surface Transportation (FAST) Act, a piece of legislation signed in December 2015, authorized the edge lettering for the numismatic editions of the 2016 American Silver Eagle and allowed the Mint great flexibility to determine the fineness of silver coins. (For more details on the FAST Act, see the 2016-W Proof entry.)

Before the passage of the FAST Act, the fineness of "certain coins" was mandated .900 fine (90 percent silver, 10 percent copper), but the legislation changed the standard to "not less than 90%" silver, allowing for the Mint to increase silver fineness. The change in fineness, which allowed the Mint to expand its supplier base and cut costs, did not impact the Proof American Silver Eagle, which was already .999 fine.

The .900 fine standard for the sets was originally legislated in 1990 (after having been used for circulating coinage from the 1830's until the mid-1960's). The first Silver Proof Sets released under the 1990 legislation and using that silver alloy were released in 1992.

According to the Mint's January 17, 2021, cumulative sales report, 146,735 2019-S Proof American Silver Eagles had sold. The Mint's cumulative sales figures from January 26, 2020, report 137 bulk packs of 2019-S Proof American Silver Eagles sold. Later Mint reports, awaiting final audit, put total sales at 192,811 coins.

2019-S, Enhanced Reverse Proof

Mintage: 29,909

GSID: 81738

Minted at San Francisco, with S mintmark

Coin commentary: American Silver Eagles with an Enhanced Reverse Proof finish, struck at the San Francisco Mint, went on sale November 14, 2019, at noon Eastern Time. The issue was limited to 30,000 coins, priced at $65.95 each ($10 higher than individual Proof coins struck at the West Point or San Francisco Mints). Some of the coins were released at the Whitman Coin and Collectibles Baltimore Expo with certificates of authenticity signed by Mint Director David Ryder.

A household ordering limit of one coin per household was imposed.

Despite the limit, the coins sold out in less than 20 minutes, stoking outrage among disappointed customers and collectors. The product-ordering page received 150,000 unique visitors and 1.6 million page views within the first hour of sale, according to Mint officials.[61] About 99,000 people were online and 4,700 on the phone waiting to purchase the coins when they went on sale.[62]

The Mint's website had to repel a cyberattack staged by unidentified users who attempted to circumvent the household ordering limit. "None of the orders attempted through the use of bots were processed," Paul Gilkes reported on the front of *Coin World*'s December 9, 2019, edition. "Known bots" accounted for 1.4 percent of the page views on November 14 and "the Mint does not believe automated 'bots' made a large number of purchases" for the 2019-S Enhanced Reverse Proof coins, according to Mint officials.

Many Mint customers reported ordering problems. When a *Coin World* staff member tried to place an order, "We were able to get onto the Mint's website less than 30 seconds after launch, select the one-coin limit for placement in the ordering 'bag,' then click the Checkout button to make payment. However, while in the process of filling in the information requested to complete the transaction, the website froze, kicked the staff member out and deselected the ordering option."[63]

The Mint acknowledged that the volume of traffic slowed the site down; for the first two minutes, the Mint was only able to process 1,800 orders per minute. Spokesperson Michael White put out a statement that explained: "Items are not automatically made unavailable to others when they are placed in a customer's cart. Instead, inventory is decremented once billing information is entered and verified. Normally, this is transparent to customers but during an event like American Eagle 2019 One Ounce Silver Enhanced Reverse Proof launch . . . it can result in items that appear in a customer's cart can be unavailable at checkout."

Some dealers found a legal way to circumvent the household ordering limit. *Coin World* Managing Editor William T. Gibbs shared in an Editor's Letter that "some firms openly circumvented the limit by publicly offering individuals a profit of $150 for any coin they might purchase."[64] Gibbs noted that the practice was not illegal but that collectors might find it "objectionable, particularly when a firm starts selling multiples of the coin at huge profits."

The coins began appearing on the secondary market almost immediately, selling for many times their issue price.

Serial-numbered certificates of authenticity were included with the coins, a first for the Mint. Mint Director David Ryder hand-signed COAs at the Whitman Coin and Collectibles Baltimore Expo from noon to 2:30 p.m. on November 14. Eight hundred coins were sold at the Whitman Expo.

A 2019-S Enhanced Reverse Proof with a signed COA (#16), certified PF-70 by PCGS, sold in an eBay auction for $14,001 on December 4.[65] Other coins brought thousands of dollars in different sales and auctions. *Coin World*'s Coin Values Spotlight estimated their February 2021 retail value at $1,500 in PF-69DC and $2,500 in PF-70DC.

By January 31, 2021, the Mint reported 29,909 coins sold. The 97 unissued coins from cancelled orders sold out again when they were offered for sale on August 5, 2020; the Mint explained that while "working to move the inventory in our system to prepare it for sale . . . an error was made and the product was made available for sale via the Mint's website and immediately sold out." On August 12, 2020, 119 more coins sold out in 10 seconds in an online sale.[66] The Mint's cumulative sales data as of early 2021 listed 29,909 coins sold.

Enhanced Reverse Proof American Silver Eagles are distinguishable from other Reverse Proof coins by the selective application of frosted and polished design elements: "What sets it apart are the multiple polished and frosted finishes applied to different isolated design elements," according to the Mint. (For more details about the appearance of the Enhanced Reverse Proof finish, see the 2019-W Enhanced Reverse Proof entry.)

The same finish was applied to the 2019-W Enhanced Reverse Proof American Silver Eagle included in the Pride of Two Nations set, issued earlier that year.

2019-W, Proof

Mintage: 372,118

GSID: 81463

Minted at West Point, with W mintmark

Coin commentary: The 2019 Proof American Silver Eagles minted at West Point were released on January 10, 2019, without mintage, product, or household ordering limits. Sales were brisk, totaling 236,442 "across all product options," according to Fern Loomis and Paul Gilkes's reporting on sales figures in *Coin World*'s February 2019 monthly edition.[67] That figure included 208,760 individual coins; 10,320 sold in 258 40-coin packs; and 17,452 sold in Congratulations Sets.

Priced at $55.95 ($56.95 in Congratulations Sets), the coins were available in discounted 40-coin bulk packs made available only to active participants in the Mint's Numismatic Bulk Purchase Program.

The Proof coins were sold through the Mint's annual subscription program, at its sales center at Mint headquarters on Ninth Street in Washington, D.C., and at gift shops in the Philadelphia and Denver Mints, in addition to thousands of coins sold at the Florida United Numismatists (FUN) show. 2019-W Proof American Silver Eagles, whether sold in the regular Proof or Congratulations Set packaging, were "the star of the numismatic products the Mint had on offer" at the FUN Show. The coins attracted a line of interested customers and dealers in advance of the noon release on January 10.

The Mint almost missed the FUN Show, as its staff faced the "possibility of being recalled to Washington, unless revised clearance would be received from the Treasury Secretary" as a result of the partial government shutdown, Gilkes reported for *Coin World*.[68] "Once Treasury executives were informed of the Mint's potential to record $2 million in numismatic sales, full travel authority was granted."

According to the Mint's January 13, 2019, sales report, 236,442 2019-W Proof American Silver Eagles had sold. By April 5, 2020, 346,366 2019-W Proof American Silver Eagles had sold, while the January 26, 2020, report lists 745 bulk packs of 40 coins sold.

The Mint hiked the price of all silver products on October 13, 2020, including all products still on sale.[69] The only product including a 2019-W American Silver Eagle that was impacted by the price hike was the 2019 Congratulations Set, which was raised to $75.

2019-W, Enhanced Reverse Proof

Mintage: 99,675

GSID: 81903

Minted at West Point, with W mintmark

Coin commentary: The United States Mint released its first American Silver Eagles struck with an Enhanced Reverse Proof finish at the West Point Mint on July 3, 2019, as part of the Pride of Two Nations set. Produced and released jointly by the U.S. and Royal Canadian Mints on July 3, the sets featured the 2019-W Enhanced Reverse Proof American Silver Eagle and a Canadian $5 silver Maple Leaf with a "modified Proof" finish.

The Mint issued 110,000 of the 2019-W Enhanced Reverse Proof American Silver Eagles—100,000 for sets in the United States and 10,000 for sets in Canada. The U.S. sets were priced at $139.95 and "reached 'currently unavailable' status" within a week of their release, according to Paul Gilkes's reporting in *Coin World*.[70] By February 2020 all were recorded sold; the Mint's website lists the set as "sold out."[71]

For more details about the Pride of Two Nations set, see its separate entry.

Enhanced Reverse Proof American Silver Eagles have frosted fields and polished devices like other Reverse Proof coins, but "what sets it apart are the multiple polished and frosted finishes applied to different isolated design elements," according to the Mint.

Dies for the Enhanced Reverse Proof coins are fully "Proof-polished," after which the designated areas receive, according to Gilkes's reporting, "different intensities of laser-frosting after being mapped out according to a computerized template."[72]

On the obverse "Proof polishing remains on the rim, date, letters of 'LIBERTY' and 'IN GOD WE TRUST,' the stars, what would be white stripes on the American flag, the strapping on Liberty's sandals, the sun and the sun's rays.

"Light frosting is applied to Liberty's body and upper garment, the branch in her left hand, and portions of her sandals. Light plus frosting appears on what would be the red stripes on the American flag as well as the canton behind the stars. Heavy frosting is used on the background."[73]

"Proof polishing remains on the rim" of the reverse, as well as on "UNITED STATES OF AMERICA and the inscription designating weight in silver, the denomination, the background on the shield, the 13 stars above the eagle, the S Mint mark, the letters of E PLURIBUS UNUM and Mint sculptor engraver John Mercanti's initials. Light frosting covers the entire eagle. Light plus frost is used on the ribbon in the eagle's beak, the branch in the right talon and arrows in left. Heavy frosting is used on the background fields as well as on the frame and vertical stripes on the shield."[74]

2019, Pride of Two Nations Set

Mintage: 99,675 U.S. sets; 10,000 Canadian sets

GSID: 315631

Minted at West Point (American Silver Eagle, with W mintmark) and Ottawa (Maple Leaf)

Set commentary: On June 25, 2019, the U.S. Mint issued a press release announcing the Pride of Two Nations Limited Edition Two-Coin Set, the first product issued jointly by the U.S. Mint and the Royal Canadian Mint (RCM). The set "commemorates both countries' nationhood with coins that capture their rich history, pride, and their close relationship as neighbors and friends."

Featured in the set are a 2019-W Enhanced Reverse Proof American Silver Eagle struck at the West Point Mint and a Canadian $5 Maple Leaf with a "modified Proof finish," struck at the Royal Canadian Mint in Ottawa. Priced at $139.95, the sets were released on July 3, 2019, at noon Eastern Time with a product ceiling of 100,000 sets and a household ordering limit of five sets.

The U.S. Mint sold 74,054 of the sets on the first day. The RCM's 10,000 sets sold out within days of their release on June 25 and the U.S. sets "reached 'currently unavailable' status" less than a week after their release, according to Paul Gilkes's reporting in *Coin World*.[75]

Canada's coin has a "serrated" edge, while the American Silver Eagle has the usual reeded edge. The "modified Proof finish" has inscriptions with the same "natural shine" as fields on a conventional Proof coin. The U.S. Mint's catalog entry for the set describes the Canadian coins: "The obverse of the Canadian One Ounce Silver Maple Leaf Coin features the effigy of Her Majesty Queen Elizabeth II by Susanna Blunt on a radial lines background with a pattern of stars and maple leaves on the perimeter.

"The reverse features a maple leaf by Walter Ott on a radial lines background with a pattern of stars and maple leaves on the perimeter."

Each country packaged the sets differently. The U.S. Mint's set was packaged in a blue box, with the American Silver Eagle positioned at left, while the RCM placed the Maple Leaf on the left in its set, housed in a black box. The symbols of the national mints on the boxes' lids and the flags within them are also reversed between the sets; the U.S. set has its mint logo and flag at left, the Canadian set the opposite.

Canada issued only 10,000 of the sets, priced at $189.95 in Canadian dollars, and did not impose ordering restrictions. Sets were sold at the RCM's outlets in Ottawa and Winnipeg and could be ordered online and over the phone.

The U.S. Mint described the packaging of the American set as "a handsome blue leatherette presentation case emblazoned with color imagery of the United States and Canadian flags on the inside cover. A classic blue outer box and matching outer sleeve cover the presentation case. A bilingual Certificate of Authenticity (COA) accompanies the set." The bilingual COA was the first of its kind issued by the U.S. Mint.

The U.S. Mint and the RCM hosted a joint release ceremony at the Philadelphia Mint, at which U.S. Mint Director David Ryder and Marie Lemay, president and chief executive officer of the RCM, signed certificates of authenticity. The pair also signed COAs at the American Numismatic Association's World's Fair of Money in Rosemont, Illinois.[76] Some of both sets were reserved for sale at the event; the Mint's press release did not specify how many sets were available, saying only that a limited number were reserved for ANA sales and signing.

Plans for an international joint product were in the works in 2018. The Bureau of Engraving and Printing and the Mint considered issuing a jointly packaged product with silver bullion coins from three countries: the U.S., Canada, and Mexico.[77] In a focus group run by a contractor, NAXION, "current and potential Mint customers across the country" were asked about silver bullion products including coins from the United States, Canada, and Mexico.[78] The set was not developed beyond exploratory phases.

2020, Bullion Strike

Mintage: 30,089,500

GSID: 81905 (Philadelphia) / 213172 (San Francisco) / 81904 (West Point)

Minted at Philadelphia, San Francisco, and West Point, without mintmark

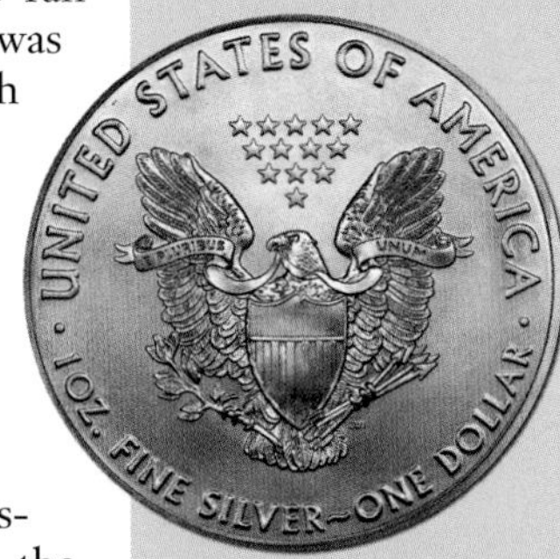

Historical context: The years-long decline in bullion-strike American Silver Eagle sales that began in 2016 ended in 2020, with sales spiking to more than double their 2019 levels.

COVID-19 made its presence felt in the precious-metals market in 2020, with a wild upswing in prices in July, August, and September after a precipitous drop early in the year.[79] The drop ran parallel to a collapse in the stock market (though silver's decline was not as sharp), after which prices rallied, marking a nine-year high for silver values.[80] "Supply disruptions have also supported silver . . . prices," and mine shutdowns as a result of COVID-19 "heavily affected" silver production, according to an article from the World Bank.[81] Silver's highest price came on September 1, at $28.88, and its lowest price was $12.00, on March 19.[82] 2020 average silver price: $20.55/ounce.

Coin commentary: Demand for the bullion-strike American Silver Eagles was "extremely strong," according to U.S. Mint spokesman Michael White, and, as in previous years with high demand, the San Francisco Mint was also pressed into service to augment the output from the West Point Mint. The Mint ran out of bullion-strike American Silver Eagles in March after a massive spike in sales, with more coins (2.32 million) sold in the first 12 days of March than the entire month of February. Sales were suspended on March 12 as a result of depleted inventory, for the first time since February 2019. Sales resumed on an allocated basis and continued increasing in the spring.

Coinage production at the West Point Mint was suspended from March 28 to 31 after an employee tested positive for COVID-19; it shut down again on April 15 and reopened on April 21.

An "emergency run" of 240,000 coins was struck between April 8 and April 20 at the Philadelphia Mint as the West Point facility closed to protect its workers from COVID. The coins were encapsulated by third-party certification services and began selling on the secondary market for prices approaching $100 in short order, with a range of labels using terms like "Emergency Issue" and "Emergency Production." The San Francisco Mint closed from March 18 to May 4 as a result of executive orders from California governor Gavin Newsom.

One million coins struck at the San Francisco Mint were offered on November 2 to the Mint's Authorized Purchasers "at a slightly higher premium per coin than that charged for the same coins struck at the West Point Mint," according to Paul Gilkes's reporting in *Coin World*.[83] The Mint's usual markup on a 2020 bullion-strike American Silver Eagle was $2.35 above the price of an ounce of silver; for the San Francisco Mint bullion strike coins, the premium was $2.65. Boxes of the San Francisco Mint coins were labeled and numbered so they could be identified as products of that facility.

2020-W, Burnished

Mintage: 154,864

GSID: 84271

Minted at West Point, with W mintmark

Coin commentary: On July 8, 2020, the U.S. Mint released Burnished American Silver Eagles struck at the West Point Mint, initially priced at $54.

Like other silver products, the 2020-W Burnished American Silver Eagle's price was increased on October 13, 2020 (to $67). The price for 40-coin bulk packs was raised to $2,680. No mintage, product, or household ordering limits were imposed.

Visually almost identical to their bullion-strike counterparts, save for the presence of the West Point Mint's W mintmark, the coins were struck on specially treated planchets and marketed as a numismatic product. The Burnished coins were sold directly to collectors and other Mint customers, unlike the bullion-strike coins, which the Mint sells to Authorized Purchasers for a small premium above their silver value. (Authorized Purchasers in turn sell the bullion coins to small distributors and to the public.)

During the first day of sales, 98,682 Burnished American Silver Eagles were sold.

According to the Mint's cumulative sales figures published on September 26, 2021, 154,264 individual Burnished American Silver Eagles had sold, in addition to 15 bulk packs.

2020-S, Proof

Mintage: 208,871

GSID: 81739

Minted at San Francisco, with S mintmark

Coin commentary: Proof American Silver Eagles struck at the San Francisco Mint were put on sale on October 13, 2020. The coins' initial price was announced at $63.25 without a mintage or household ordering limit.

Originally a mintage limit of 200,000 was announced. Minting was delayed as a result of COVID-19 restrictions, which interrupted production at the San Francisco Mint from March 18 to May 4.[84] The price for the individual coins was raised to $73 on the day the individual coins were released, and both of the products in which they were to be included also had price increases.[85]

The Mint sold 169,564 2020-S Proof American Silver Eagles, individually and as part of two other products, on the first day.

The Mint later acknowledged that the initial mintage limit of 200,000 was incorrect. More than 260,000 coins were actually struck, but the Mint did not include the coins sold in dealer discount bulk packs and the Limited Edition Silver Proof Sets. Mint spokesman Michael White announced: "This year due to COVID-19 and Plant Production capacity, a decision was made to conduct only one production run of 200K units for the individual American Eagle One Ounce Silver Proof Coin (S), limiting the production mintage to 200K, but the mintage limit should not have been reported as 200K. We have corrected the Mintage Limit to list as 'None.'"

Secondary market prices for the 2020-S Proof American Silver Eagles were strong in the weeks after issuance; *Coin World* reported that certified coins were being sold for $100 to $300 or more by a number of retailers.[86]

As in previous years, the 2020-S Proof American Silver Eagle was included in the Limited Edition Silver Proof Set, issued on December 10, 2020. The Mint increased the set's price to $201, a large increase from the year before; 2019's set had been priced at $149.95. As with the 2019 set, all of the coins included in the 2020 Limited Edition Silver Proof Set had a .999 fine silver composition.

First-day sales of the 2020 Limited Edition Silver Proof set totaled 33,928. A household ordering restriction of two sets was imposed.

The Mint's September 26, 2021, cumulative sales report shows that 191,271 individual coins and 440 bulk packs (of 40 coins each) had sold.

2020-W, Proof

Mintage: 359,511

GSID: 81464

Minted at West Point, with W mintmark

Coin commentary: The first Proof American Silver Eagles of the 2020's were released on January 9, 2020, bearing the West Point Mint's W mintmark. The U.S. Mint charged $64.50 for the coins, an $8.55 price hike from 2019, when the 2019-W Proof was sold for $55.95. Prices for other Mint products were increased again in 2020, with the American Silver Eagle Proof raised on October 13, 2020, to $73.

No mintage, product, or household ordering limits were applied to the 2020-W Proof American Silver Eagle; the coins could be purchased at Mint sales centers in Washington, D.C., Philadelphia, and Denver.

2020 Congratulations Sets, which included the 2020-W Proof American Silver Eagle, were released the same day as individual coins, January 9. The Mint charged $65.50 for the sets, a $1 markup from the individual coin.

In its September 26, 2021, cumulative sales figures the Mint reported 357,111 individual coins and 600 bulk packs (of 40 coins each) sold.

2020-W, World War II Privy Mark, Proof

Mintage: 74,709

GSID: 82111

Minted at West Point, with W mintmark

Coin commentary: To honor the 75th anniversary of the Allies' victory in World War II, the United States Mint applied privy marks to several different denominations of 2020 coinage. Proof American Silver Eagles struck at the West Point Mint in 2020 were among the coins to sport the privy marks, which had the characters V75 (for the 75th anniversary of victory) set within an incuse cartouche, in the shape of the "aerial view of the Rainbow Pool located at West Potomac Park in Washington D.C., now an integral part of the World War II Memorial."[87]

American Gold Eagles in the $50 denomination had the privy marks applied, too.

A limited number of Proof American Silver Eagles were struck with the V75 privy marks and sold to the public individually. The price was announced as $69.50 but was raised on October 13 to $83, ahead of the coins' release on November 5.

The privy mark was "digitally engraved" into the master die, appearing in the upper-right field on the obverse. Aside from the privy marks, the coins were identical to the other Proof struck at the West Point Mint that year.

The mintage of the 2020-W Proof American Silver Eagle with the V75 privy mark was capped at 75,000. (The gold coins' mintage was capped at 1,945 and sold out in about 90 minutes, enraging disappointed Mint's customers.)

By November 29, a quantity of 74,969 American Silver Eagles had sold.

As with the release of the 2019-S Enhanced Reverse Proof American Silver Eagles, dealers tried to find ways around the household ordering limit. Collectors were furious as they scrambled to buy the coins and the Mint's website was overwhelmed. More than 390,000 people tried to access the website in one "time frame," according to U.S. Mint Director David Ryder.[88] Bots were also an issue that the Mint had to contend with. Collector outrage was palpable in comments sections and forums around the Web and in letters to the numismatic media. Comparisons were drawn between the V75 situation and the release of the 2019-S Enhanced Reverse Proof American Silver Eagles.

Coin World's managing editor, William T. Gibbs, wondered in an editorial "whether [the Mint's] marketing decisions are deliberately aimed at shrinking the Mint's customer rolls."[89]

Coins began appearing for multiple times their issue price on the secondary market, with prices crossing the $1,000 threshold. The coins went back on sale November 29 after "order reconciliations" made another undisclosed number available.[90]

Director Ryder put out a statement addressing the quick sellout and customer anger on November 18, committing to improve the ordering process. "As many of you are aware, a slowdown of the Mint's online sales website caused frustration for many of our loyal customers, who were unable to purchase their desired product. . . . I can also tell you that our solutions to prevent automated purchases by 'bots' also put an immense strain on our website and can lead to unintended issues for other legitimate purchasers. The overwhelming demand for these products outpaced our website capacity in ways that we are still trying to better understand and remedy."[91]

2021, Variety 1, Bullion Strike

Mintage: 13,306,500
GSID: 85128 (Philadelphia) / 85054 (San Francisco) / 213362 (West Point)
Minted at Philadelphia, San Francisco, and West Point, without mintmark

Historical context: The COVID-19 pandemic that swept the world in 2020 continued into 2021. Health authorities in the United States and many other nations began administering vaccines to millions of people to help mitigate the most serious symptoms of the deadly illness. A gradual return to a semblance of normalcy ensued as the year rolled on. However, inflation ticked upward due to many factors, including supply-chain interruptions and persistent staffing shortages across many industries. America's social scene wasn't just disrupted by pandemic woes. Deepening sociopolitical divisions sparked a deadly riot at the Capitol Building in Washington, D.C., on January 6, 2021, along with wide-reaching rebukes against newly inaugurated President Joe Biden. In other news, a 12-story condominium tower collapsed in Surfside, Florida, killing 98 residents and prompting reforms on building inspection laws in the Sunshine State and beyond. A Midwest tornado outbreak spawning 71 twisters led to the deaths of 95 people and $3.9 billion in damages. The price of silver saw its 2021 high of $29.59 per ounce on February 1 and dipped to as low as $21.53 on September 30. Silver saw an average price of $25.14 for the year.

Coin commentary: It was the end of an era and the beginning of a new one for the long-running American Eagle program. The gold and silver coins saw changes to their reverse designs during the 35th anniversaries of these two oldest arms of the popular U.S. bullion program, which launched in 1986. John Mercanti's Heraldic Eagle motif on the American Silver Eagle was supplanted by a flying eagle device. The new design was created by Emily S. Damstra, an esteemed member of the Mint's Artistic Infusion Program. Her new Silver Eagle design was sculpted by U.S. Mint engraver Michael Gaudioso. The mid-year transition from the Variety 2 design to the Variety 2 truncated the output of the former subtype, which saw just over 13 million bullion strikes. Mint Director David Ryder struck the final Variety 2 emission, which hammered for $85,000 in a September 2022 Stack's Bowers Galleries auction. According to a *Coin World* report quoting Todd Martin, deputy chief of the Mint's Office of Corporate Communications, the Mint struck the bullion Variety 1 Silver Eagles at three facilities, with West Point producing 11,811,000, San Francisco producing 1,000,000, and Philadelphia emitting 495,500. None of these coins have mintmarks and are not distinguishable as to their origin except for markings on sealed, bulk-sized "monster boxes." Many pieces have been positively identified as originating from the Philadelphia and San Francisco Mints and encapsulated with labels declaring them "emergency" issues.

2021-W, Variety 1, Proof

Mintage: 327,339

GSID: 85060

Minted at West Point with W mintmark

Coin commentary: The Mint released the 2021-W Variety 1 Proof Silver Eagle on February 11 for $73. Demand was high for the last Proof Variety 1 Silver Eagle. The coin became unavailable on the Mint's website within three minutes, due mainly to advance dealer sales and retail enrollments. *Coin World* reported that first-day sales of individual Proofs registered a whopping 284,272 coins. Meanwhile, the Congratulations Set, which contained a 2021-W Variety 2 Proof in ornate packaging, managed first-day sales of 35,715 despite its slightly higher $75 issue price. The coin was also available in the 2021 Limited Edition Silver Proof Set, which saw 48,374 sold at an original issue price of $235.

2021-W, Variety 1, Reverse Proof

Mintage: 124,822

GSID: 152461 / 152463 (set)

Minted at West Point with W mintmark

Coin commentary: The Mint produced a two-piece offering known as the 2021 American Eagle Silver Reverse Proof Two-Coin Designer Edition Set. This set, originally issued for $175, was intended to launch on August 24, 2021. However, the U.S. Mint moved the release date back to September 13 in a schedule reshuffling that affected several products; Mint officials were working to combat technologically disruptive bots that caused website issues and artificially quick sellouts. The two-coin reverse proof set, containing a Variety 1 Reverse Proof from the West Point Mint and a Variety 2 from San Francisco, had a maximum authorized mintage of 125,000. As CoinNews.net noted in an article published on the day of the coin's eventual release, "The set's mintage/product limit is capped at 125,000. This instantly makes both coins key issues in the entire American Silver Eagle series." The same outlet reported days later that the two-coin offering became unavailable on the U.S. Mint website within three hours of the set's release. Examples that were broken out of their original government packaging and encapsulated by mainline third-party graders did well on the marketplace thanks to high demand from registry set collectors and investors.

The Dawning of a New Era: The Variety 2 American Silver Eagle

By David J. Ryder

An Innovative Coin Took Flight in Turbulent Skies

In 2021, the American Silver Eagle welcomed a new reverse motif that was designed by Emily S. Damstra and engraved by Michael Gaudioso. It depicts a majestic flying eagle clutching an oak branch in its talons. It's simple enough to say that the implementation of the new design was a ceremonious way to mark the 35th anniversary of the American Silver Eagle, which debuted in 1986 with John Mercanti's stately Heraldic Eagle reverse.

However, a succinct summary like that glosses over the complex and compelling story that led to the creation of a new American Silver Eagle design. There were many challenges we at the U.S. Mint overcame in the process. Ultimately, revamping the American Silver Eagle wasn't merely about changing the design for the sake of change. It was about inspiring collectors, infusing new life into our hobby, and paying homage to the past while looking ahead to a brighter future—all, perhaps, when we needed that glimmer of optimism the most.

New Realities, New Opportunities

When I returned to serving as the U.S. Mint director in 2018, I found a lot had changed in the numismatic world since my previous term at the helm of the Mint from 1992 through 1993. For one? There were far fewer coin collectors subscribing to United States Mint coin programs in the late 2010's than there were a generation earlier. Back in the early 1990's, we had more than 2.3 million active collectors buying U.S. Mint products each year. By 2018, there were closer to 425,000 on the rolls.

It was a brave new world in which society had become reliant on using plastic cards and phone apps to pay for goods and services. That meant young kids weren't necessarily growing up using coins anymore like children would have a generation or two earlier. And adults? Many had moved away from collecting coins and instead were mostly spending their disposable incomes on various other recreational pursuits—generally none having to do with numismatics. For the coin collectors who remained, many had grown tired of the "same ol', same ol'."

I was coming into the U.S. Mint as director for round two ready to do something different. I wanted to inspire people to collect coins again!

And what a time to return to the U.S. Mint as its director. Little did I or anyone else know the multitude of challenges—and opportunities—that would come our way over the next few years. I kicked off a variety of initiatives that I thought would help enthuse collectors again, chief among these being a run of limited-edition W mintmarked America the Beautiful Quarters. These

2019-W and 2020-W coins were struck at the West Point Mint to the tune of just two million each. The kicker? They were available only through circulation channels. Therefore, collectors had to look through rolls and pocket change to find these scarce coins—they couldn't just buy them from the U.S. Mint for a price. That program caused a media sensation, and for two years there were all kinds of cool stories online and on social platforms about people around the country finding the "W quarters." There were even a couple of famous folks who made the news when they found their first West Point quarters in change.

That helped to get people talking about coins again. And that wouldn't be the end of it. Around the time the first W-Mint America the Beautiful Quarters were hitting circulation, many were in the midst of recognizing the 75th anniversaries of various battles and significant events relating to World War II—a subject near and dear to my heart. Both of my parents were World War II veterans, as were so many others close to me in my life. Sadly, millions of World War II veterans had already passed away by the 75th anniversary of the international conflict, but I—like so many others—wanted to honor those who were still with us. And there was a grand opportunity to do just that with the 75th anniversary of victory, when the United States and Allied Forces won the war in 1945.

The big anniversary would arrive in 2020, and I knew that Congressman Stephen Scalise of Louisiana was working diligently to get a "Victory 75" commemorative coin program passed. It just couldn't get the votes. That prompted me to go into action. I thought one of the best ways to numismatically honor World War II veterans while circumventing bureaucratic hurdles was by way of employing a privy mark. It was something the U.S. Mint had never done before, and I was certain it would appeal to many collectors.

It was settled that the privy mark would appear on the American Silver Eagle and the $50 American Gold Eagle. But we just couldn't seem to get the right design for the privy mark. It was on one of my routine bicycle rides around the Washington, D.C., mall on my way to work that I was struck with inspiration. As I was bicycling around the famous World War II Memorial, I came upon its reflecting pond, known as the Rainbow Pool, and said to myself, "*That's* the privy mark!"

Overcoming Challenges

When I arrived at Mint headquarters that morning, I went directly to the office of April Stafford, who was the head of design management for the Mint. I proceeded to show her the pictures I took of the World War II Memorial, and that's when we decided that using the outline of the Rainbow Pool was the right thing to do. Design sketches soon came together. But there was an obstacle to carrying out that design. The overall concept of the World War II Memorial Rainbow Pool was technically the intellectual property of the Department of the Interior. So, we couldn't just interpret the shape of the pool in the privy mark without obtaining the necessary clearances to do so.

I consulted with attorneys who helped me and my colleagues at the Mint navigate intellectual property rights and acquire permission to use the shape of the World War II Memorial Rainbow Pool as the basis for the privy mark. Once we cleared that hurdle, we decided to emblazon the privy mark with the letter V (for "victory") and the number 75 (referencing the 75th anniversary of the end of World War II) within the shape of the pool. Before long, the design of the privy mark was ready for prime time. We struck 75,000 of the 2020-W American Silver Eagles with the V75 privy mark and 1,945 one-ounce American Gold Eagle $50 coins with the same feature. The coins proved to be instant hits when they sold out in a matter of moments upon their release on November 5, 2020.

However, by November 2020 we at the U.S. Mint were dealing with a challenge unlike any other we had ever experienced. That challenge, of course, was COVID-19.

A New Era

I don't think there are too many of us who would choose to relive the trying times that we all faced in 2020, when the COVID-19 pandemic swept the globe, killing some seven million and infecting nearly 1 billion. Yet, amid the darkness and danger of the pandemic came glimmers of hope, sparks of innovation, and moments of triumph. For us at the U.S. Mint and for the numismatic community at large, it's when a number of inspiring changes began taking shape and where the story behind the Variety 2 American Silver Eagle (and Gold Eagle) really begins taking flight.

In the spring of 2020, when the pandemic began dealing blows in the United States, millions spent seemingly countless hours at home. In many cases, they had little choice—workplaces and schools shut their doors, community events and family get-togethers where canceled, and even restaurants and grocery stores dimmed their lights. Many Americans did what they could from home, and for many it meant a return to the things they used to do but for which they had dedicated little time: starting backyard vegetable gardens, making household repairs, reading books, and returning to hobbies they put aside long ago. In many cases, that meant dusting off old Whitman coin folders and delving back into the world of coin collecting; many others began their numismatic journeys for the first time, often inspired by online videos or hobby websites touting rare and valuable coins.

We at the U.S. Mint were taking notice of this extraordinary phenomenon: that more and more people were coming into numismatics—some for their first time in many years, others for their first time ever. It was uplifting, especially at a time when so many of my colleagues were cloistered within their homes, while I continued to show up every day at Mint headquarters managing the many day-to-day challenges at the Mint. We met only by video conferences or commiserating by phone or email. I worked with safety personnel and many others to maintain full operating crews who were tasked with producing our nation's coinage. They did an outstanding job producing record levels of circulation and other numismatic products. It was those incredible employees who kept the United States Mint up and running while most international mints were forced to shut down.

Even still, we never stopped working on new ideas to invigorate the numismatic community—especially during the uncertain times we all faced together as a nation. Three projects were about to unfold in quick succession at the Mint that highlight the innovations we embarked upon, including the new reverse designs that grace the American Eagle silver and gold coins.

Going the Distance

Numismatists are keenly aware of history. That was certainly the case with the building interest in marking the centennial of the last Morgan dollar and first Peace dollar, both of which had last been struck in 1921. Tom Uram and Mike Moran from the Citizens Coinage Advisory Committee (CCAC) had a meeting with me to explain their strong desire to have the U.S. Mint produce Morgan and Peace silver dollars for the 100th anniversary. During that meeting it was decided that they would get together and write a piece of legislation to develop a commemorative coin program for the Morgan silver dollar, which they did.

The problem was that, because time was short, we simply couldn't get enough traction in congress to get a commemorative coin passed, as there was not enough interest. At that point we reconvened, and I realized that it would be a tremendous opportunity for the coin-collecting community if we could get a Morgan 100th anniversary silver dollar produced. At that point, the U.S. Mint decided to undertake the challenge of developing brand-new legislation that was going to require congressional support. Uram, Moran, director of Legislative Affairs Jennifer Warren, and I went as a team to the offices of Kentucky Congressman Andy Barr and Nevada Congressman Mark Amodei.

Both Barr and Amodei were very receptive to our plan to introduce our proposed legislation and gave us plenty of time to present our case. However, I really felt we had a champion in Congressman Amodei, as he was from Nevada, and the Carson City Mint was in his congressional district. He had just one condition: that there be an option for Morgan dollars to be struck bearing the CC mintmark of Carson City, Nevada. There was just one problem with that: the building that had once housed the Carson City Mint was no longer a mint. It was a museum. That was also the case with the New Orleans Mint, which—like the Carson City Mint—had once struck millions of Morgan dollars but ceased operations more than a century earlier. Thankfully, we had a viable workaround: privy marks. We decided that we could honor both the Carson City and New Orleans Mints with CC and O privy marks on the new Morgan dollars.

Congressmen Amodei and Barr moved quickly on our proposed legislation for the introduction of H.R. 6192, the 1921 Silver Dollar Coin Anniversary Act, for the introduction of the modern Morgan and Peace silver dollars to Congress. All of us worked tirelessly, especially Congressman Amodei and the Mint's legislative staff, in order to get the necessary votes. Without this tremendous effort the new 100-year anniversary Morgan and Peace coins would have ever been minted!

The legislation was passed, and President Donald J. Trump signed it into law just as he was leaving his first term in office. We cleaned up the Morgan and Peace dollar designs and prepared the new silver dollars for production. The Morgan and Peace dollar can now be struck by the U.S. Mint in perpetuity for as long as Mint brass wants to have them available for the public. I also had the privilege to host Congressman Amodei at the Philadelphia Mint, where he assisted me in striking the first Carson City Morgans. What better way to say "thank you" to a person who went the distance to help get this incredible undertaking done?

Thinking Outside the Box

It's one thing to resurrect the silver dollars of yesteryear for 21st-century coin collectors. Yet I learned it's entirely another to reimagine the concept of what "liberty" looks like. I received word from the Mint's marketing team that it was time to choose another design for the American Liberty High-Relief Gold Coins. I realized the importance of staying with the tradition of depicting "liberty" in the form of Lady Liberty. But I also felt it was equally important to do something new.

I asked the many talented artists in the United States Mint Artistic Infusion Program (AIP) to come up with renditions of what they felt freedom meant to them. I gave them complete latitude to come up with whatever they thought was appropriate. When all the designs were finished, the CCAC committee got together with the Mint, and we chose five designs that were emblematic of this new design for the American Liberty gold coin. It was at that point that Beth Zaiken's Bucking Bronco motif took center stage. It just caught all our imaginations as an absolutely beautiful design.

The incredible design features a horse throwing off its saddle. But upon seeing it for the first time I said to the people in the room that there was one thing that bothered me about it. To me, someone who grew up in Montana and Idaho, I felt the wild horse was being broken from his freedom and liberty—it was a depiction of a horse throwing off a saddle in an effort to not lose its freedom. It's being tamed by someone that wants to ride it and break its freedom.

It was then that Zaiken revealed the deeper meaning of the design. She described to me the horse was throwing off the yoke of British rule, the latter represented by the saddle. Once that was explained, I understood the intention of the artist's design, and I fully embraced it. The 2021 Bucking Bronco American Liberty piece went on to win the coveted Coin of the Year award in 2023.

Fly, Eagle, Fly

What a ride it has been . . . From bucking broncos, we now look to flying eagles. And yet, like so many of the important changes that transpired during my colorful second term as Mint director, this is one that arose somewhat spontaneously yet left a lasting impact on the numismatic community. The new reverses that appeared on the American Eagle silver and gold coins in 2021 have a rather humble origin. They emerged from an ordinary marketing meeting, where it was mentioned as an aside that the U.S. Mint and Treasury had the latitude to bypass Congress and change coin designs more than 25 years after their debut.

This began an informal debate on whether the Mint should even embark on changing the designs of the American Eagle gold and silver coins, which at the time had retained the same motifs they were born with back in 1986. Some people thought we should change the designs, while others thought we shouldn't. Those who thought we should've left the designs alone often pointed to the Canadian Maple Leaf and South African Krugerrand, just two of many popular bullion coins that had never seen major design changes.

I then called John M. Mercanti, because I wanted his take on the matter of replacing his Heraldic Eagle motif that had appeared on the reverse of the Silver Eagle for so many years. He was enthusiastic about giving another artist the chance to make their mark on the Silver Eagle. "It would be wonderful if a new artist had the same design opportunity that I had back in 1986," said Mercanti. I was also pleased that Miley Busiek-Frost, whose Family of Eagles motif had appeared on the reverses of the four American Gold Eagle designs since 1986, agreed with taking the coins in a new artistic direction.

Minting a New Legacy

My goal in recreating the reverses of the American Eagle silver and gold coins was to capture the beauty and majesty of the eagle while also showcasing this beloved national symbol as the embodiment of American strength and resilience. What followed were hundreds of hours of work by many people in creating the fresh, innovative designs that were soon to grace the reverses of the American Eagle program's world-renowned silver and gold coins. The flying eagle design by AIP artist Emily S. Damstra and eagle head motif by Jennie Norris, also of the AIP, were introduced for consideration. They won overwhelming approval from the secretary of the Treasury, the CCAC, and the Commission of Fine Arts, as well as that of the global coin-collecting community.

Damstra's design was engraved by retired U.S. Mint medallic artist Michael Gaudioso, while Norris's work was sculpted by U.S. Mint medallic artist Renata Gordon. It took a lot of ambition, especially as so many of us on the Mint team were working from home during the height of the pandemic. But we got the job done. We even navigated through a challenging silver-planchet shortage, allocating enough supply to support ample runs of both the new Variety 2 American Silver Eagle and the 2021 Morgan and Peace silver dollar program I mentioned earlier.

We debuted the new American Eagle designs mid-year in 2021, providing a novel opportunity to close out the 35th anniversary of the old designs while ushering in the new ones during the same production year. This resulted in a highly successful marketing campaign for the U.S. Mint and offered an exciting variety of coins for collectors and investors, who clamored for all iterations of the American Eagles in terrific numbers.

I was at the West Point Mint with Ellen McCullom, the outstanding and longtime West Point Mint superintendent, and Tom Dinardi, the West Point Mint deputy superintendent, along with John Mercanti, the Mint's former chief engraver, and Joe Menna, the Mint's new chief engraver, all standing at the press to strike the last of the Variety 1 designs and the first of the Variety 2, filled with such pride about what we at the U.S. Mint were able to achieve. It wasn't just the realization that we were embarking on a new chapter of the American Eagle program. It was that we did it amid one of the most challenging times of our entire generation. It showed us how far we could go and how much we could do when we put our minds to it. It's true when they say, "Where there's a will, there's a way."

We were faced with an extraordinary test. Yet, not only did we at the U.S. Mint cross the finish line, but I believe coin collectors won, too. Just as John M. Mercanti's modern Heraldic Eagle did for the Silver Eagle in 1986, Emily S. Damstra's innovative Flying Eagle captures the spirit of what it means to be an American and to believe in liberty. It's a symbol for these times, and—indeed—for all time.

2021, Variety 2, Bullion Strike

Mintage: 14,968,500

GSID: 213173 (San Francisco) / 213363 (West Point)

Minted at San Francisco and
West Point, without mintmark

Coin commentary: The first Silver Eagle bullion strikes bearing Emily S. Damstra's Flying Eagle design rolled off the presses on April 10, 2021. The new design proved popular with collectors and investors, who clamored for the new coin. Many collectors saw the introduction of the Variety 2 design as a reason to begin building sets of the silver bullion coin for the first time, while others who had long been assembling sets of the Silver Eagle pivoted toward the new Damstra design with great enthusiasm. Mass promoters were also fond of the new design, featuring the Variety 2 issue in multitudes of print and online advertisements either as standalone pitches or paired with the 2021 Variety 1 design for two-coin "last and first"–type offers. According to a *Coin World* story citing the Mint's deputy chief of the Office of Corporate Communications, West Point struck 13,968,500 and San Francisco produced 1,000,000 without mintmarks; the San Francisco emissions are not distinguishable from their unmintmarked West Point kin except for pieces still contained within their Mint-assembled "monster boxes" bearing labeling that identifies them as such. Many confirmed San Francisco strikes are encapsulated and labeled "emergency" strikes. Among the headlines generated by the Variety 2 motif was one made in September 2022, when Stack's Bowers Galleries sold the first-ever Variety 2 example, struck by Mint Director David Ryder, for $80,000.

2021-W, Variety 2, Burnished

Mintage: 185,791

GSID: 193325

Minted at West Point, with W mintmark

Coin commentary: The 2021-W Burnished (or "Uncirculated," in U.S. Mint terminology) Silver Eagle became the first such satin-style issue in the series to carry the new reverse design by Emily S. Damstra. The 2021-W Burnished Silver Eagle was released on September 9, 2021, and was issued for $67. While the coin wasn't an immediate sellout, it quickly reached its allotted distribution of 175,000 individual units and saw hundreds of 40-coin bulk orders.

2021-S, Variety 2, Proof

Mintage: 272,181
GSID: 121152
Minted at San Francisco, with S mintmark

Coin commentary: The first of the San Francisco Proof emissions with the Variety 2 reverse, this issue was offered for $73 upon its release on August 12, 2021. According to *Coin World,* inventories of the 2021-S Variety 2 Proof were "nearly" exhausted "in less than 10 minutes" after the coin became available for sale. The coin was also available in the 2021 Limited Edition Silver Proof Set, which saw 48,374 sold at an original issue price of $235.

2021-S, Variety 2, Reverse Proof

Mintage: 124,822

GSID: 152462 / 152463 (set)

Minted at San Francisco, with S mintmark

Coin commentary: Part of the two-piece 2021 American Eagle Silver Reverse Proof Two-Coin Set, Designer Edition, this S-Mint emission became the first Reverse Proof bearing the Silver Eagle's new design. The set, released on September 13 for $175, was a quick sellout that soon fetched significantly higher prices in the secondary market. Like its set-sibling, the Variety 1 W-Mint Reverse Proof, the Variety 2 Reverse Proof performed remarkably well on the secondary marketplace when broken out of its original government packaging and encapsulated by major third-party grading companies. Proof-70 examples are highly sought after by set collectors and investors alike.

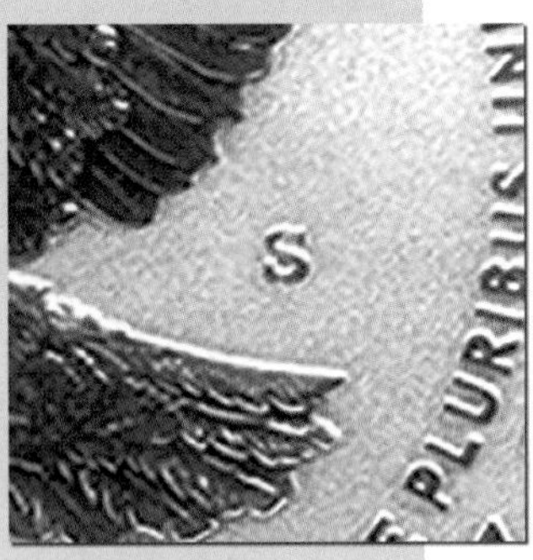

2021-W, Variety 2, Proof

Mintage: *385,776 (final mintage not yet audited)*

GSID: 121151

Minted at West Point, with W mintmark

Coin commentary: The Variety 2 Silver Eagle was originally slated for release on July 1, 2021, but the date was pushed back to July 20 in light of rescheduling so the U.S. Mint could properly address the problem of bot traffic on its website. The Variety 2 Proof was issued for $73, which was the same price the Mint charged for the last of the Variety 1 Proofs earlier in the year. Similar to other hot Mint items of the day, inventories of the Variety 2 Proof were quickly depleted. The coin had a household ordering limit of three and was unavailable via the website within minutes.

2022, Bullion Strike

Mintage: 16,000,000
GSID: 213174
Minted at West Point, without mintmark

Historical context: The COVID pandemic continued making headlines in 2022 as variants going by names like Omicron infected millions and killed thousands. The economy was dogged by the ongoing pandemic, leading to inflation rates not seen in the United States since the early 1980's. Overseas, tensions flared as Russian military forces invaded Ukraine, leaving hundreds of civilians dead and laying waste to towns and cities throughout the Eastern European nation. A mass shooting at an elementary school in Uvalde, Texas, left 19 children and two teachers dead. Queen Elizabeth II of the United Kingdom died at the age of 96 after serving 70 years on the throne and appearing on billions of coins struck around the world. Silver prices reached the year's high of $26.18 per ounce on March 9 and dipped to as low as $17.77 on September 1, with an average closing price of $21.79.

Coin commentary: For the American Silver Eagle, 2022 was the first full production year with the newly implemented Flying Eagle reverse by Emily S. Damstra and Michael Gaudioso. Given that just one design was employed on the Silver Eagle in 2022, the year saw fewer product offerings than in the previous year, which spawned the two reverse designs. The bullion offering yielded 16 million strikes, which was down significantly from 2021, when a total of nearly 28 million bullion strikes were produced. Softer numbers were likely a result of lower silver prices in 2022 and less collector demand for the coin, as the novelty of its new reverse design had worn off somewhat.

2022-W, Burnished

Mintage: 219,640
GSID: 194492
Minted at West Point, with W mintmark

Coin commentary: The 2022-W Burnished American Silver Eagle, widely marketed by the U.S. Mint as "Uncirculated," was released on June 1, 2022. It was issued for $67, a price unchanged from the previous year. By this time, enrollment purchases had become very popular for those ordering annual products like the Burnished Silver Eagles. CoinNews.net reported on April 5 that, according to a Mint notice, "the American Eagle Silver One Ounce Uncirculated Coin (W) inventories [among other Silver Eagle products] have all been depleted. This marks the first time that all American Eagle silver coins have been depleted through enrollments."

2022-S, Proof

Mintage: 366,366
GSID: 200004
Minted at San Francisco, with S mintmark

Coin commentary: This San Francisco Proof was officially released on August 9, 2022, at an issue price of $73, which was the same amount charged for individual Proofs of the previous year. However, as CoinNews.net noted, there was relatively little rush from the public to buy the coins on its release date because, by then, the allotted inventory had already been purchased through the U.S. Mint's preorder enrollment program. Those who managed to order by way of cancellations were subject to an ordering limit of three coins per household during the first 24 hours of the coin's release. An alternative for buying the 2022-S Proof Silver Eagle was the Limited Edition Silver Proof Set. It was released on October 26 with an issue price of $201; the reported mintage for that set was 47,094—a little shy of its authorized maximum production limit of 50,000.

2022-W, Proof

Mintage: 663,762
GSID: 194491
Minted at West Point, with W mintmark

Coin commentary: The 2022-W Proof Silver Eagle was released on April 14, 2022, and issued for $73, identical to the sales price of the similar individual offering in 2021. By that time, the allocated individual units were already accounted for by retail customers through the Mint's popular preorder enrollment program. For $2 more, collectors could also purchase the 2022-W Proof in that year's Congratulations Set. As *Numismatic News* reported on April 22, 2022, the Congratulations Set "promptly sold out of its 30,000 limit."

2023, Bullion Strike

Mintage: 24,750,000

GSID: 213175

Minted at West Point, without mintmark

Historical context: Tensions flared in the Middle East as a group of militants led by Palestinian political-militant group Hamas attacked Israel on October 7, 2023, killing some 1,200 civilians, including 40 Americans. Another 251 people, among them 12 Americans, were taken hostage. This prompted military responses by Israel, which continued operations in the Palestinian territory's Gaza Strip into 2024. Five people onboard an OceanGate Expeditions submersible were killed when their vessel imploded while descending to the wreckage site of the *Titanic.* Eyes turned skyward in North America as a high-altitude Chinese balloon drifted over Alaska, western Canada, and much of the contiguous United States. The balloon was shot down by the United States Air Force after it drifted aloft off the coast of South Carolina, but it was eventually determined to have not sent any intelligence information back to China. The World Meteorological Organization found 2023 to be the hottest year on record, with natural disasters ranging from massive typhoons in Asia and raging floods in California to wind-driven wildfires on the Hawaiian island of Maui, destroying the town of Lahaina. Inflation softened to 3.4% by the end of the year, though concerns over rising prices led many speculators to hard assets like bullion. Silver saw an average closing price of $23.41 per ounce, reaching $26.05 on May 4 and dipping as low as $20.05 on March 7.

Coin commentary: The bullion arm of the Silver Eagle saw its highest mintage since 2020, owing to continued trepidation over inflation and fervent activity on the bullion tickers. While the buzz over the new American Silver Eagle design had largely subsided by 2023, the large silver coin remained extremely popular with collectors and investors.

2023-W, Burnished

Mintage: 199,533

GSID: 213629

Minted at West Point, with W mintmark

Coin commentary: The 2023-W Burnished Silver Eagle, sold by the Mint as "Uncirculated," hit the scene at noon Eastern on May 25, 2023, with the usual fanfare. One big difference this year was the issue price of the coin, which stood at $76—an increase of $9 over the similar 2022 offering.

2023-S, Proof

Mintage: 242,667

GSID: 226242

Minted at San Francisco, with S mintmark

Coin commentary: The 2023-S Proof was released on October 10 at an issue price of $80, an increase of $7 more than its equivalent offering in the previous year. A higher issue price for the coin didn't dissuade buyers, who snapped up more 157,953 examples by the end of the first day of sale alone, as reported by *Coin World* and inclusive of advance orders. The coin was also available in the 2023 Limited Edition Silver Proof Set, which hit the scene on November 28 for an initial issue price of $220 and had a maximum authorized production of 50,000.

2023-W, Proof

Mintage: 213,357
GSID: 198248
Minted at West Point, with W mintmark

Coin commentary: The 2023-W Proof was offered for sale on March 2 as both a standard offering and in the annually produced Congratulations Set. The Proof in standard packaging was issued for $80, an increase of $7 from the previous year. The Congratulations Set was sold for $82, also $7 higher in price than seen the previous year.

2024, Bullion Strike

Mintage: 22,860,000

GSID: 347656

Minted at West Point, without mintmark

Historical context: The Israeli-Hamas war continued into 2024 with thousands of innocents killed or injured, prompting large protests throughout the United States against government-backed funding of the ongoing conflict. These protests played into the 2024 presidential election, which initially saw incumbent Democratic President Joe Biden face off against his Republican predecessor, Donald Trump. A contentious political situation unfolded in the summer, when many Democratic party officials pressured President Biden to end his bid for a second term in the Oval Office. Vice President Kamala Harris was lifted to the fore as the 2024 Democratic presidential nominee. She and her running mate, Governor Tim Walz of Minnesota, ran an ambitious campaign as they tried making names for themselves in the closing months of a presidential campaign that saw at least one assassination attempt against Trump. Ultimately, the fledgling Harris-Walz team lost against Trump and his running mate, Senator J.D. Vance (Ohio). During the last weeks of the campaign, stormy weather derailed many campaign plans for both parties, with all eyes turning toward the paths of destruction left by Hurricanes Helene and Milton. Both storms inundated the Southeast United States with damaging winds and torrential floods. Hurricane Helene unleashed historic floods in the mountains of North Georgia, western North Carolina, and eastern Tennessee; Hurricane Milton raked a path of destruction through Central Florida that damaged many major landmarks and caused widespread floods due to historically heavy rainfall. Farther up the Eastern Seaboard, in Baltimore, Maryland, the Francis Scott Key Bridge collapsed on March 26 after a container ship struck a support structure and caused the 1970's arch-truss span to fall into the water, killing six. A multitude of turbulent events, including political nerves and continued economic apprehensions, caused bullion prices to generally ascend over the course of the year. Silver prices averaged \$28.27 per ounce, dropping as low as \$22.01 on February 13 and climbing as high as \$34.46 on October 29.

Coin commentary: A hectic 2024 caused many investors to embrace hard assets like silver, as demonstrated by silver prices that peaked more than 40% higher at one point in the year than seen just months earlier in the same calendar year. This led to a rush in demand for coins like the American Silver Eagle bullion strikes, which saw brisk sales throughout the course of the year. Nearly 23 million were struck, putting the 2024 bullion emission about on par with output with the previous year and substantially ahead of 2022.

2024, Bullion Strike, Star Privy Mark

Mintage: 500,000 authorized

GSID: 376845

Minted at Philadelphia, without mintmark

Coin commentary: As the U.S. Mint ventured into collaborations with private entities, one that excited American Silver Eagle collectors was an agreement with Nice Gang. The mobile technology company launched a free game called Eighth Era, in which players could win the opportunity to purchase limited-edition collectibles graded by Numismatic Guaranty Company. The star of that game quite literally became the Star Privy Silver Eagle, which showcases a five-pointed star on the bottom right area of the obverse just below and to the right of Adolph A. Weinman's AW monogram. The coin had a maximum authorized mintage of 500,000, making it the lowest-mintage regular bullion strike of the entire series. It became a hot collectible both inside and outside the gaming community, and it certainly did so in the numismatic world. Many believe the 2024(P) Star Privy Silver Eagle is required to complete a series set, pushing prices for this special issue into the hundreds of dollars.

2024-W, Burnished

Mintage: 113,130

GSID: 374796

Minted at West Point, with W mintmark

Coin commentary: The 2024-W Burnished (or "Uncirculated," in U.S. Mint parlance) Silver Eagles were released on June 6. The coin was issued with a $76 sales price, unchanged from the previous year. The availability of this perennially popular coin at the same price as its last outing spurred much demand, and an initial household ordering limit of 10 coins was imposed before being lifted after the first 24 hours of sale. *Coin World* reported that a whopping 89,273 units had been sold by June 9, just three days after the coin hit the scene. The coin saw a reported mintage of 113,130, making it a notably scarce entry as compared to other Burnished Silver Eagles.

2024-S, Proof

Mintage: 151,190
GSID: 375535
Minted at San Francisco, with S mintmark

Coin commentary: The 2024-S Proof was released on August 7, 2024, with an issue price of $95, a whopping $15 higher than in the previous year. Orders were limited to 25 coins per household during the first 24 hours of sale, although these restrictions were lifted 24 hours after initial sales commenced (as customary for such offerings by the Mint). The coin was also sold in the 2024 Limited Edition Silver Proof Set, which went on sale on November 5 for $255.

2024-W, Proof

Mintage: 333,863

GSID: 346867

Minted at West Point with W mintmark

Coin commentary: The 2024-W Proof was released on January 16, 2024, at an issue price of $80, unchanged from the previous year. While orders were initially limited to 25 per household for the first 24 hours after the coin's release, there was no mintage limit. The 2024-W Proof was also available in the Congratulations Set, released on January 16 and priced at $82.

2025, Bullion Strike

Mintage: not available as of press time
GSID: 376287
Minted at West Point, without mintmark

Historical context: President Donald J. Trump was sworn into office on January 20, 2025, to become the first commander-in-chief since Grover Cleveland in the late 19th century to serve two nonconsecutive terms in the White House. President Trump ordered several executive actions or recommendations that affected the United States Mint, including the termination of the one-cent coin on the grounds that it cost nearly four times the denomination's face value to produce and distribute. In April 2025, the White House announced reciprocal tariffs on various goods, but at that time specifically exempted bullion from those duties. This exemption was widely understood to include gold, silver, platinum, and palladium, and therefore these precious metals, including coins, were largely unaffected by the tariffs. Deadly wildfires raged in California throughout January, killing dozens and destroying thousands of homes and businesses in the Greater Los Angeles metropolitan area and in San Diego County. The first fatal commercial jet crash in the United States since 2009 occurred on January 29, when a U.S. Army Black Hawk helicopter collided with American Airlines Flight 5342 on approach for Ronald Reagan Washington National Airport. All 64 people onboard the commercial flight and the three soldiers in the military helicopter perished in the nighttime crash over the Potomac River in Washington, D.C. Changes in domestic and international economic policy, including impending trade wars with a multitude of nations, pushed bullion prices skyward. Gold crossed the $3,000-per-ounce threshold for the first time ever on March 14, while silver ticked persistently upward past the $30-per-ounce mark.

Coin commentary: Production of the 2025 American Silver Eagle kicked off in frenzied fashion, with more than 5 million units reportedly sold through the first quarter of the year. Bullish Silver Eagles sales reflected much uncertainty in domestic and global economic policy as well as socioeconomic turbulence at home and abroad. As historically typical, investors turn to physical safe-haven assets like silver (and gold) when economic futures look cloudy. Silver's persistent trend north of $30 per ounce early in the year led many to purchase 2025 Silver Eagles as well as older dates in the series on the secondary market. The American Silver Eagle program marked its 40th anniversary of authorization, as the Liberty Coin Act that brought the series to life was signed into law by President Ronald Reagan four decades earlier on July 9, 1985.

2025, Bullion Strike, Eagle Privy Mark

Mintage: 500,000 authorized

GSID: 393377

Minted at Philadelphia, without mintmark

Coin commentary: The second emission stemming from the collaboration between the United States Mint and game company Nice Gang became a sought-after collectible. It was struck at the Philadelphia Mint sans mintmark but with a flying-eagle privy mark above the motto IN GOD WE TRUST on the obverse. Some 500,000 strikes were authorized, making it among the scarcest of all bullion strikes. Numismatic Guaranty Company had an exclusive deal to encapsulate a run that was distributed through the game Eighth Era, featuring real collectibles that players could win the opportunity to purchase. Many collectors wanted examples of their own, causing some coins to sell for hundreds of dollars.

2025-W, Burnished

Mintage: not available as of press time

GSID: 376288

Minted at West Point, with W mintmark

Coin commentary: The 2025-W Burnished (termed "Uncirculated" by the Mint) American Silver Eagle went on sale May 20. With its issue price of $91, the 2025-W Burnished Silver Eagle cost substantially more than in the previous year, when that year's similar offering was pitched to the public for $76. Sales of the coin nevertheless remained strong on the heels of ardent bullion speculation and the enduring popularity of the American Silver Eagle program among numismatists and precious-metals investors.

2025-S, Proof

Mintage: not available as of press time

GSID: 376290

Minted at San Francisco, with S mintmark

Coin commentary: The 2025-S Proof Silver Eagle was slated for release in summer 2025, though an issue price was unavailable at the time this book went to press. In addition to the standard individual offer, the 2025-S Proof was also expected to be available in the 2025 Limited Edition Silver Proof Set.

2025-W, Proof

Mintage: not available as of press time

GSID: 376289

Minted at West Point, with W mintmark

Coin commentary: The 2025-W Proof was released for sale on January 9, 2025, with an original issue price of $95, which was an increase of $15 from the initial cost of the previous year's offering. The coin was also available in the Congratulations Set for an initial price of $97 in special gift-themed packaging.

2025-W, United States Army 250th Anniversary, Proof

Mintage: 100,000 authorized

GSID: 393460

Minted at West Point, with W mintmark

Coin commentary: Few details were available about this special coin, which was the first of three Silver Eagles issued in 2025 to honor the 250th anniversaries of three branches of the United States Armed Forces. This coin was projected to be released in summer 2025.

2025-P, United States Marine Corps 250th Anniversary, Proof

Mintage: 100,000 authorized

GSID: 393458

Minted at Philadelphia, with P mintmark

Coin commentary: Following up on the Army 250th Proof is this special Marine Corps 250th entry. As with the Army-themed coin, the media and the Mint's product page for the Marine Corps 250th Anniversary Proof yielded few details when this book went to print. The coin was expected to be released in fall 2025.

2025-S, United States Navy 250th Anniversary, Proof

Mintage: 100,000 authorized

GSID: 393459

Minted at San Francisco, with S mintmark

Coin commentary: This third of three military-themed 2025 Silver Eagle Proofs features a tribute to the Navy's 250th anniversary. Upon publication of this book, there were few details known to the public about this coin or its two related Armed Forces entries, including maximum authorized mintages or actual production figures, details on designs or the presence of privy marks, or other important information.

A
Check List of American Silver Eagles

Use this appendix as a check list and record book of your American Silver Eagle collection. A "Quantity" column is included because many collectors purchase multiples of each coin.

Coin	GSID	Quantity	Purchase Price	Notes
1986, Bull. †	10644			
1986-S, Pf	10657			
1987, Bull.	10645			
1987-S, Pf	10659			
1988, Bull.	10646			
1988-S, Pf	10660			
1989, Bull.	10647			
1989-S, Pf	10661			
1990, Bull.	10648			
1990-S, Pf	10662			
1991, Bull.	10649			
1991-S, Pf	10663			
1992, Bull.	10650			
1992-S, Pf	10664			
1993, Bull.	10651			
1993-P, Pf	10665			
1994, Bull.	10674			
1994-P, Pf	10682			
1995, Bull.	10675			
1995-P, Pf	10683			
1995-W, Pf †	10684			
1996, Bull. †	10676			

† Ranked in the *100 Greatest U.S. Modern Coins* (Schechter and Garrett).

Coin	GSID	Quantity	Purchase Price	Notes
1996-P, Pf	10685			
1997, Bull.	10677			
1997-P, Pf	10686			
1998, Bull.	10678			
1998-P, Pf	10687			
1999, Bull.	10679			
1999-P, Pf	10688			
2000, Bull.	10680			
2000-P, Pf	10667			
2001, Bull.	10681			
2001-W, Pf	10668			
2002, Bull.	10652			
2002-W, Pf	10669			
2003, Bull.	10653			
2003-W, Pf	10670			
2004, Bull.	10654			
2004-W, Pf	10672			
2005, Bull.	15388			
2005-W, Pf	15391			
2006, Bull.	68740			
2006-W, Burn.	70901			
2006-P, RevPf	68427			
2006-W, Pf	65333			
2007, Bull.	68989			
2007-W, Burn.	68986			
2007-W, Pf	68606			
2008, Bull.	68913			
2008-W, Burn., Rev of 2007 †	197930			
2008-W, Burn., Rev of 2008	68999			
2008-W, Pf	68914			
2009, Bull.	69445			
2010, Bull.	71049			
2010-W, Pf	71050			
2011, Bull.	84266 / 84267			

† Ranked in the *100 Greatest U.S. Modern Coins* (Schechter and Garrett).

Coin	GSID	Quantity	Purchase Price	Notes
2011-S, Burn.	74464			
2011-W, Burn.	71303			
2011-P, RevPf	71375			
2011-W, Pf	71046			
2012, Bull.	71114 / 84272			
2012-W, Burn.	71116			
2012-S, Pf	71644			
2012-S, RevPf	71592			
2012-W, Pf	71492			
2013, Bull.	71551 / 71554			
2013-W, Burn.	71493			
2013-W, Enh. Unc.	71533			
2013-W, Pf	71505			
2013-W, RevPf	74465			
2014, Bull.	84273 / 84274			
2014-W, Burn.	74223			
2014-W, Pf	74074			
2015, Bull.	213361 / 84275			
2015-W, Burn.	74224			
2015-W, Pf	74075			
2016, Bull.	213171 / 84276 / 84277			
2016-W, Burn.	74225			
2016-W, Pf	74076			
2017, Bull.	198090 / 84278 / 84279			
2017-W, Burn.	74226			
2017-S, Pf	84294			
2017-W, Pf	74077			
2018, Bull.	81693			
2018-W, Burn.	84269			
2018-S, Pf	81462			
2018-W, Pf	74078			
2019, Bull.	81694			
2019-W, Burn.	84270			
2019-S, Pf	81737			

Coin	GSID	Quantity	Purchase Price	Notes
2019-S, Enh. Rev Pf	81738			
2019-W, Pf	81463			
2019-W, Enh. Rev Pf	81903			
2020, Bull.	81905 / 213172 / 81904			
2020-W, Burn.	84271			
2020-S, Pf	81739			
2020-W, Pf	81464			
2020-W, V75 Pf	82111			
2021, Var. 1, Bull.	85128 / 85054 / 213362			
2021-W, Var. 1, Pf	85060			
2021-W, Var. 1, Rev Pf	152461			
2021, Var. 2, Bull.	213173 / 213363			
2021-W, Var. 2, Burn.	193325			
2021-S, Var. 2, Pf	121152			
2021-S, Var. 2, Rev Pf	152462			
2021-W, Var. 2, Pf	121151			
2022, Bull.	213174			
2022-W, Burn.	194492			
2022-S, Pf	200004			
2022-W, Pf	194491			
2023, Bull.	213175			
2023-W, Burn.	213629			
2023-S, Pf	226242			
2023-W, Pf	198248			
2024, Bull.	347656			
2024, Bull., Star Privy Mark	376845			
2024-W, Burn.	374796			
2024-S, Pf	375535			
2024-W, Pf	346867			
2025, Bull.	376287			
2025, Bull., Eagle Privy Mark	393377			
2025-W, Burn.	376288			
2025-S, Pf	376290			

Coin	GSID	Quantity	Purchase Price	Notes
2025-W, Pf	376289			
2025-W, Pf, U.S. Army Privy Mark	393460			
2025-W, Pf, U.S. Marine Corps Privy Mark	393458			
2025-W, Pf, U.S. Navy Privy Mark	393459			

Coin	GSID	Quantity	Purchase Price	Notes
1993 Philadelphia Mint Bicentennial	79849			
1997 Impressions of Liberty Set	376892			
2000 United States Millennium Coinage and Currency Set	70996			
2006 American Eagle 20th Anniversary Silver Coin Set	70815			
2006-W American Eagle 20th Anniversary Gold & Silver Coin Set	65332			
2011 American Eagle 25th Anniversary Silver Coin Set	71571			
2012 American Eagle San Francisco Mint Two-Coin Silver Proof/Reverse Proof Set	71491			
2012 Making American History Coin and Currency Set	393505			
2012 Limited Edition Silver Proof Set	72534			
2013 American Eagle West Point Two-Coin Silver Set	76851			
2019 Pride of Two Nations Two-Coin Set	315631			
2021 American Eagle Reverse Proof Two-Coin Set, Designer Edition	152463			
2021 Silver Proof Set—American Eagle Collection	193289			

B

Illustrated Catalog of John Mercanti's Numismatic Work

This catalog illustrates some of the U.S. coins (and a sampling of the medals) designed and/or sculpted by John Mercanti during his employment as a sculptor-engraver (and, from 2006 to 2010, chief engraver) with the U.S. Mint. "We are all classically trained," Mercanti said of the Mint's staff, in an interview in the December 25, 2006, issue of *Fortune* magazine, "and we demand a lot [of ourselves] because the Mint is known for its beautiful coins. . . . The best part of my job is seeing the finished product—holding the coin in my hand. It's satisfying seeing them all over the country."

Mercanti's work has been featured on silver, gold, and platinum bullion coins and medals; circulating coins (State quarters); copper-nickel, silver, gold, and bi-metallic (gold/platinum) commemorative coins; and a variety of national commemorative medals.

1970's FBI Director J. Edgar Hoover medal, reverse

The shield of the Federal Bureau of Investigation surmounts the life and death dates of the late FBI director.

1979 U.S. Mint Director Stella Hackel medal, reverse

A charming view of the Mint director's native Vermont is the central motif of this commemorative medal.

1982 Louis Armstrong American Arts gold medallion, obverse

This relaxed portrait of the "Ambassador of Jazz" is from the third year of the American Arts gold medallion program.

1982 Louis Armstrong American Arts gold medallion, reverse

Mercanti featured a trumpet—Louis Armstrong's famous musical instrument—on the medallion's reverse.

1982 Netherlands–America Friendship and Commerce medal, reverse

This medal was issued to celebrate, in President Ronald Reagan's words, "the longest unbroken, peaceful relationship that we have had with any other nation."

1983 Los Angeles Olympiad silver dollar, reverse

Designed by Elizabeth Jones and engraved by Mercanti, this motif features the head and upper body of an American eagle.

1983 Secretary of the Treasury Donald T. Regan medal, reverse

Symbols relevant to Regan's life are arranged underneath the emblem of the secretary of the Treasury.

1983 Fred Waring Congressional Gold Medal, obverse

Mercanti's portrait captures the warmth of composer, musical director, and educator Fred Waring, "America's Singing Master."

1983 Leo Ryan Congressional Gold Medal, obverse

Congressman Leo Ryan was posthumously honored after his assassination in Jonestown, in Guyana, where he was investigating on behalf of the U.S. government.

1984 John Steinbeck American Arts gold medallion, obverse

In American Gold and Silver, *Dennis Tucker describes Mercanti's "finely sculpted portrait of Steinbeck, nearly photographic in its execution."*

1984 Helen Hayes American Arts gold medallion, obverse

Mercanti's portrait of the famous actress is beautiful and elegant.

1984 Helen Hayes American Arts gold medallion, reverse

The reverse design of Hayes's gold medallion features the classical Greek theatrical masks of Comedy and Tragedy.

1984 Los Angeles XXIII Olympiad gold $10, obverse

Mercanti modeled a scene of two runners holding aloft the Olympic torch, from a concept by James Peed.

1984 Los Angeles XXIII Olympiad gold $10, reverse

The reverse of the coin is an adaptation of the Great Seal of the United States.

1984 Vice President Hubert H. Humphrey medal, obverse

This commemorative medal features a profile portrait of the late senator and vice president.

1984 Harry S Truman Centennial medal, reverse

Mercanti's design features the longtime home of President Harry Truman, in Independence, Missouri.

1986 Statue of Liberty Centennial silver dollar, obverse

Liberty Enlightening the World, *more popularly known as the Statue of Liberty, rises in the foreground, with the Ellis Island immigration center—the "Gateway to America"— behind her.*

1986 Statue of Liberty Centennial silver dollar, reverse

Liberty's torch, held aloft, sends its rays outward; surrounding this motif is an inscription from Emma Lazarus's famous poem, The New Colossus.

1986 American Silver Eagle, reverse

A bold heraldic eagle holds an olive branch, symbolizing peaceful intentions, and arrows, representing national strength and defense.

1989 President George H.W. Bush inaugural medal, obverse

A profile portrait of the nation's 41st president is superimposed on a finely detailed view of the White House.

1989 Congress Bicentennial gold $5, obverse

The Annual Report of the Director of the Mint *described Mercanti's work: "a spectacular rendition of the Capitol dome."*

1989 Congress Bicentennial gold $5, reverse

The coin's reverse shows a dramatic portrait of the majestic eagle atop the canopy overlooking the Old Senate Chamber.

1990 Eisenhower Centennial silver dollar, obverse

Mercanti depicted Dwight D. Eisenhower in two profile portraits: one as a five-star general during World War II, and the other as United States president.

1991 Korean War Memorial silver dollar, obverse

Featured are two F-86 Sabrejet fighters, a soldier climbing a hill, and five Navy ships, representing America's action in the Korean conflict of 1950 to 1953.

1991 Mount Rushmore Golden Anniversary gold $5, obverse

An American eagle flies above Mount Rushmore, carrying sculpting tools representing the labor and talents of artist Gutzon Borglum and his staff, who created the national monument in South Dakota.

1991 United Service Organizations silver dollar, reverse

Mercanti's design honors the USO, a private non-profit group that provides entertainment and other services to members of the nation's armed forces.

1991, General Norman Schwarzkopf Congressional Gold Medal, obverse

A facing portrait of the retired Gulf War commander is flanked by legends DESERT SHIELD and DESERT STORM.

1992 Christopher Columbus Quincentenary silver dollar, obverse

Explorer Christopher Columbus is shown holding a scrolled map and a flag in front of a globe, with his ships, the Nina, Pinta, *and* Santa Maria, *in the distance.*

1992, Persian Gulf Veterans National Medal, reverse

A heraldic American eagle and a ribbon at the bottom of this design identify the medal as being awarded by Act of Congress to servicemembers in the Persian Gulf Conflict.

1994 World Cup Tournament half dollar, obverse

A soccer player runs with a ball at his feet in this motif designed by Richard T. LaRoche and modeled by Mercanti.

1994 Vietnam Veterans Memorial silver dollar, obverse

A hand reaches out to touch the Vietnam Veterans Memorial, with its thousands of names of the war's dead and missing in action; the Washington Monument is in the background.

1994 U.S. Capitol Bicentennial silver dollar, reverse

Mercanti's rendering of a shield decorated with American flags and surmounted by an eagle is based on the central area of a stained-glass window near the House and Senate grand staircases.

1994 Rabbi Menachem Schneerson Congressional Gold Medal, obverse

A stylized line-art–style portrait celebrates the benevolence, ethics, leadership, and scholarship of The Lubavitcher Rebbe.

1994 U.S. Mint Director Philip N. Diehl medal, obverse

Mercanti captures the 35th director of the United States Mint in a strong profile portrait on a plain background.

1995 Civil War Battlefields silver dollar, reverse

A quotation by Joshua Chamberlain, a Union hero of the Battle of Gettysburg, surmounts a landscape of the war field's consecrated ground.

1995 Centennial Olympic Games Track and Field silver dollar, obverse

Mercanti's dynamic scene shows two Olympic athletes competing in track and field.

1995 Centennial Olympic Games Cycling silver dollar, obverse

Three Olympic cyclists race toward the viewer.

1995 Centennial Olympic Games Eagle gold $5, reverse

A standing eagle bears a banner with the centennial dates of the modern Olympic Games (1896–1996); designed by Frank Gasparro and modeled by Mercanti.

1996 Centennial Olympic Games Eagle gold $5, "Flag Bearer" obverse

An athlete carries the U.S. flag, followed by a cheering crowd; designed by Patricia L. Verani and modeled by Mercanti.

1996 Smithsonian Institution 150th Anniversary silver dollar, reverse

An allegorical goddess sits atop the world holding a scroll embodying Art, History, and Science—specialties of America's national museum, the Smithsonian.

1997 to date, American Platinum Eagle, obverse

The Statue of Liberty is featured in a facial close-up; this design is used on all denominations in the platinum bullion program.

1998 Little Rock Nine Congressional Gold Medal, reverse

In a simple design, the nine students involved in the 1957 civil-rights case are cited by name for their courage and bravery.

1998 American Platinum Eagle, Proof, reverse

Mercanti's "Eagle Over New England" is the first entry in the platinum bullion program's Vistas of Liberty series.

1998 Black Revolutionary War Patriots silver dollar, obverse

Mercanti's portrait of Crispus Attucks, the 1770 Boston Massacre's first victim, is an artistic conception—no historical images of Attucks exist.

1999 Rosa Parks Congressional Gold Medal, reverse

A globe and the scales of justice symbolize the importance of civil-rights icon Rosa Parks, along with legends noting her quiet strength, pride, dignity, and courage.

1999 American Platinum Eagle, Proof, reverse

Mercanti's "Eagle Above Southeastern Wetlands" is the second entry in the platinum bullion program's Vistas of Liberty series.

1999 Pennsylvania State quarter, reverse

The central elements are the goddess Commonwealth holding an eagle-surmounted standard, and a pebbled bas-relief keystone, symbolizing Pennsylvania's status as the "Keystone State."

2000 Library of Congress Bicentennial silver dollar, reverse

Featured is the dome of the main Library of Congress building in Washington, D.C.

2000 Library of Congress bimetallic (gold/platinum) $10, obverse

The Torch of Learning, held by Minerva, ancient Roman goddess of wisdom, is raised above the Library of Congress's Thomas Jefferson Building.

2000 Leif Ericson Millennium silver dollar, obverse

The helmeted bust is Mercanti's conception of Leif Ericson—no contemporary portraits of the Viking explorer exist.

2000 Bicentennial of the White House medal, reverse

A view of the presidential mansion is surrounded by laurels and the bicentennial dates 1800–2000.

2000 John Cardinal O'Connor Congressional Gold Medal, obverse

Mercanti designed and engraved a warmly personal portrait of John Cardinal O'Connor—priest, chaplain, humanitarian, and archbishop of New York.

2001 U.S. Capitol Visitor Center silver dollar, obverse

The original U.S. Capitol and the later Capitol building are featured in a motif designed by Marika Somogyi and modeled by Mercanti.

2001 U.S. Capitol Visitor Center silver dollar, reverse

A heraldic eagle is surrounded by rays and a ribbon reading "U.S. Capitol Visitor Center."

2001 North Carolina State quarter, reverse

From a design submitted by Mary Ellen Robinson, Mercanti modeled a view of the Wright Brothers' famous first manned flight, at Kitty Hawk, North Carolina.

2002 Louisiana State quarter, reverse

Louisiana is represented by a brown pelican (the state bird), a textured map of the 1803 Louisiana Purchase territory, and a trumpet symbolic of New Orleans jazz.

2002 Salt Lake City Olympic Games silver dollar, obverse

The crystal emblem of the 2002 Olympic Winter Games sits atop the "rhythm of the land" emblem and Olympic rings.

2002 West Point Bicentennial silver dollar, reverse

Mercanti's design is an adaptation of the seal of the U.S. Military Academy at West Point, with an ancient Greek helmet and a sword.

2002 Ronald and Nancy Reagan Congressional Gold Medal, obverse

Mercanti honored the former president and first lady with conjoined profile portraits.

2002 General H. Hugh Shelton Congressional Gold Medal, reverse

The reverse of the medal honoring the chairman of the Joint Chiefs of Staff highlights his sterling leadership qualities.

2003 Arkansas State quarter, reverse

From a design by Ariston Jacks, Mercanti modeled a collage of Arkansas motifs: a faceted diamond, stalks of rice, a sylvan river scene, and a mallard in flight.

2003 First Flight Centennial half dollar, obverse

Depicted is the monument at Wright Brothers National Memorial in Kill Devil Hills, North Carolina.

2003 National Wildlife Refuge System Centennial medal, Salmon reverse

Mercanti's salmon reverse was one of four designs in this popular U.S. Mint silver medal series—the first to use laser technology in their production.

2004 Iowa State quarter, reverse

Illustrating the theme of "Foundation in Education," a teacher and children plant a tree in front of a clapboard one-room schoolhouse.

2004 Thomas Alva Edison silver dollar, reverse

An 1879-style light bulb mounted on a base is surrounded by arcs of light, "emblematic of . . . the many inventions made by Thomas A. Edison throughout his prolific life."

2004 Dr. Dorothy Height Congressional Gold Medal, reverse

Mercanti's design features the National Council of Negro Women's building in Washington, D.C., with the U.S. Capitol in the background and an inspirational quote by social activist Dorothy Height.

2005 Chief Justice John Marshall silver dollar, obverse

Mercanti's portrait of Marshall is adapted from an 1808 likeness by French artist Charles Balthazar Julien Févret de Saint-Mémin.

2005 West Virginia State quarter, reverse

West Virginia's New River Gorge Bridge and its scenic environment are the focus of this design.

2005 Jackie Robinson Congressional Gold Medal, reverse

An inspirational quote from the baseball Hall of Famer, who broke the sport's racial barrier in the 1940's and 1950's, graces Mercanti's design.

2006 South Dakota State quarter, reverse

Mount Rushmore is the central motif, flanked by stalks of wheat and surmounted by a flying ring-necked pheasant.

2007 Jamestown 400th Anniversary gold $5, obverse

Captain John Smith, English explorer and settler of Jamestown, Virginia, is shown with Indian chief Powhatan in the New World.

Other Medals

In addition to the medals illustrated in this appendix, John Mercanti designed and/or engraved these medals while working for the United States Mint: 19xx Second U.S. Mint, obverse (unissued); 1984 U.S. Mint Set filler token, obverse; 1989 Mary Lasker Congressional Gold Medal, reverse; 1993 U.S. Mint Director David J. Ryder, reverse; 1997 Frank Sinatra Congressional Gold Medal, obverse; and 1998 U.S. Mint Service Award pin, obverse.

NOTES

The reader may view reference citations, if desired, via the QR code at right.

ABOUT THE AUTHORS

John M. Mercanti

John M. Mercanti is an American sculptor and engraver, best known to numismatists as the 12th chief engraver of the United States Mint and the designer of many circulating and commemorative coins and medals. He created the original (1986–2021) Heraldic Eagle reverse design of the American Silver Eagle coin.

Mercanti was born in Philadelphia. It was there that he received his artistic training, at the Pennsylvania Academy of Fine Arts, the Philadelphia College of Art, and the Fleisher Art Memorial School. He began his career as an illustrator and in 1974 joined the U.S. Mint as a sculptor-engraver under the legendary Frank Gasparro. In 2006 Mercanti was named chief engraver (supervisory design and master tooling development specialist), a position he held until his retirement in late 2010.

John Mercanti has produced more coin and medal designs than any other employee in the history of the U.S. Mint. Among his works (in addition to the American Silver Eagle) are gold and silver commemorative coins honoring the Statue of Liberty, the Olympic Games, Dwight D. Eisenhower, the Smithsonian Institution, and other important people, places, and events from American history; more than a dozen Congressional Gold Medals; five circulating State quarters; and numerous commemorative and bullion medals.

Mercanti resides in New Jersey, across the Delaware River not far from his workplace of nearly 40 years, the Philadelphia Mint.

David J. Ryder

David J. Ryder served as the 34th director of the U.S. Mint from 1992 to 1993 under President George H.W. Bush and President William J. Clinton. He returned to the Mint as its 39th director from 2017 to 2021 under President Donald J. Trump. Ryder is the only two-time director of the Mint in more than a century.

Prior to returning to the Mint, Ryder was the global business-development manager and managing director of currency for Honeywell's Authentication Technologies group. Previously, Ryder served as CEO of Secure Products Corporation, a spin-off from the Sarnoff Corporation, which developed highly advanced anti-counterfeiting technologies for the protection of global currencies and other valued documents. The Honeywell Corporation acquired Secure Products in 2007.

Ryder's prior government positions include Deputy Treasurer of the United States, Deputy Chief of Staff to Vice President Dan Quayle, and special assistant to Vice President George H.W. Bush. Ryder was also the Commissioner General–Director, U.S. Pavilion at the Louisiana World Exposition, United States Department of Commerce.

Ryder was born in Billings, Montana; grew up in Boise, Idaho; and attended Boise State University. Currently the president of the Aureus Group, LLC, a consulting company in Alexandria, Virginia, Ryder is married with two children.

Credits and Acknowledgments

Creative Director and Cover Designer, Matt Jeffirs
Editorial Director, Diana Plattner
Graphic Designers, Matt Heller and Thinh Bui

Index

2x2 coin holders, x

America the Beautiful quarters, W-Mint, 165
American Arts gold medallions, 5, 201, 202
American Buffalo gold coins, 5
American Gold Eagle, 5
American Liberty High-Relief Gold Coins, 168–169
American Numismatic Association (ANA), xi
American Palladium Eagle, 5
American Platinum Eagle, 5, 205, 206
American Silver Eagles
  2021 reverse redesign, v–vi, 169–70
  buying, x–xi
  check list of *(see appendix A)*
  coin-by-coin study *(see chapter 3)*
  how to collect, vii–xii
  launch of, 1, 9–10
  Variety 1 (*see* Variety 1 Silver Eagle [Heraldic Eagle])
  Variety 2 (*see* Variety 2 Silver Eagle [Flying Eagle])
Amodei, Mark, 167, 168
Anthony, Susan B., dollar, 12, 21
Antonucci, Steve, 39, 42
Architect of the Capitol, 20
Arkansas State quarter, 207
Armstrong, Louis, American Arts gold medallion, 201
Art Students League of New York, 24
Artistic Infusion Program (AIP), 15, 168
Australia, 4
autographed labels, ix

Baker, James, 9–10
Barr, Andy, 167, 168
Black Revolutionary War Patriots dollar, 205
Bostomatic milling machine, 39
Bowers, Q. David, 13
Britannia (bullion coin), 4
British Royal Mint, 43
Bucking Bronco American Liberty gold coin, 168–169
Buffalo nickel, 18
bullion coins, international, 4
Bush, George H.W., inaugural medal, 203
Busiek-Frost, Miley, 169

Canada, 4
capsules, x
Carson City Mint, 167–168
Carter, Jimmy, 6
Cather, Willa, American Arts gold medallion, 5
Certified Acceptance Corporation (CAC) Grading, xi
certified coins, vii
certified holders, x
China, 4
Churchill, Winston, 12
Citizens Coinage Advisory Committee (CCAC), 20, 167, 168
Civil War Battlefields dollar, 204
Claybrook, Barry, 39, 42, 43, 44
coin albums, x
coin holders, types of, x
Coin of the Year, 18, 169
Coin World, xii
collecting strategies, vii, viii–ix
Collins, Ron, 42–43, 44
Columbus Quincentennial commemoratives, 204
Congress Bicentennial commemorative, 203
Congressional Gold Medals, 20
Cooper Union, 24
counterfeits, xi
COVID-19, 166–167
Craig, Larry, 8

Dalai Lama, Congressional Gold Medal, 19
Damstra, Emily S., v, 10, 169–170
dealers, reputable, xi
Defense Logistics Agency, 6
Defense National Stockpile Center, 6
Department of Defense, 8
design selection process, 20–21
die preparation, 36–37
Diehl, Philip N., Mint director medal, 204
digital technology, 39–43
display cases, x
Donato, Giuseppe, 12

eagle, as a design element, 32–33, 34
Edison, Thomas Alva, dollar, 208
Eisenhower Centennial dollar, 203
Eisenhower dollar, 12, 13
emergency-issue labels, ix
Energy and Natural Resources Committee, 8
engraving, 36–37
epoxy models, 29–30
Ericson, Leif, dollar, 206
error coins, 43
Everhart, Don, 19
Executive Order 3524, 21
Executive Order 6102, x, 2–3

Federal Arts Administration, 12
federal debt, 6
Filipino Veterans of World War II, Congressional Gold Medal, 21
First Flight dollar, 207
first-strike / first-release labels, ix

Flanagan, John, 19
Fleisher Art Memorial School, 12, 13
flips, x
Flying Eagle design. *See* Variety 2 Silver Eagle (Flying Eagle)
Ford, Gerald, 3
Fore, Henrietta Holsman, 39
Fort Knox, 1
Fowler, Philip J., 15, 36
Franklin half dollar, 12
Fraser, Laura Gardin, 19
Freedom of Information Act. *See chapter 3*
Freeform (software), 40
French, Daniel Chester, 24

galvano process, 29
Garrett, Jeff, 26, 27
Gasparro, Frank, 12–16
  chief engraver, 11
  early life, 12
  Iacocca medal, 36
  Mint career, 12
  obituary, 13
  Presidential medals, 15–16
  teaching, 13
Gaudioso, Michael, v, 170
Gerber polisher, 43–44
gesso, 12–13
Gilkes, Paul, xii
Gold Bullion Coin Act of 1985, 5
Gold Certificates, 1
Gold Reserve Act of 1934, 3
gold standard, 3
gold surrender, 1
gold, historical value, 1
Gordon, Renata, 170
Great Depression, 1–2
Greysheet, the, xi
GSID numbers, xii
Guth, Ron, 26, 27
Hackel, Stella, medal of, 201
Hayes, Helen, American Arts gold medallion, 202
Height, Dorothy, Congressional Gold Medal, 208
Hemphill, Phebe, 19
Heraldic Eagle design. *See* Variety 1 Silver Eagle (Heraldic Eagle)
Hoover, J. Edgar, medal, 15–16, 201
House Armed Services Committee, 8
Humphreys, Hubert, Vice Presidential Medal, 202

Iacocca, Michael G., 14
  and Gasparro medal, 36
Idaho, influence on silver markets, 8
Illustrator (software), 34
Individual Retirement Account, 10
Interior Department, 8
Iowa State quarter, 208
IRA. *See* Individual Retirement Account
Iskowitz, Joel, 19

Jamestown commemorative, 208
Janvier reducing lathe, 28–30, 38, 39
Johnson Atelier, 40
Johnson, Lyndon, Presidential medal, 12
Jones, Elizabeth, 43

Karlsruhe (city), 24
Keck, Charles, 24
Kennedy half dollar, 12, 27–28
Korean War dollar, 203
Krugerrand (bullion coin), 4

labels, on coin slabs, ix
laser technology, 42–44
Lasker, Mary, Congressional Gold Medal, 208
Libertad (bullion coin), 4
Liberty Cap half cent, 18
Liberty Coin Act, 8–9, 22–23
Liberty Walking half dollar, 26–27
Library of Congress commemoratives, 206
Lincoln cent, 12, 13
Little Rock Central High School Desegregation silver dollar, 18
Little Rock Nine Congressional Gold Medal, 205
Los Angeles Olympiad commemoratives, 201, 202
Louisiana State quarter, 207

MacArthur, Douglas, 12
Maple Leaf (bullion coin), 4
Marshall, John, dollar, 208
Martiny, Philip, 24
Masters, Richard, 18
McAdoo, William Gibbs, 26
McClure, James, 8
McFarlane Toys, 19
Menna, Joseph, 41
  Dalai Lama medal, 19
Mercanti, John M., 16–19, 20–21, 23, 24–31, 34–35, 44, 169, 170
  applying to the Mint, 11–12
  breakthrough into engraving, 11–13
  coin and medal designs *(see appendix B)*
  design process, 15
  early career, 11
  family, 11
  and Frank Gasparro, 11–14
  and Heraldic Eagle design, 10, 203
  Mercury dime, 24
  sculpture of Ronald Reagan, 7
Mexico, 4
Michelangelo, 12
milk spots, xi–xii
Mint director medal, 40
mintmarks, 39–40
Moran, Mike, 167
Morgan and Peace commemorative silver dollars, 167–168
Mount Rushmore Golden Anniversary commemorative, 203

National Coin and Bullion Association (NCBA), xi
National Defense Stockpile, 8
National Numismatic Collection, 21
National Wildlife Refuge System medal, 207
Netherlands-America medal, 201
New Orleans Mint, 167–168

Nicolardi, John, 37–38
Niehaus, Charles, 24
Nixon, Richard
  and gold standard, 3
  plan to sell stockpiled commodities, 6
Norris, Jennie, 169
North Carolina State quarter, 207

Nugget (bullion coin), 4
Numismatic Guaranty Company (NGC), xi

O'Connor, John Cardinal, Congressional Gold Medal, 206
Olympic coinage, 204–205, 207

Panda (bullion coin), 4
parenthetical mintmarks, ix
Parks, Rosa, Congressional Gold Medal, 205
Peloso, Matthew, 15, 36
Pennsylvania Academy of Fine Arts, 12
Pennsylvania State quarter, 206
Persian Gulf Veterans National Medal, 204
Philharmonic (bullion coin), 4
Photoshop (software), 34
plaster preparation, 24–29
privy marks
  CC (Carson City Mint), 168
  O (New Orleans Mint), 168
  V75, 165–166
Professional Coin Grading Service (PCGS), xi
Professional Numismatists Guild (PNG), xi
Proof polishing, 43–44
PVC (polyvinyl chloride), x

raw (uncertified) coins, vii
Reagan, Nancy, Congressional Gold Medal, 207
Reagan, Ronald, v, 7, 8, 9
  Congressional Gold Medal, 207
  plan to sell stockpiled commodities, 6
  Presidential medal, 12
  signing the Liberty Coin Act, iv
Regan, Donald T., medal, 201
registry sets, viii
Roberts, Gilroy, 12, 27
Robinson, Jackie, Congressional Gold Medal, 208
Rodin, Auguste, 12
Roosevelt dime, 12
Roosevelt, Franklin D., x, 1–2
Ryan, Leo, Congressional Gold Medal, 201
Ryder, David J., 164–170
  Mint director medal, 208
  return as 39th Mint director, 164–165
  See also the foreword
Saint-Gaudens, Augustus, 24
Salt Lake City Olympic Games dollar, 207
San Francisco Assay Office, 9
Scalise, Stephen, 165
scanners, 42
Schneerson, Menachem, Congressional Gold Medal, 204
Schwarzkopf, Norman, Congressional Gold Medal, 203
Sheldon, H. Hugh, Congressional Gold Medal, 207
Shrek, 41
silver stockpile, 6, 8
Sinatra, Frank, Congressional Gold Medal, 208
Sinnock, John R., 12
slabbed coins, vii
  labels on, ix
  See also certified holders
Smithsonian Institution, 21
Smithsonian Institution dollar, 205
South Africa, 4
South Dakota State quarter, 208
Stafford, April, 165–166
Statue of Liberty, 9, 202, 205
Statue of Liberty–Ellis Island Commemorative Coin Act, 8–9
Steever, Edgar Z., 14, 36
Steinbeck, John, American Arts gold medallion, 202
storing Silver Eagles, x–xi
strike formats, viii

toned coins, viii–ix
transfer engravers, 38
Treasury secretary, and coin design selection, 20
Truman, Harry S, medal, 202
Tucker, Dennis, 5
Twain, Mark, 5

U.S. Capitol Bicentennial dollar, 204, 206
U.S. Capitol Visitor Center dollar, 206
U.S. Commission of Fine Arts, 20, 21. *See also appendix D*
U.S. Mint packaging, x
U.S. Mint Service Award, 208
United States Mint, 164
Uram, Tom, 167
USO dollar, 203

Variety 1 Silver Eagle (Heraldic Eagle), 164–170
  collecting, vii
  designer of, 10, 23 (*see also* John M. Mercanti)
  See also chapter 3 listings for 2021
Variety 2 Silver Eagle (Flying Eagle), 170
  designer and engraver, 164 (*see also* Damstra, Emily; Gaudioso, Michael)
  See also chapter 3 listings for 2021
Vermeule, Cornelius, 27
Vietnam Veterans Memorial dollar, 204

Wales, 43
Wall Street Journal, 6
Wallop, Malcolm, 8
Waring, Fred, Congressional Gold Medal, 201
Warner, Olin, 24
Warren, Jennifer, 167
Washington quarter dollar, 19, 28
Watt, James, 8
Wayne, John, national medal, 12
Weinman, Adolph A., 10, 24, 26–27
West Point Bicentennial dollar, 189
West Point Mint, 165
West Virginia State quarter, 208
White House Bicentennial medal, 206
Winter, Sherl Joseph, 14, 36
Women Airforce Service Pilots Congressional Gold Medal, 19
World Cup commemoratives, 204
World Trade Center labels, ix
World War I, 26
World War II
  anniversaries of, 165
  Victory 75 commemorative coin program, 165
  Memorial Rainbow Pool, 165, 166

Zaiken, Beth, 168–169
Zechariah, 12

American
Silver Eagles
1986-2021
Bullion Strikes, by Year
THE OFFICIAL RED BOOK
A Guide Book of
AMERICAN
SILVER EAGLES
AMERICAN
SILVER
EAGLE
ORDER NOW

SETTING THE
MODERN STANDARD
1995-W S$1
CAC PR70DCAM
Eagle
2025 S$1
CAC MS70
Eagle
First Delivery
2025 G$50
CAC MS70
Eagle
First Day of Delivery
Traditional grading for modern coins makes CAC the collector's choice. No need to take our word for it; our coins speak for themselves.
Calling all collectors! Ensure your collection achieves its fullest potential by joining the CAC Grading Club.
Scan the QR code now!
CAC®
"Confidence in a Coin's Quality is Priceless"
www.CACgrading.com